T0330628

ROUTLEDGE LIBRARY EDITIONS:
SOVIET ECONOMICS

Volume 15

SOVIET CENTRAL ASIA

SOVIET CENTRAL ASIA

'A Tragic Experiment'

BORIS Z. RUMER

Routledge
Taylor & Francis Group

LONDON AND NEW YORK

First published in 1989 by Unwin Hyman, Inc.

This edition first published in 2023
by Routledge
4 Park Square, Milton Park, Abingdon, Oxon OX14 4RN

and by Routledge
605 Third Avenue, New York, NY 10158

Routledge is an imprint of the Taylor & Francis Group, an informa business

British Library Cataloguing in Publication Data
A catalogue record for this book is available from the British Library

ISBN: 978-1-032-48466-2 (Set)
ISBN: 978-1-032-48486-0 (Volume 15) (hbk)
ISBN: 978-1-032-48513-3 (Volume 15) (pbk)
ISBN: 978-1-003-38942-2 (Volume 15) (ebk)

DOI: 10.4324/9781003389422

Publisher's Note
The publisher has gone to great lengths to ensure the quality of this reprint but
points out that some imperfections in the original copies may be apparent.

Disclaimer
The publisher has made every effort to trace copyright holders and would
welcome correspondence from those they have been unable to trace.

SOVIET CENTRAL ASIA

"A Tragic Experiment"

Boris Z. Rumer

Boston
UNWIN HYMAN
London   Sydney   Wellington

Unwin Hyman, Inc.
8 Winchester Place, Winchester, Mass. 01890, USA

Published by the Academic Division of
Unwin Hyman Ltd
15/17 Broadwick Street, London W1V 1FP, UK

Allen & Unwin (Australia) Ltd,
8 Napier Street, North Sydney, NSW 2060, Australia

Allen & Unwin (New Zealand) Ltd in association with the
Port Nicholson Press Ltd,
Compusales Building, 75 Ghuznee Street, Wellington 1, New Zealand

First published in 1989
First published in paperback in 1990

Library of Congress Cataloguing in Publication Data

Rumer. Boris Z.
Soviet Central Asia: "A tragic experiment"/Boris Z. Rumer
p. cm.
Bibliography: p.
Includes index.
ISBN 0-04-445146-0
ISBN 0-04-445896-7 (pbk.)
1. Soviet Central Asia—Economic policy.   2. Soviet Central Asia—
Economic conditions.   3. Soviet Union—Economic condition—1976—
Regional disparities.   I. Title
HC336.9.C45R85 1989
338.958′ 4—dc 19
88–28608 CIP

British Library Cataloguing in Publication Data

Rumer, Boris Z.
Soviet Central Asia: "A tragic experiment".
1. Soviet Central Asia
I. Title
330.958′40854

ISBN 0-04-445146-6
ISBN 0-04-445896-7 (pbk)

Typeset in 11 on 12 point Goudy by Columns (Caversham) Reading and
' ' C----t Britain by Billing and Sons Ltd. London & Wor---'-

To Natasha

CONTENTS

Preface   xiii

Acknowledgments   xix

CHAPTER 1
Introduction: Regional Economic Policy in the USSR   1

CHAPTER 2
Central Asia's Role in the Soviet Economy and Its
    Economic Structure   27

CHAPTER 3
Problems of Industrialization   43

CHAPTER 4
Cotton   62

CHAPTER 5
Water   76

CHAPTER 6
Labor and Employment   105

CHAPTER 7
The Standard of Living   123

CHAPTER 8
The Shadow Economy and Organized Crime   144

CHAPTER 9
The Impact of the Gorbachev Reforms on Central Asia 160

CHAPTER 10
Conclusion   184

Notes   188
About the Author   199
Index   200

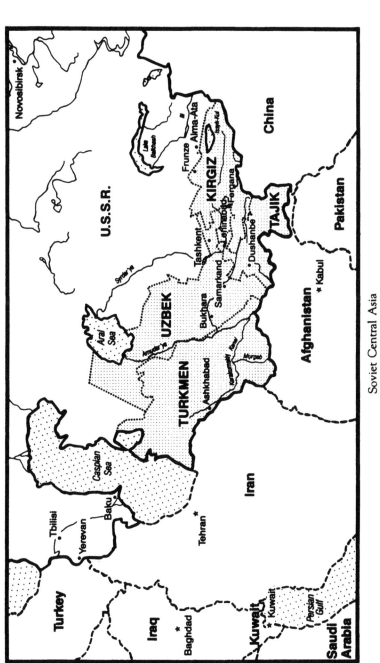

Soviet Central Asia

PREFACE

At a conference held at the University of London in 1987, I discussed the Central Asian question with a high Soviet official who is also a leading specialist on the Islamic East. I asked him whether he would not agree that the new Kremlin leadership shows too little flexibility in its nationality policy, underestimates nationality discontent, and failed to draw the right conclusions from the unrest in Alma Ata. I added that the liberalization of public life and glasnost must inescapably stir up nationalist movements in the Soviet republics (Central Asia included), creating an explosive situation. The official smiled ironically and, in reply, asked whether I seriously think that the Soviet leaders will put a nationalist outburst like that in Alma Ata higher on the agenda than other, more important, problems. "We have quite different 'sore points' right now. So far as the discontent of Uzbeks, Kazakhs, and the others is concerned, we'll quickly put things in order with them. That is what the local authorities are for; they are to prepare the bread and butter; that's their function."

His explanation was stated with such self-assurance, in a tone of such superiority, that I seemed (even in my own eyes) to have been naive. Really, I thought to myself, all these nationality problems are overdramatized by Sovietologists in the West. For 70 years Moscow has reliably regulated the temperature in the multinational caldron of its empire and will not permit it to reach the boiling point. Events in Alma Ata and other petty outbursts of nationalism represent nothing more than minor disturbances, whose significance should not be exaggerated.

Subsequent events, however, have demonstrated that my Soviet interlocutor was too optimistic: the explosive nationality issue exists not only in the imagination of Western experts, and Moscow is by no means able to control the development of nationalist movements on the periphery of its empire. The sudden eruption of the violent Armenian–Azerbaijanian conflict revealed the Kremlin's lack of preparedness and its confusion. And the Armenian–Azerbaijanian conflict is nothing more than a small ripple on the surface; the real storm will come from the Islamic peoples of Central Asia.

Certainly the Soviet press provides ample material to chart the gravity of the problems in that part of the Soviet Union. The waves of an Islamic renaissance have rolled as far as Soviet Central Asia. After the 70 years that Moscow has devoted to the extirpation of Islam, Igor Beliaev, a Soviet specialist on Islam, wrote the following on May 20, 1987, in *Literaturnaia gazeta*: "Facts of a truly horrifying character are continually coming to light in our Central Asian republics. This area provides a very hospitable environment [for Islam]; [it has] a kind of Islamic infrastructure—regardless of whether one calls it religious or nationalistic." That kind of acknowledgment in the Soviet press is without precedent.

Interest in Central Asia has been sharpened by the events in Alma Ata. For the most part, attention has focused on a variety of phenomena—eruptions of nationalist or Islamic fervor, the appointment of outsiders to replace the aging and corrupt cadres from the local nationality, and the criminal prosecution of local mafias. That focus on the sensational, however, has led to "an excessive stress on complexity and excessive interest in the exotic."[1] Such material may generate good journalistic copy, but it manifestly fails to provide a structured analysis of the fundamental issues and dynamics that underlie the unrest and instability. It is not the mere replacement of Kunaevs with Kolbins that matters; rather, it is a far more pervasive "repression"—a complex of social and economic policies—that has caused Central Asia's economic level, social sphere, and living standard to fall ever further behind those in the non-Moslem regions of the USSR.

To counteract such sentiments, Soviet propagandists have trumpeted the achievements of Soviet Central Asia and compared them with conditions in such Moslem countries as

Afghanistan and Egypt. It is obvious why the comparison conveniently forgets Saudi Arabia or Kuwait; what is more telling is that it also omits other republics and regions in the USSR. So far as the population of this Moslem region is concerned, the propagandists' artful comparisons with Egypt or Pakistan are an empty abstraction. Far more relevant is that Central Asia is fully aware that in Kiev one can easily purchase meat in government stores, whereas in Ashkhabad it must be bought at the market—and at three times what it costs in state shops. And the Uzbeks and Tajiks know that in Minsk, because of the labor shortage, one can easily obtain a good job and in a modern specialty but in Tashkent or Dushanbe hardly anyone can do that. They know too that it is no problem to buy an automobile in Sverdlovsk, whereas one must wait years to obtain one in Samarkand. Such glaring contrasts evoke a feeling of discrimination among Uzbeks, Tajiks, Turkmens, and others.

Central Asia now has an active stratum of nationalistically minded scholars, intellectuals, economists, and sociologists who shape the thinking in broader circles of each nationality's intelligentsia. These people hold prominent positions in the republic establishment and thus are well informed on Moscow's economic and nationality policy. As a result, they understand that the top-priority goals of the new regime (namely, accelerated replacement of fixed capital in industry; concentration of modernization resources in existing factories, primarily machine-building plants, with minimal construction of new enterprises) mean an increased investment quota for the western regions of the USSR, where 80 percent of Soviet industrial production (and 90 percent of machine building) are currently concentrated. The very terms of this policy mean that the resolution of economic problems in Central Asia will be deferred to some indefinite future.

The demographic problem is of particular concern: Central Asia has the highest population growth of any area in the USSR. But, in making regional allocations of investment, Moscow disregards this demographic factor, declining to increase accordingly that region's share of the country's investment resources, to develop labor-intensive industries and create new employment opportunities, or to increase investment in the consumer sphere and social infrastructure.

Gorbachev said recently that the economic situation in the USSR is "on the verge of crisis." Even that language, however, is hardly adequate to describe the gravity of the situation in the Central Asian economy. But the Gorbachev regime has thus far failed to address the Central Asian problem; its economic program (embodied in the current five-year plan) gives no reason to anticipate higher investment in Central Asia. Although Gorbachev in his speech to the Central Committee plenum in June 1987 called for a strengthening of the regional approach to economic planning, this appears to have been more idle rhetoric. The role of national republics in deciding on the allocation of investment (and other economic resources) remains insignificant.

In the foreseeable future, economic problems in Central Asia will continue to worsen. This region will fall further and further behind the rest of the country, and that will inevitably create dissatisfaction (among ethnic cadres as well as the general populace) with Moscow's policy. Only if the Gorbachev regime undertakes radical economic reform could one expect substantial improvement in conditions in Central Asia. But that kind of reform—tantamount to the establishment of a market economy—seems highly improbable, at least as long as the existing political structure is preserved.

•   •   •   •

The term "Central Asia," as used in *Soviet Central Asia: "A Tragic Experiment,"* embraces the four Soviet republics of Uzbekistan, Tajikistan, Turkmenistan, and Kirghizia. In Soviet economic and geographic usage, these republics constitute a single, separate economic region. In the geographic literature, there is a much broader concept of Central or Inner Asia that includes not only this part of the Soviet Union, but also other landlocked Asian areas such as Afghanistan, Western China (with Tibet), and Mongolia. Those areas are obviously beyond the scope of this book, which is concerned only with the Soviet Union.

Some Western writers on the USSR extend the definition

of Soviet Central Asia to cover not only the four republics considered here, but also Kazakhstan'. There is some justification for this, since the Kazakhs are closely related to the Uzbeks, Tajiks, Turkmens, and Kirghiz by ties of proximity, shared historical experience, culture, and (except in the case of the Iranian Tajiks) language. On the other hand, Russian immigration has made the Kazakhs a minority in their own republic, much of whose vast territory (twice that of the other four republics taken together) is settled almost exclusively by Russians and other European nationalities.

For the sake of clarity and simplicity, I have chosen here to follow the Soviet definition of "Central Asia," but the reader should be aware of its alternative uses.

The Central Asian economic region, then, occupies an area of 1.3 million square kilometers (approximately half a million square miles) or the equivalent of Great Britain, France, Germany, and Greece combined. The population of the four republics in 1986 was 31.4 million, of which about four-fifths consisted of nationalities of Moslem origin. This region, which until the 1920s was know as Turkestan (Land of Turks), was conquered by Russia in the nineteenth century. Following the October Revolution, it, became a target of Sovietization.

There are two irreconcilable pictures of how Soviet power came to Central Asia. The current Soviet version stresses the "voluntary" nature of this process, depicting it as an exercise in self-determination based on a fundamental community of interests between the oppressed ex-colonial peoples of the territory and the Russian proletariat. Western specialists, by contrast, have emphasized the role of force and violence in establishing Soviet rule in the territory.

An earlier Soviet version of how Soviet rule was imposed on Central Asia tends to substantiate Western views. In 1920, a writer in *Zhizn' Natsional'nostei* (no. 16, June 2), the organ of the People's Commissariat of Nationalities (then headed by Joseph Stalin), admitted that Moscow's approach resembled nothing less than an "attitude of plundering colonizers accustomed to looking down on the native population 'like cattle'!" The writer, who signed with the initials "V.K.," added that, "Totally unjustified mass exterminations of the local population, unfortunately, took place in this struggle," concluding that the result was conversion of a class struggle into a national war of liberation. (There is some evidence that the author of these words was none other than Valerian V. Kuibyshev, who had been one of a troika appointed by Lenin to deal with Central Asian matters, and who is still enshrined in the pantheon of Soviet Communist saints.)

This study draws on a wide variety of published sources. The backbone of hard analysis derives from a careful sifting and collating of official statistics that, for all their taciturnity and deliberate lacunae, nevertheless reveal the underlying structural problems that resist facile reformism and political dissimulation. To these statistical data that Western Sovietologists have long used (if not always with sufficient care and skepticism), glasnost has added an important new source: the rich commentaries that appear in enormous volume in the Soviet press. The first-hand descriptions, relatively candid statements by central and regional economists, and periodic "discussions" shed valuable light on the problems and politics of reform in Central Asia's economy.

This study does not pretend to be an exhaustive, definitive analysis of the Central Asian economy and its problems. Rather, it addresses the fundamental issues that seem most important and peculiar to that region. Chapter 1 describes the historical background and distinctive features of Soviet economic policy making, to delineate how Central Asia fits into the larger scheme of center-local decision making. Chapter 2 examines the special (and extremely specialized) role of Central Asia in the Soviet economy. The next four chapters then consider in detail key aspects of the Central Asian economy—industrial development, cotton production, water resources, and labor. Chapters 7 and 8 explore the social ramifications of this region's economy, examining the effects on living conditions and on the development of the "shadow economy." Chapter 9 examines the impact of the new Gorbachev policies on the region, and the final chapter considers the prospects for development in Central Asia.

ACKNOWLEDGMENTS

This book is based on research funded by the National Council for Soviet and East European Research.

It is my pleasant duty to thank Messrs. Paul A. Goble, Ed A. Hewett, and Vladimir I. Toumanoff for their valuable comments on the manuscript.

I would also like to express my gratitude to Alec Nove and Gertrude Schroeder for their pioneering work on the Central Asian economy.

The book greatly benefitted from discussions with Central Asia specialists including Donald Carlisle, James Critchlow, William Fierman, James Gillula, Lubomyr Hajda, Nancy Lubin, Beatrice Manz, Aleksandr Nekrich, Martha Brill Olcott, Teresa Rakowska-Harmstone, and S. Enders Wimbush. Lastly, it would be difficult to exaggerate the influence of the academic atmosphere of the Russian Research Center at Harvard, where it has been my good fortune to work for many years. Of course, the final responsibility for the work is entirely my own.

CHAPTER 1

Introduction: Regional Economic Policy in the USSR

The conflict between regionalism and centralism in the economic development of the USSR is a contradiction that neither theory nor practice has been able to resolve in the 70 years that the Soviet state has been in existence. All efforts to find an optimal relationship between these two poles of economic organization have come to nought. In the first years of the Soviet state, it was quite popular to cite the Leninist dictum about the exceptional importance of "the model organization of the small, integral unit"—with the stress on the "integral unit," that is, not a single enterprise, not an individual branch of the economy, but an aggregate of all economic relations, "the sum of the entire economy, if only for a small area."[1] Still more to the point is another of Lenin's dicta: "Democratic centralism (a euphemism for the Soviet political system) in no wise excludes but, on the contrary, presupposes, the most complete freedom of various localities and even various collectivities or communes (*obshchiny*) in the state to work out the diverse forms of state, public and economic life."[2]

It is significant that, among the plethora of Leninist quotations bandied about by Soviet leaders and the Soviet mass media in the last two decades, one does *not* find these two theses, which bear so fundamentally on economic and nationality policy. And that is hardly surprising: the entire practical activity of the regime is based on two principles diametrically opposed to the Leninist dicta—lack of freedom for local areas and communal collectives, and their subordination to Moscow.

1

In an authoritarian state of the Soviet type, it is natural for the interests of the state to diverge sharply from those of local society. The command structure of economic management, the all-encompassing planning for every sphere of economic activity by a single center, the rigidly centralized distribution of economic resources, the enormous territorial expanse of the USSR—all this deprives particular territorial economic entities of any substantial independence. For ideologists of Soviet economic planning, the insolubility of the problem rests in the incompatibility of two basic conceptions—that of proportional development of regional economies and that of the superior interests of a single national economy (which are determined less by economic than by political considerations). Since the 1920s, countless publications on this question have offered nothing more than verbal tightrope walking and, as we shall see, have had little impact on the actual practice of planning.

Territorial Economic Planning in the Era of Industrialization and the Prewar Years

The first Soviet five-year plan (1928–1932) contained a special section on regional economics. It addressed general problems of the regional economy and its specialization, interregional relations, growth rates, and the role of regions in the national economy. It also presented an exhaustive analysis of the economy in each region in the USSR and outlined the prospects for its development. The first five-year plan incorporated twenty-four territorial units, formed by merging economic and administrative divisions of the country.

This was the apogee of regionalism in Soviet economic planning. A statement by Valerian Kuibyshev (then the chairman of Gosplan, the state planning agency) in May 1931 illustrated the prevailing attitude: "Only attention to the complex development of the entire economy of a given region will yield a literate, economically defensible plan for a given district, for a given region, and hence for the entire national economy of the Soviet Union. . . . A territorial or

2

regional division must be sustained as a principle from the very beginning."[3] Never again did a five-year plan give so much attention to the regional dimension of the economy.

The second five-year plan (1933–1937) was constructed according to purely administrative-territorial principles. As a result, economic regions and their problems received considerably less attention. This plan did allow for 32 regional units (union and autonomous republics, and districts), but these were administrative-territorial, not economic, units.

The end of the second five-year plan inaugurated a process of specialization and centralization in industrial administration, and the division of industry into branches and subordinate units. In the administrative sphere this process led to the enlargement of VSKNKh (All-Russian Council of the National Economy) and the formation of additional economic ministries ("people's commissariats"). The emergence of departmentalism in administration and planning in industry meant a corresponding retreat from the regional conception of economic planning. Interest in the complex economic development of individual geographic areas declined noticeably.

As the third five-year plan (1938–1942) was being prepared, primary responsibility for the regional dimension devolved on union republics. The preceding plan had amply demonstrated, however, that effective planning to resolve large-scale territorial problems required the demarcation of regions larger than administrative areas (which then numbered about 70). To address that need, the plan distinguished, in addition to the union republics, nine main economic regions, but this had little effect on the growth of centralized, production-branch planning and management.

The further centralization of administration in the third five-year plan resulted in planning that was increasingly simplified and determined by the branches of industrial production and by the administrative units subordinate to the people's commissariats. Regional economic planning was relegated to a low priority; the complex economic development of regions and union republics remained only an idea, devoid of practical expression.

During World War II, Gosplan developed a new territorial

3

division that split the country into 13 economic regions. Its basis was a set of nine economic regions of the Russian Soviet Federal Socialist Republic (RSFSR) which had been established as the third five-year plan was being prepared. To these were added four supplementary regions, created by clustering the other union republics (Central Asia and Kazakhstan; Transcaucasus; the South; the West). This regional division lasted until 1960.

From Postwar Recovery to Khrushchev's Sovnarkhozy

In the first years after World War II, economic administration was centralized still further. Less and less attention was given to complex, multifaceted development of the economy in regions and republics. Although the fourth five-year plan (1946–1950) still set goals for the reconstruction of the economy in union republics, the fifth plan (1951–1955) altogether lacked a section devoted to the economy of the republics or the economic regions.[4] Planning focused only on sectors and branches of the economy on a national level; the plan allocated resources not by region or republic, but by ministerial branch. It assigned an insignificant share of industries to union republics and gave them control over a mere 5 percent of new investment capital.[5] The remaining 95 percent was allocated to all-union ministries, which, in turn, distributed these funds across the country, but without concern for the economic development of republics. In short, the allocation of investment took into account only the interests of branch development for the national economy, without regard to the regional aspect, and, in many cases, positively inflicted harm on such local interests.

This situation changed radically in the sixth five-year plan (1956–1958), which marked a transition to a territorial system of economic administration, the establishment of *sovnarkhozy* (regional economic boards), and the abolition of various ministries. In 1961 the share of industry under the control of *sovnarkhozy* reached 93 percent, and their share of capital investment amounted to 77 percent.[6]

It would be wrong, however, to exaggerate the effect of

4

the *sovnarkhozy* in improving the territorial balance of the economy. The majority of newly established economic regions were merely administrative-territorial formations, not authentic economic units. At the same time, as the *sovnarkhozy* endeavored to ensure full development of a self-contained economic unit, they often established enterprises that were not economically viable, that did not mesh with the existing industrial structure and substructure, that were alien to the economic traditions and skills of the local population, or that failed to match the raw material and energy endowments of a given region. The artificial separation of regions that had long been closely linked in economic terms caused the economy of each to become disjointed and isolated.

To overcome these and many other shortcomings, an effort was made at the end of 1962 to merge the *sovnarkhozy* into larger units. Thus, the 105 economic administrative regions originally foreseen in 1957 were reduced to just 47 units. But this change came only at the end of the *sovnarkhoz* experiment and hence did not have time to produce tangible results. In addition, the *sovnarkhozy* were stripped of their control over the construction industry, which was transferred to the governments of union republics; that change, however, disrupted the nexus between industry and construction and led to complete disorder in the planning process. As a result of these ill-advised experiments (initiated by Khrushchev), the positive elements in regional planning and the opportunities created by a territorial organization of the economy were compromised and lost.

The Post-Sovnarkhoz Era: Centralism Triumphant

The liquidation of the *sovnarkhozy* and the return to production-branch administration of the economy in 1965 raised the specter of a retreat to economic planning that, in effect, would totally ignore regional interests. Aleksei Kosygin, who was premier at the time, foresaw this danger and noted in his report at a Central Committee plenum in September 1965 that a system of production-branch administration increased "the significance of reconciling the development of various economic branches and the economic regions of the country."[7] Leonid Brezhnev addressed this issue still more pointedly in his report to the twenty-third congress of the Communist Party of the Soviet Union (CPSU) in 1966: "I would like to discourage people in the ministries from attempting to revive the *narrowly ministerial, special-interest approach* [emphasis added] which was committed by previous ministries."[8] Brezhnev had in mind the hypertrophy of the production-branch approach to economic planning that had prevailed before the formation of the *sovnarkhozy*. But as the centralized production-branch system of economic administration gained control over operational plans and the five-year plan, the goals of a proportionate, complex development of regions and republics became increasingly remote.

To be sure, the theory of territorial planning continued to develop, and economic-mathematical methods suitable for economic regionalization ostensibly played an ever greater role. In practice, however, the regional approach figured only in planning exercises for the long-term economic development of the country. The fact is that no one—neither ministries (operating through their subordinate scientific and research centers) nor Gosplan itself—paid any serious attention to the twenty- and thirty-year horizons of these so-called general schemes for development and distribution. Rather, they regarded these exercises as an expensive game, conducted to gratify the fantasies of Soviet leaders and to create the illusion that optimal planning actually exists and determines economic development in the USSR.

In the 1970s a new conception of "territorial production complexes" was put forward. Scholars such as Viktor Krasovskii and Viktor Bogachev developed the idea of "large territorial investment programs." Many publications, discussions, and conferences were devoted to pursuing this line of territorial planning.

But this activity never went beyond the realm of pure theory and, for all practical purposes, had no effect on current, short-term planning. The latter was dictated, rather, by the interests of the ministries; hence, the territorial structure of industry was modified only insofar as a given ministry deemed it profitable or not to place a certain production capacity in a particular area. One might well argue that never before in Soviet history had economic planning been so totally sacrificed to the dictates of a rigid, centralized production-branch administration; never before had regional proportions been so disregarded as in the era of "mature Brezhnevism."

To be sure, there were some activities that intersected the economic-geographic map of Soviet Asia. Such interministerial, large-scale territorial projects included the Siberian fuel and energy complex, BAM (the Baikal-Amur railway line), and the South Tajikistan complex. But all these projects were based on ideas that antedated the Brezhnev era.

Thus the basic contours of the gigantic project for BAM were presented in a five-year plan for railway construction adopted in November 1916—still in the tsarist period. This plan foresaw the construction of a railway line from the northern extremity of Baikal to the Amur; the line was incorporated in the plan under the name of the Great Northern Route.

Responsibility for preparing this plan was assigned to the distinguished Russian scholar Petr Semenov-Tian-Shanskii, and at the time he wrote: "The enormous state and world significance [of this railway line] is so self-evident that its construction must in any event be given a high (if not the highest) priority."[9] But the revolutionary turmoil that erupted soon afterward prevented construction of the railway and caused the entire proposal to be tabled for several decades. Not until the 1940s and 1950s were geologic and geodesic investigations on individual parts of the planned line undertaken, and not until the 1970s, after the Soviet leadership recognized the very real possibility of armed conflict with China, was the decision to construct BAM finally made.

It is fair to assume that the Soviet leadership fully understood what a return to the ministerial system of industrial production meant: a renewed predominance of departmentalism—with all the negative consequences for the national economy that were all too familiar. Particular anxiety was reflected in Kosygin's statements on this subject after he became chairman of the Council of Ministers in October 1964. Kosygin attempted to prevent the concentration in the hands of the ministries of responsibility for planning the regional distribution 'of industry, and, at his initiative, Moscow defined the powers of union republics in planning, construction, and other sectors of the economy.

Under the new rules, union republics (besides preparing plans for the economy directly under their jurisdiction) were to prepare recommendations (but not plans) for the development of industries directly subject to the central ministries but located in their territory. In addition, union republics were given the right to "review" certain intersector problems of industrial development and long-range planning that were being worked out by the ministries. "In this way," Kosygin declared at the Central Committee plenum in September 1966, "the Gosplans of union republics will become active organs in solving questions of industrial development in the republic as a whole, even as the interests of the national economy are taken into account. This will permit union republics to avert the manifestation of a tendency toward vested interests by particular central ministries."[10]

The attempts to strike a compromise, however—between the production-branch and territorial approaches to planning and administration, between departmentalism and regionalism —failed once again. Control of industrial production was largely concentrated in the ministries, which—as ever—pursued their own vested interests. It should also be emphasized that the republic Gosplans had no capacity for serious work on plans for the development and distribution of industry, because the majority of scientific and engineering institutes and economic planning centers active in such work were under the direct jurisdiction of the ministries. Hence, the republic organizations had neither the authority nor the apparatus to pose a serious challenge to the central organs.

In practice, the heads of all-union ministries listened politely to the proposals from union republics and made a show of taking their criticisms and wishes into account. But

8

because the union republics' recommendations were nonbinding, central ministries had no need to pay them much heed. And this was the limit of regional input into planning; only union republics, not economic regions, had even a formal right and a planning organization (the main link in territorial planning at the present time).

In assessing the relationship between production-branch and territorial planning, one must keep in mind the role of regional party committees in defending their regions' economic interests against Moscow's demands. By using personal influence, the head of a particular republican or oblast committee can often obtain approval for the construction of an enterprise even when this runs contrary to the wishes of the responsible ministry. In general, the party organizations play a primary role in the development of regional and republic economies. This role often brings them into conflict with the industrial-branch ministries, and they frequently emerge the victor in such clashes.

Not all of the 15 union republics, however, have the same influence in planning their economic development. The Ukraine has considerable power, republics in the Transcaucasus much less. (I leave aside the RSFSR, which only in formal terms can be placed in the same category with the other republics.) Still, even the Ukrainian leadership has limited freedom to make decisions about the reconstruction of existing facilities and the creation of new ones; the dictates of central ministries are almost irresistible. It would likewise be wrong to equate the economic regions of the RSFSR in this respect, for some—most notably, Western and Eastern Siberia and the Far East—have far greater clout than do the European regions.

Econometric Models in Regional
Economic Planning

Plans for the optimal development and distribution of industrial branches have also had a destructive influence on the balance of economic growth in the RSFSR and union republics. These plans enjoyed extraordinary favor in

Gosplan and the production-branch ministries in the 1960s and 1970s and played a major role in shaping Soviet economic policy. The plans derived from the work of Vasilii Nemchinov, the founder of the contemporary Soviet econometric school. Nemchinov tackled the problem of the rational distribution of production forces but defined the problem on an all-union scale, to be solved through economic-mathematical methods. In other words, he proposed to construct a model for the optimal combination of natural resources with centers for production and consumption.

Nemchinov's basic idea, however, failed to become the basis for an integrated plan. One reason was poor preparation of these plans, which, above all, suffered from insufficient coordination at the level of the national economy. Second, the Nemchinov conception was bedeviled by unresolved methodological problems that posed a major impediment to its practical application. Third, it was weakened by contradictions in determining investment strategy and norms. In brief, it replaced the regional approach with the all-union production branch, but the sum of branch projects (given the lack of coordination, the vague criteria for optimization, and the unreliable information base) could not provide the basis for current or long-range territorial planning of industry. As a result, the idea proved stillborn. What was worse, many scientific and planning institutes were forced to play this game, and these included such leading scientific centers as the Central Economic-Mathematic Institute (Moscow), the Institute for Economics and the Organization of Industrial Production (Novosibirsk), and Gosplan's Council for the Distribution of Production Forces. As a result, significant human and financial resources were diverted from real regional research.

A second approach to the application of mathematic models to territorial planning—which, in theory, held greater promise—consisted of the preparation of territorial (regional) balances for production among branches and for the distribution of output. These models determine, in quantitative terms, the proportion of development among branches, the structural characteristics of the economy, and the interaction among economic branches within union

10

republics and economic regions, as well as the economic ties among them.

This approach underwent significant development. In 1970 a series of theoretical works on regional balances among sectors and on optimal planning for regional economies was published; in addition, many variants of interregional and interbranch models were published.

Despite this work, the development of economic-mathematical modeling did not have a major impact or lead to an improvement in the territorial distribution of industry in the USSR as a whole or in the individual republics and regions. Although many factors explain the failure of repeated efforts to apply econometric methods to Soviet territorial planning, the most fundamental is the contradiction between departmentalism and localism—that is, between the interests of central ministries and those of particular regions.

The difficulty of applying the new methods is greatly compounded by the shortage of reliable statistical data. That problem is particularly acute for republic and regional economies, because the republican statistical volumes contain exceedingly sparse data on the regional economy. Indeed, that fund of data has been shrinking with each passing year. For example, since 1975 the statistical volumes for the RSFSR have ceased to publish statistics on its component economic regions. Likewise, many of the republican statistical volumes lack even such basic information as data on the national income.

A listing of the indicators for which statistical information is lacking and that are essential for serious regional planning (through the application of either econometric modeling or more traditional methods) would occupy considerable space. A good example is the statistics on transportation and territorial economic ties. The current statistics on transportation are considerably less complete than those available in the 1920s, when the linkages between divisions and stations on the railway line were worked out. Now, to the best of my knowledge, the transportation flows are published only for five aggregated groups of mass cargoes (coal, oil and petroleum products, iron ore, timber products, and cement). Annual statistical data on the shipping of all forms of transportation (with distribution according to the region of import and export) are prepared for 22 categories of cargo, but 15 of these simply comprise different types of steel. Data on the shipment of machines and equipment, or the products of the chemical, food, light, and other industries are exceedingly sparse. Statistical data in monetary terms are altogether lacking for territorial economic relations, for the redistribution of wealth among various regions, and for inter-regional imports and exports. Given this data base, it is not surprising that nothing significant can be achieved by optimizing, balancing, or other calculations, however sophisticated the methods might be.

Economic Regions: Theory and Practice

It is important to discuss briefly the basic conception of "economic region" (*ekonomicheskii raion*) within the context of contemporary Soviet usage and classification of areas.

A Soviet economic encyclopedia offers the following definition of this basic term: "An economic region represents a part of the national economy that is characterized by a definite territory, distinct natural and economic conditions, and a historically based specialization of production based on a territorial social division of labor." In addition, official Soviet reference works draw a clear distinction between the formation of economic regions under capitalism and under socialism: "Under capitalism, the formation and development of economic regions occur spontaneously and are accompanied by an acute competitive struggle; the development of a given sector in one district often results in the demise in others. But under socialism economic regions attain *a complex, planned development* [emphasis added], their specialization is coordinated with the rational distribution of productive forces, with the development in districts of a complex of branches and production—which raise the efficiency of the economy and provide for the multisided use of natural, human, and technical resources of a region in the interests of increasing the general economic capacity of the country. As the productive capacities of the country develop, so too is

12

there a further improvement in the development of regional economies, *in the formulation of new economic regions through the aggregation of existing ones*" [emphasis added].[11]

Two points are important here: (1) the notion that economic regions should have proportionate development, that is, that their economic structure should be improved in a rational, planned fashion; and (2) that economic planning for regions should be dynamic, changing in response to geographic shifts in the national economy.

Most Soviet economists and planners see the conception of an economic region in somewhat abstract terms. In their opinion, the goals for the development of an economic region are simultaneously to increase harmony with other regions and the complexity of the region's own economy.

To what degree does the present division of the country into economic regions correspond to this view? Very little: the definition of economic regions in the USSR derives less from the establishment of objective territorial and economic complexes than from noneconomic goals. How else can one explain the fact that the network of economic regions created a quarter of a century ago has gone unchanged to the present day? That network has remained astonishingly rigid despite substantial changes in the geographic distribution of industry and despite statements by leading Soviet specialists (including specialists from the Council on Productive Forces of Gosplan USSR) that it would be useful to recast regions into larger aggregates, or even to reconstruct the network.

Before World War II, the economic regions of the country were considerably more flexible, reflecting a genuine search for optimal relations between territorial and industrial planning. Both in the first plan for economic development (the GOELRO plan for electrification) and in the early five-year plans, the regional structure of the economy was subordinated to established territorial structures or new ones established in remote regions. The 1920s constituted a period of intensive theoretical and methodological exploration in this sphere. Representatives of the "nomographic" school sought to establish quantitative correlations and to devise mathematical relationships among territorial elements of the economy. To do so, they produced a large number of detailed studies on the economic geography of various regions and national republics. Many of these studies were incorporated in the 1928 methodological guidelines for the preparation of the first five-year plan. These guidelines included long-term prospects for the development of the economy in republics and newly established regions (oblasts) as well as the distribution of goals among economic regions.

One primary goal of Gosplan's regional economic policy was to achieve unity and integrity in its system of economic and administrative divisions. That goal, however, was never achieved. As the administrative and territorial decisions were implemented, attention was given to a variety of factors, including nationality policy. But relatively little attention was given to the economic regionalization of the country. More important to Soviet leaders was something quite different— administrative and management considerations. There is little point here in speculating how much policy was shaped by the doctrine of "divide and rule." But one finds decisions that appear highly illogical in terms of regional economic policy or physical geography. It was highly anomalous, for example, to assign the Chimkent oblast to Kazakhstan and not to Central Asia; or the eastern Donbas (Rostov oblast) to the RSFSR rather than to the rest of the Donbas in the Ukraine. One could adduce many more such examples where natural economic and geographic bonds were sundered by the drawing of arbitrary administrative borders.

The first plan based on economic regionalization, prepared by Gosplan for GOELRO in 1921–1922, divided the RSFSR (excluding Siberia and the Far East) into 21 regions. The economic region was set apart as a combined production aggregate, constructed broadly in terms of its energy resources and designed with the optimal level of a complete (but not closed) economy. This first plan also produced the following formulation of an economic region, which, in my view, is still the best to appear in Soviet literature: "In form, a region (*raion*) should be distinguished as a unique and (so far as possible) an economically complete territory of the country, which, because of a combination of natural peculiarities, cultural accumulations from the past, and population (with its preparation for productive activity),

14

would constitute one of the links in the general chain of the national economy."[12] Over the ensuing decades, however, interest in regionalism gradually atrophied as centralized, production-branch planning came to dominate planning and management.

In April 1961, Soviet authorities tackled the problem again and adopted a new scheme to reshape the network of economic regions. It first established 17 such regions and, after minor adjustments in September 1963, settled on 18 regions. This network, which still exists, divides the territory of the USSR for purposes of economic planning into the following regions: the Northwest, Central, Volga-Viatka, Central Blacksoil, Volga, North Caucasus, Urals, West Siberian, East Siberian, Far East (in the RSFSR); Donets and Dnieper, Southwest, and South (in the Ukraine); Beloruss (in Belorussia); and Kazakhstan. Republics that have smaller territories and close ethnic and economic ties were combined into larger aggregates—the Baltic region (Lithuania, Latvia, and Estonia), Transcaucasus (Georgia, Azerbaijan, Armenia), and Central Asia (Uzbekistan, Tadjikistan, Turkmenistan, and Kirghizia). Curiously, this system over-looked the small agrarian republic of Moldavia, which stands independently as a union republic. The sole change since 1963 was the creation of the Northern economic region, as distinct from the Northwest region, in 1982.

The striking fact is that this basic structure has remained virtually intact, notwithstanding substantial changes in regional economies over the last 25 years. Objective changes in the geographic distribution of industry (with the emergence of new industrial zones and elimination of old ones) between the 1960s and the 1980s should have resulted in corresponding changes in economic regionalization. Such adjustments were essential, if for no other reason than for the preparation of long-term plans. In fact, Soviet economic geographers did prepare and propose to Gosplan many projects for new economic regions.[13] Western Siberia can serve as a good example. It was, above all, senseless to combine the southern and northern zones of this area into a single economic district. But why, notwithstanding this, has this network of economic regions remained unchanged?

The Overlap of Military and
Economic Regions

When I raised this question with Professor Lev Iudovich, he advanced a hypothesis that deserves closer attention: namely, the 1961 network of economic regions coincides almost exactly with the system of military districts within the USSR. The overlap strongly suggests that Soviet military-economic doctrine envisages a wartime division of the country into military-economic territorial complexes; that it has devised its plans for mobilization and operation of the economy under wartime conditions.

Let us examine the comparative structure of military and economic regions in the USSR. As Table 1.1 shows, the country is divided into 16 military districts and 19 economic regions.[14] The coincidence is remarkable.

An examination of the Northern economic region reveals how profoundly extraeconomic considerations have intruded into the structure of regional economies. In November 1982 this area was divided in two—the northern and western regions. The western region (whose heart is Leningrad, with its vast scientific and military resources (corresponds to the Leningrad Military District. The question naturally arises why it was necessary to distinguish and separate precisely this Northern Region (which included the Arkhangel'sk, Vologda Murmansk oblasts and the autonomous republics of Komi and Karelia). Did significant changes in industrial development transpire in this northern section of the European part of the USSR? If so, they were far less significant than those in many other regions of the USSR where the economic network remained unaltered. This example leads to the conclusion that the structure of economic regions is subordinate to the goals of military-economic policy. In other words, the Northern economic region was created as an economic structure to support the Arctic military theater, including the Northern Fleet, which, it seems, acquired particular importance in Soviet strategic planning in the 1970s. To be sure, Soviet publications provide no explicit evidence to substantiate this hypothesis. But it bears noting that the arguments advanced in the press about the utility of

16

Table 1.1   Geographic Structure of Military Districts and Soviet Economic Regions

Military District	Economic Region
Baltic	Baltic (Estonia, Lithuania, Latvia, and Kaliningrad)
Leningrad	Western, Northern
Belorussian	Belorussian
Moscow	Central, Central-Blacksoil and Volga-Viatka
Kiev	Donets-Dnieper
Carpathian	Southwestern (Ukrainian)
Odessa	Southern (Ukrainian)
North Caucasus	North Caucasus
Urals	Urals
Volga	Volga
Siberian	West Siberian
Baikal	East Siberian
Far Eastern	Far Eastern
Transcaucasus	Transcaucasus (Georgia, Armenia, and Azerbaijan)
Turkestan	Central Asian (Uzbekistan, Tadjikistan, Turkmenistan)
Central Asian	Kazakhstan; Kirghizia (part of Central Asian Econ. Region)

this economic region (relating to the task of exploiting the natural resources of the Kola Peninsula) are simply not persuasive. The task of exploiting the natural resources in the northern part of Western Siberia is no less great, yet there have been no changes in the economic regionalization of this enormous territory.

Central Asia as a Single Economic Region

Is it valid to regard Central Asia as an integrated economy, when in fact it consists of four separate administrative units

17

(union republics)? Do the separate Uzbek, Tadjik, Kirghiz, and Turkmen republics constitute a monolithic economic unit? How indeed did the political-administrative structure in Central Asia develop in the Soviet era?

Moscow established its first administrative division for Central Asia (Turkestan) in 1924–1925. Given the general religious (Islamic) and social homogeneity of the region, it seems that the dominant motive behind Moscow's decision to create four republics was the venerable principle of *divide et impera.* That strategy was doubtless helpful in the campaign to suppress the rebellions and uprisings that persisted in this region after the civil war had been officially terminated.

But the configuration of the four republics that finally emerged was—with the exception of Turkmenia—highly complicated and arbitrary, failing to coincide with any natural frontiers or boundaries. The result was something similar to the medieval open-field agrarian system, with parts of one republic wedged inside another to form all kinds of islands and peninsulas. Although the territory of Central Asia was ostensibly divided on the basis of nationality, the ethnic composition was actually mixed in a number of localities. For instance, the population of Fergana valley was administratively part of Uzbekistan but included almost equal numbers of Uzbeks, Tadjiks, Kirghiz, and other indigenous groups.

Another example of this process is offered by the South Kazakhstan oblast, with its capital in Chimkent: although the area formed an organic part of Uzbekistan (in ethnic composition, natural features, and economic ties), it was artificially assigned to Kazakhstan. Other cases could be cited as well. [15]

Contiguous regions within the Central Asian republics, as a rule, have similar natural conditions, similar economic structures, common irrigation systems, and often a similar ethnic composition. The economic integration of Central Asia has promoted, at various times, the emergence of higher party and state economic organs that encompass the entire region. Examples include the Central Asian Bureau of the CPSU (first established in 1924, then revived in

18

1962–1965); the Central Asian *sovnarkhoz*; the State Committee for Cotton Cultivation; the State Committee for Construction and Building in Central Asia; the Ministry of Construction and Building in Central Asia; and a host of regionwide organs established in the Khrushchev era and dismantled by Brezhnev. Two of their major functions were to overcome the lack of coordination among departments and republics and to create an integrated Central Asian economy. From a strictly economic point of view, there are good grounds for regarding the Central Asian republics as a unified region, with its own particular tasks in the economic development of the USSR.

•   •   •   •

The present study compares various aspects of the economy of Central Asia with the economy of the USSR as a whole and the economies of other regions, the Baltic and Transcaucasus in particular. All three might justifiably be called national regions, to distinguish them from the economic regions of the RSFSR, the Ukraine, and Belorussia, which are populated primarily by Slavs—the dominant ethnic group in the USSR, with a common ethnic heritage no weaker than that between Uzbeks and Turkmens.

Kazakhstan represents a special case. Although it borders on Central Asia, it was not incorporated in this study, for several reasons. First, the majority of the population in Kazakhstan is not Kazakh, but a motley of non-Moslem peoples—Russians, Ukrainians, Germans (resettled from the Volga during World War II), and others. Hence, in this important respect, Kazakhstan is quite distinct from Central Asia, where 80 percent of the population consists of indigenous ethnic groups. Second, Kazakhstan is also sharply distinguished from Central Asia in its natural resources as well as its economic geography.

Third, an analysis of the contemporary economic structure of Kazakhstan shows persuasively that it should be treated as a separate economic region. The leading industrial sectors in Kazakhstan are ferrous and nonferrous metallurgy and coal mining (which plays the main role in the energy balance). In Central Asia, the main industrial sectors are cotton processing and related machine building and also oil and gas extraction. The structure of agriculture in Kazakhstan, similarly, is different from that in Central Asia: Kazakhstan concentrates on animal husbandry and cereal culture (in the virgin lands); cotton, the staple in Central Asia, is produced only in Chimkent oblast.

Nevertheless, there is a significant commonality between the contiguous oblasts in Kazakhstan and Central Asia—especially the Kazakh oblasts of Chimkent, Dzhambul, and Alma Ata. These areas are quite similar to neighboring Central Asian republics (in natural resources and economic conditions) and are linked by water resources, by a single energy system, and by the use of mineral resources and pasturelands.

Equalization of Economic Development among Regions and Republics

A key step in improving territorial proportions in the Soviet national economy would be to equalize, or level, economic development among the various regions and republics. The goal of leveling was reiterated in the resolutions of every party congress from the 1920s to the end of the Stalin era. It was reiterated in the program of the CPSU adopted at the twenty-second party congress in 1961. At the next congress, in 1966, Brezhnev declared that "in recent years much has been done so that the political equality of union republics and the friendship of the peoples of the USSR . . . are reinforced by an *equalization* [emphasis added] of the levels of their economic development."[16] In his report on the fiftieth anniversary of the formation of the USSR in 1972, Brezhnev reported that "the goal of equalization of levels of economic development of national republics has been essentially attained. . . ."[17] Paradoxically, the twenty-fifth party congress in 1976 endorsed the following declaration: "On the basis of the unity of our planned socialist economy and the broad initiative of republics, . . . the further equalization of levels of economic development will continue."[18] The realism of the latter assessment found confirmation at the twenty-sixth party congress in 1981, when Brezhnev once again spoke of the need for "more" equalization.[19] It is remarkable that, at

20

the twenty-seventh party congress, neither Gorbachev's report nor any other material emanating from the meeting says anything about this *equalization*.

The core concept of equalization is that the economies of backward republics should be raised to the level of more developed ones. This problem is fraught with enormous political significance, for the promised economic equality among national republics remains a basic slogan in Soviet nationality policy.

But before analyzing the real state of affairs, it is essential to clarify the term *level of economic development* as it is used in Soviet economic geography and in regional economic planning, and what methods are used to measure it.

This term is widely used both in practice and in scholarly literature, but it is given the most disparate definition, depending on the circumstances and the author. The lack of precise definition has inevitably given rise to contradictory conclusions about the economic development in particular regions, and no less important, the methods for achieving this goal.

Thus the *Soviet Economic Encyclopedia* defines "level of economic development" as the "condition of the economy [social production] of a country (or group of countries, or economic region) at a given historical point. The level of economic development is a generalizing concept and is characterized by several sets of indices: the production of the aggregate social product, material prosperity, per-capita national income; by the structure of social production (respective shares of industry and agriculture in the national economy; the share of production of the means of production; the share, volume, and rate of development of advanced sectors of industry); by the quantitative and qualitative level of employment of the population; the level of exploitation of natural resources; by the organization and efficiency of social production. A small country may possess a small economic potential yet, at the same time, have a high level of economic development."[20]

This definition, for all its detail, is nevertheless useless for a comparative analysis of the economic level of countries and regions, for it is too abstract, includes too many indices, and makes no allowances for differential levels in various indices. In brief, it does not provide clear guidelines for assessing the level of economic development in a given territorial economic formation.

Indices of the Level of Economic Development

Soviet authorities have, however, devised more precise indices to compare the level of economic development among regions. In the early 1960s specialists created a list of 240 indices to compare the USSR with other countries.[21] At the same time, central authorities endeavored to reduce the set of indices for internal development and even to provide a single synthetic index. This approach gained wide acceptance among specialists in the 1970s, although individual works still make comparisons based on multiple indices. Thus, the statistical yearbooks of the Central Statistical Administration compare the economic development of the USSR and the United States on the basis of the following indices: national income, industrial production, agricultural production, turnover of goods for all forms of transportation, volume of capital investment, and labor productivity in industry and agriculture. The operative idea here is basic indices, not the *level* of economic development. The distinction, however, is fundamental.

Specialists have devised several methods for measuring the level of economic development. One approach is to base the assessment on the "production of the means of production." By contrast, in a 1964 discussion in *Ekonomicheskaia gazeta*, other specialists countered with the suggestion that the level of economic development be measured by the standard of living, which is regarded as the end result of production.[22] The latter position seems reasonable enough. After all, it corresponds to the goal of development in the Soviet economy as officially proclaimed in the program of the CPSU: the maximum improvement of the population's standard of living.

Level of economic development in a region encompasses both production and consumption. Accordingly, the index used to measure and quantify this level should take into account both of these dimensions. One synthetic index that does so is per-capita national income, which—at least in theory—includes the final output from regional production (the numerator) and potential consumption (in the denominator). Such an index is exceedingly simple; it is used for all kinds of international comparisons, including the multistate comparisons made by the United Nations. It is meaningful, however, only when national income is calculated in terms of the national economy. Its application is significantly more problematic when it is used to measure the economic development of various regions in an open regional economy. To this difficulty must be added the problems arising from the peculiarities of Soviet excise policy and the Soviet system for setting prices.

Problems of Assessing Production Level in Terms of per-Capita Income of the Republic

The main difficulty concerns the peculiarites inherent in the Soviet system of price-setting: Soviet calculations include not only the real expenditure of resources for production, but also the norms set by the state for profitability. The catch is that these norms vary significantly, thereby distorting the true magnitude of per-capita income of the republic.

Nor do these profitability norms (and hence profits) bear a significant relationship to the real economic results for a given industrial sector or, frequently, the demand for a given product. Very often, they reflect neither the efforts of the enterprise, nor technological improvements, nor expenditure of resources. In essence, profitability norms represent a mechanism that state organs use to stimulate the development of some production and retard the development of other production, all in accord with considerations of economic strategy (and frequently the interests of defense or foreign policy). But the main point is that this kind of profit manipulation detaches the development of production from real economic results, and that in turn introduces substantial distortions into the indices of national income. Obviously, when a particular region is highly identified with a particular economic sector, its per-capita income will be profoundly affected by the profit norms set in Moscow.

A further problem is caused by the turnover tax. The amount of tax added to the per-capita income of union republics is proportionate to the taxable goods produced in their territory. This turnover tax is calculated by the Central Statistical Administration of the USSR and then transmitted to the statistical bureaus in the union republics. In general, it is added to the end production of light and food industries and also to certain forms of fuel and energy resources.

In essence, the turnover tax is a device that allows the national budget to confiscate profit from the production of consumer goods. The high profitability from this production is explained by the high prices the state sets for such goods, not by objective technological and economic factors. Hence, as a result of the existing excise system and the state's redistribution policy, the magnitude of per-capita income in official statistics does not provide a reliable index to real production. Further, under Soviet political economic theory, the per-capita income does not include services or the shadow, or second, economy. (The shadow economy encompasses both permitted private transactions and underground economic activity.) These factors affect the calculation of per-capita income not only at the republic, but also at the national, level.

In economic terms, the turnover tax and profit represent pure income. Insofar as the turnover tax is not included in the production price of the producer enterprise, the volume of the tax in the republics does not depend mainly on the volume of pure income that they really produce, but rather on taxable production in other regions as well. As a result, approximately half of the pure income that has actually been produced is not calculated according to its place of origin. This method creates a significant statistical redistribution of pure income that cannot help but distort the magnitude of per-capita income produced in the republics. Obviously, when national income is calculated in this manner, it cannot measure the level of development in production in a given republic. Given the present system for setting prices and the centralized distribution of the turnover tax, the optimal way to maximize per-capita income in a given republic would be to produce the greatest possible amount of alcohol.

In short, Soviet calculation of per-capita income at the regional level provides a highly imperfect index for measuring the level of production.

Problems in Calculating the Level of Consumption

Measuring the consumption level in a region is likewise fraught with significant problems, for it is very difficult to isolate the region from the larger national economy. To be sure, the level of consumption refers simply to consumption within the borders of a given region. But it is impossible to separate that region from the dynamics of consumption in the country as a whole, since the latter are largely determined by the general material resources of the country (taking into account their redistribution among regions).

As is true for production levels, what is needed here is an integral index that gives an objective picture of regional differentiation in consumption. Many Soviet publications recommend using the "real incomes of the population" on the grounds that this index characterizes the real volume of acquired goods and services (taking into account the changes in retail prices and expenditures for the payment of taxes and other obligatory payments).[23] Revenues of the population include payment for labor, public funds for consumption, and revenues from auxiliary individual economic activity. This index has the advantage of reflecting the potential for *personal* consumption and also the volume of a population's consumption (regardless of where a given good was consumed).

But this index also has shortcomings. Above all, it conveys only the consumption *potential*—and, at that, a potential ascertained statistically. This calculation does not include the underground economy, the scale of which varies considerably within a given region. It also fails to take account of the real possibilities for satisfying demand for one or another good; these are very uneven in the different regions of the country. Finally, this index also has a statistical problem: Soviet statistical annuals present the real incomes of the population in union republics only as growth rates, not in absolute terms. Hence one can make only an analysis of growth rates—and, furthermore, only for union republics, not for the national economic regions.

Another possible method for studying consumption levels would be to use data on the consumption funds in a region's national income. This would be easy to do in national regions, for the statistical yearbooks of most national republics provide such information. But there are good reasons that this approach would not provide a reliable index. The most important is that, under conditions of an acute shortage of consumer goods and of unsatisfied demand (which varies sharply among regions of the country), consumption in fact is not localized within the boundaries of a given region. In contrast to productive activities, the consumption of goods and services in an open regional system is much less fixed and permits some migration of material and monetary resources to other regions. The shortage of goods in various regions is a catalyst to interregional transfer.

In analyzing regional levels of consumption, one must consider the differences in natural conditions, the specific characteristics of the structure of consumption, the role of auxiliary economic activity, national traditions, and the demographic peculiarities of the population. A particularly important role is played by demographic factors, such as the population's sex and age structure and its family size. Only by taking into account these regional factors can one make generalizations about the comparative level of consumption.

•　　•　　•　　•

The foregoing examination of problems in measuring regional economic development reveals that one cannot simply apply synthetic indices (national income as an index for production, or real income of the population as an index of consumption). Rather, it is necessary to advance beyond these indices and draw on a series of other economic indicators—to be sure, within the realm of the feasible, given the limits of Soviet regional statistical information.

26

CHAPTER 2

Central Asia's Role in the Soviet Economy and Its Economic Structure

Central Asia's economy is among the most specialized in the Soviet Union. In Central Asia, cotton is king.

This specialization developed as a result of the region's climatic conditions and its land and water resources, which favor cotton cultivation. The Turan Lowland, which is distinguished by its warmth and abundant sunlight, makes up approximately 70 percent of the region. It has 180 to 250 frost-free days a year; the average daily temperature exceeds 20 degrees Celsius on 120 to 150 days. But rainfall in the Lowland amounts to no more than 70 to 200 mm annually, of which only 20 to 50 mm occurs in June, July, and August (the growing season for cotton).[1] Under these conditions cotton cultivation requires artificial irrigation.

But no more than 6 or 7 percent of the region's arable land is irrigated.[2] If the unused land were brought under irrigation, cotton production and related crops could be greatly expanded. The result has been to create a specialized infrastructure to serve the cotton industry: irrigation networks, branches of machine-building (to manufacture equipment such as cotton sowers, cultivators, harvesters, and tractors), the chemical industry (to produce mineral fertilizers and pesticides for cotton growing), cotton-processing plants (to clean the cotton and produce cottonseed oil), textile mills, and some garment factories. Central Asia produces approximately 95 percent of the USSR's raw cotton and cotton fibers, 15 percent of its vegetable oils, 100 percent of its machinery and equipment for cotton growing, more than 90 percent of its cotton gins, a large quantity of looms, and equipment needed for irrigation.[3]

Although cotton still predominates, research and geological discoveries of the 1950s and 1960s showed that Central Asia has much greater energy resources than previously believed. These discoveries, in turn, radically altered views about the region's potential economic development. In gas, oil, and hydroelectric power, Central Asia now ranks as one of the richest, most promising regions in the USSR. Subsequent exploration during the second half of the 1970s expanded the potential gas reserves significantly, especially in Turkmenia. When the new reserves are added to the deposits discovered earlier, Central Asia stands second only to Western Siberia in the volume of its holdings in natural gas.[4]

Thus, the traditional orientation of the Central Asian economy toward almost exclusive reliance on cotton no longer corresponds to the region's economic potential. Its rich energy potential would permit the development, alongside the cotton complex, of energy-intensive industries. Such a development would, obviously, mean a dramatic rise in the industrial role and significance of Central Asia within the larger Soviet economy.

Central Asia's Role in the National Economy

Central Asia's place in the economy of the USSR is clear from Table 2.1, which reveals significantly lower indices per capita here than in the USSR as a whole. Soviet specialists on regional economies explain this phenomenon chiefly by alluding to two factors: (1) the legacy of economic backwardness from prerevolutionary times; and (2) the "demographic peculiarities" of the region (that is, "extremely high rates of population growth and increased proportion of the employable population that does not work in public production"). But history is more an excuse than explanation;

after all, seven decades have elapsed since Central Asia came under Soviet control. The high proportion of nonworking population is an effect, not a cause, and is a consequence of the economic development of the region as dictated from Moscow.

Table 2.1 Central Asian Share of Soviet National Economy (1985)

Territory	5.7%
Population	10.9
National Income	4.0
Number of People in Labor Force	7.5
Basic Capital of Production Sphere	6.0
Capital Investments	6.4
Industrial Production	4.5
Agricultural Production	8.3*

*1984 data
Sources: *Narodnoe khaziastvo SSSR v 1985 godu*, 8, 12, 409, 390, 394, 48, 363, 93; *Narodnoe khoziaistvo SSSR v 1985 godu*, 229; *SSSR i soiuznye respubliki v 1985 godu* (Moscow, 1986), 88, 89, 221, 222, 237, 238, 270, 271.

To judge from official statistics, Central Asia is seemingly developing with sufficient dynamism, particularly if compared with growth rates for the USSR as a whole (see Table 2.2). Although these data speak for themselves, it should be underlined that Kirghizia and Uzbekistan have had absolutely no growth in capital investment, even though these two republics account for more than two-thirds of Central Asia's national product.

If, however, one examines Central Asia's role in the Soviet national economy, the data in Tables 2.3 and 2.4 give still less reason for optimism. The disproportion between Central Asia's rankings in population and fixed capital is a characteristic feature of its economy. When Central Asia is compared with two analogous regions, one finds that the fixed capital in the Baltic region exceeds the

Table 2.2 Indices of Economic Growth in Central Asia and the USSR (1985 as a Percentage of 1984)

	USSR	Uzbekistan	Kirghizia	Turkmenistan	Tadjikistan
National Income	3.1	3.9	2.7	4.8	4.6
Ind. Production	3.9	7.3	3.7	2.0	4.3
Agr. Production	1.6	—	-4.3	2.8	2.2
Cap. Investment	3.0	0.2	0.1	4.0	4.0
Workers, Employees	0.6	0.8	2.2	3.3	2.1

Sources: SSSR i soiuznye respubliki v 1986 godu, 3, 88, 89, 221, 222, 237, 238, 270, 271.

population, whereas in the other two regions the relationship is just the reverse. More important, this discrepancy is particularly great and growing in Central Asia. It constitutes the region's main economic problem and has a decisive influence not only on the rate and character of economic growth, but also on social development.

Another important feature of Central Asia's backwardness is the disproportion between its share of population and its share of national income. If the regional statistics on national income are taken seriously, then the fact that the region's share of population is twice as great as its share of national income can only mean that labor productivity is sharply lower in Central Asia.

Let us look more closely at the region's labor productivity, both in comparison with the USSR as a whole and in comparison with our two control examples (the Baltics and Transcaucasus). As a measure of labor productivity, we use the ratio between a region's total income and the aggregate size of its labor force. As Table 2.5 illustrates, labor productivity is lower in Central Asia than in the USSR as a

Table 2.3   The Role of Central Asia in the Soviet Economy (as a Percentage of National Economy)

	1971–75	1976–80	1981–84
National Income	6.0	6.0	6.0
Industrial Production	4.0	4.0	4.0
Agricultural Production	8.0	8.0	9.0
Capital Investment	6.0	6.0	6.0
New Fixed Capital	6.0	6.0	6.0
Population (end of period)	9.2	10.0	10.7
Share of Population Growth	26.0	29.0	30.0

Note: Calculated on the basis of average annual indicators for the periods of the index and given in comparable prices. The 1984 data for Tadjik SSR and Turkmen SSR were interpolated.

Sources: Narodnoe khoziaistvo SSSR v 1984 godu, 56; Narodnoe khoziaistvo Uzbekskoi SSR v 1984 godu, 23, Narodnoe khoziaistvo Tadzhikskoi SSR v 1982 godu, 30, Narodnoe khoziaistvo Kirghizskoi SSR v 1984 godu, 13, 14.

Table 2.4 Central Asian Share of Population and Fixed Capital Compared with other National Regions (in Percent)

Area	1975 Pop.	1975 Fixed Capital	1980 Pop.	1980 Fixed Capital	1984 Pop.	1984 Fixed Capital
USSR	100	100	100	100	100	100
Baltics	2.8	3.5	2.8	3.25	2.8	3.2
Transcaucasus	5.3	3.7	5.4	3.7	5.5	3.8
Central Asia	9.2	5.5	10.0	5.7	10.7	5.9

Note: Fixed capital is based on comparable prices from 1973.

Sources: Narodnoe khoziaistvo SSSR v 1984 godu, 61; *Narodnoe khoziaistvo Uzbekskoi SSR v 1981 godu,* 26; *Narodnoe khoziaistvo Turkmenskoi SSR v 1980 godu,* 44; *Narodnoe khoziaistvo Kirghizskoi SSR v 1980 godu,* 10; *Narodnoe khoziaistvo SSSR v 1984 godu,* 8.

whole and the two other national regions. This pattern, moreover, has remained constant for the entire period. In 1970–1974, when labor productivity rose both at the all-union level and among national economic regions, this growth was smallest in Central Asia. Table 2.5 also presents an index called "coefficient of labor activity," which correlates the region's share of the total national income with its share of total population. This indicator likewise suggests that the "level of labor activity" in Central Asia is less than that in the two other national economic regions.

Although statistics on the labor force create no problems, the other constituent of our index of labor productivity is more difficult to establish. As already noted in Chapter 1, Soviet methods of calculating these indices distort the true magnitude of a region's national income. It is important to determine how significant these distortions are and how they affect data on the national income produced in Central Asia.

As pointed out earlier, the main difficulty in computing national income for particular regions is that many products are finally used outside the regions in which they are produced. We have noted the problems in determining a republic's national income that are due to the turnover tax.

Table 2.5 Labor Productivity in Central Asian, Transcaucasus and Baltic National Regions

	Nat. Income in Real Rubles	Share of USSR Nat. Income (%)	Ave. Annual Workers	Share Ave. USSR Workers (%)	Labor Produc. (103 rubles/ person)	Coeff. Lab. Prod. Activ. (2:4)
	1	2	3	4	5	6
1970						
USSR	289.9	100.0	106.8	100.0	2.7	—
Baltics	10.1	3.5	3.3	3.1	3.1	1.13
Transcaucasus	10.2	3.5	4.1	3.8	2.5	0.92
Central Asia	15.2	5.2	6.2	5.8	2.4	0.90
1975						
USSR	363.3	100.0	117.2	100.0	3.1	—
Baltics	12.7	3.5	3.6	3.6	3.6	1.14
Transcaucasus	14.0	3.8	5.0	4.3	2.8	0.88
Central Asia	20.7	5.7	7.4	6.3	2.8	0.90
1980						
USSR	462.2	100.0	125.6	100.0	3.7	—
Baltics	14.9	3.2	3.8	3.0	3.9	1.07
Transcaucasus	22.3	4.8	5.7	4.5	3.9	1.07
Central Asia	27.4	5.9	8.6	6.8	3.2	0.86
1983						
USSR	548.1	100.0	129.9	100.0	4.2	—
Baltics	17.8	3.2	3.8	3.0	4.6	1.07
Transcaucasus	26.3	4.8	6.0	4.6	4.4	1.04
Central Asia	33.6	6.1	9.4	7.2	3.6	0.85

Sources: *Narodnoe khoziaistvo Uzbekskoi SSR v 1982 godu*, 188, 194; *Narodnoe khoziaistvo Kirgizskoi SSSR v 1970 godu*, 126; *Narodnoe khoziaistvo Kirgizskoi SSR v 1980 godu*, 154; *Narodnoe khoziaistvo Kirgizskoi SSR v 1984 godu*, 99; *Narodnoe khoziaistvo Kirgizskoi SSR 1982 godu*, 159, 170; *Narodnoe khoziaistvo Tadzhikskoi SSR v 1982 godu*, 178; *Narodnoe khoziaistvo Turkmenskoi SSR v 1976 godu*, 129; *Narodnoe khoziaistvo Turkmenskoi SSR v 1982 godu*, 128, 137; *Narodnoe khoziaistvo Turkmenskoi SSR 1924-1984*, 144; *Narodnoe khoziaistvo Estonskoi SSR v 1984 godu*, 144, 154; *Narodnoe khoziaistvo Litovskoi SSR v 1984 godu*, 144, 152; *Narodnoe khoziaistvo Latviiskoi SSR v 1984 godu*, 210, 226; *Narodnoe khoziaistvo Gruzinskoi SSR v 1984 godu*, 172, 165, 103, 107; *Narodnoe khoziaistvo Azerbaidzhanskoi SSR v 1970 godu*, 221; *Narodnoe khoziaistvo Azerbaidzhanskoi SSR v 1984 godu*, 145, 151; *Narodnoe khoziaistvo Armianskoi SSR v 1980 godu*, 151, 169; *Narodnoe khoziaistvo Armianskoi SSR v 1984 godu*, 227, 213, 146, 154.

Data for a few missing years have been interpolated or extrapolated.

According to present methods, regions that have more industry of the so-called B type (that is, production of consumer goods) and therefore produce goods subject to the turnover tax, have accordingly a higher index for national income. Under these conditions, the region's share of the total national income in the USSR is artificially inflated. Conversely, regions that produce more intermediate products (serving as raw materials or semifinished components for final products manufactured in other regions and subject to the turnover tax) find themselves disadvantaged. It is precisely to this last category of regions that Central Asia belongs.

In Central Asia, especially among cadres from the indigenous peoples, it is widely believed that their region makes a much greater contribution to Soviet national income than that depicted in the official statistics. They blame the underassessment on distortions caused by the system of price-setting, methods of adding on the turnover tax, and the existing economic relations between Central Asia and other regions and republics. In their view, Moscow's method of calculating national income and interregional economic relations place Central Asia at a disadvantage and reduce its role in the overall economy of the USSR. For example, the director of the Institute of Economics at the Tadjik Academy of Sciences, Rashid Rakhimov, contends that if the national income were computed on the basis of intersec or balances, "it could turn out that currently dominant conceptions of the relative and absolute levels of the production of national income in the Tadjik republic would be corrected." Rakhimov adds (with due circumspection) that the revised data could lead to changes "in assessments of the region's level of development and in *demands for the development and distribution of its productive forces*" [emphasis added].[5]

Until now, however, the region's productive forces have been focused almost exclusively on the production of cotton. Central Asia serves as the cotton producer for the entire USSR, and hence cotton is its main export. Approximately 96 percent of the raw cotton produced in Uzbekistan is shipped out for processing and manufacturing to the RSFSR, the Ukraine, Belorussia, and other republics, to the countries of Comecon (the Council for Mutual Economic Aid, which includes Hungary, Czechoslovakia, Poland, East Germany, Bulgaria, and Rumania), and elsewhere. The industrial processing of one ton of raw cotton yields 3,400 meters of cloth, 94 kilograms of vegetable oil, 6 kilograms of soap, and so forth. The crucial difference is the rate of turnover tax imposed at the various stages: 410 to 600 rubles is assessed on one ton of raw cotton, whereas 1,260 to 1,700 rubles is added to the products obtained from the industrial processing of each ton of raw cotton.[6] Obviously, if a more significant part of the cotton raised in Central Asia were also processed there, the region's national income as well as its share in the total national income of the USSR would be greater.

How much greater? Enough to raise its labor productivity significantly in comparison with other national economic regions and the USSR as a whole? According to calculations by the Uzbek economist Z. Solokhiddinov,[7] the real volume of national income produced by Uzbekistan in 1976–1980 was 7.8 percent higher than that reported in official statistics. Moreover, Uzbekistan's share of the national income of the USSR should be corrected to read not 3.80 percent, but 3.86 percent—that is, it should be increased by 0.06 percentage points. This correction can probably be extended to the entire region, for Uzbekistan accounts for about 70 percent of the national income in Central Asia. Still, although the revised data improve the picture slightly, Central Asia nevertheless continues to lag behind the indices for other national regions and the USSR as a whole.

Another distinctive feature of Central Asia is the structure of national income—that is, the relationship of current consumption to accumulation. Unfortunately, data are not available for the entire region, but only for Uzbekistan; similarly, data are unavailable for some republics in the Transcaucasus and Baltic regions. Hence, one is limited to a comparison of certain republics (Uzbekistan, Azerbaijan, Estonia) with the USSR as a whole (see Table 2.6). As these data demonstrate, the share of consumption in the national income of Uzbekistan has remained lower than that in the USSR as a whole and the other two national regions.

Table 2.6   Percentage Share of Consumption in National Income
(in Prices of Corresponding Years)

	1970	1975	1980	1984
USSR	70	74	76	73
Uzbekistan	65	73	72	70
Azerbaijan	74	75	73	71
Estonia	74	—	80	76

Sources: *Narodnoe khoziaistvo SSSR v 1970 godu*, 535; *Narodnoe khoziaistvo SSSR v 1975 godu*, 565; *Narodnoe khoziaistvo SSSR v 1980 godu*, 380; *Narodnoe khoziaistvo SSSR v 1984 godu*, 426; *Narodnoe khoziaistvo Uzbekskoi SSR v 1984 godu*, 232; *Narodnoe khoziaistvo Azerbaydzhanskoi SSR v 1984*, 152; *Narodnoe khoziaistvo Estonskoi SSR v 1984 godu*, 155.

Capital Investment

The investment quotient allocated for Central Asia, in the course of the entire Soviet era, has undergone considerable change, as the data in Table 2.7 indicate. For the entire period of Khrushchev's experiment with *sovnarkhozy*, Central Asia's share in Soviet investment remained in the range of 3.6 to 4.1 percent. Then came the dramatic spurt in the 1960s. That increase can be explained by increasing investment activity by the *sovnarkhozy*, which gained control over the distribution of investments within their territories. The growth of the late 1960s (after the dismantling of the *sovnarkhozy*) resulted from the heavy investment supplements made to overcome the devastation resulting from the 1966 earthquakes in Tashkent. The increase in capital investment can be further traced to the development of gas and petroleum industries in the region.

As a result of all this investment, the construction capacities of the region were augmented significantly, which encouraged a number of production-branch ministries in Moscow to look favorably on further investments in Central

Table 2.7 Central Asia's Share of Capital Investment (Based on Prices for the Given Period)

1921–1928	3.6%
1928/29–1932	3.8
1933–1937	3.7
1938–June 1941	4.1
1941–1945	4.0
1946–1950	3.7
1951–1955	3.9
1956–1960	3.9
1961–1965	5.3
1966–1970	6.5
1971–1975	6.1
1976–1980	6.3
1981–1985	6.6
1984	6.6
1985	6.3

Sources: *Kapital'noe stroitel'stvo v SSSR* (Moscow, 1961), 74; *Narodnoe khoziaistvo SSSR v 1970 godu*, 488; *Narodnoe khoziaistvo SSR v 1975 godu*, 513; *Narodnoe khoziaistvo SSSR v 1980 godu*, 343; *Narodnoe khoziaistvo SSSR v 1985 godu*, 369.

Asia in subsequent years. This outlook apparently explains why the region's investment quota did not fall in later years. Nevertheless, it has ceased to rise for the last four five-year plans (1966–1985) and hence has remained virtually unchanged over a 20-year period. This investment quotient is but half of the region's share of total population in the USSR.

In the last five-year plan, growth in investment in Central Asia was smaller than in the USSR at large and less than in any other region in the country, except Kazakhstan (which had the same rate of growth). Between 1980 and 1985, investment increased by 19 percent for the entire Soviet economy, 18 percent in the RSFSR, 18 percent in the Ukraine, 26 percent in Belorussia, 34 percent in the Baltic region, 39 percent in the Transcaucasus, but only 16 percent in Central Asia (in adjusted prices).

Table 2.8 Distribution of Capital Investment per Economic Sector (Percentage, Based on Adjusted Prices)

	Industry	Agriculture	Transportation and Communication	Construction	Social Sphere*
Central Asia					
1971–75	28.2	29.5	10.5	3.6	28.2
1976–80	28.2	31.5	9.4	3.1	27.8
1981–85	28.5	33.2	8.3	3.2	26.8
Caucasus					
1971–75	37.0	17.7	10.2	3.8	31.3
1976–80	38.0	18.8	10.9	3.7	28.6
1981–85	39.5	19.3	11.4	3.7	26.1

Baltics					
1971–75	26.6	29.1	9.2	2.7	32.4
1976–80	26.9	27.5	9.4	3.4	32.8
1981–85	30.1	23.5	8.9	3.4	32.8
Belorussia					
1970–75	32.6	27.5	7.1	3.2	29.6
1976–80	32.7	27.5	9.4	3.3	28.5
1981–85	32.2	25.3	9.2	3.2	30.1
RSFSR					
1970–75	39.2	11.7	12.4	4.2	32.5
1976–80	38.9	12.4	14.3	4.4	30.0
1981–85	38.9	11.9	15.2	4.0	30.0

• Housing, health services, recreation, science, and education.

Sources: Narodnoe khoziaistvo Turkmenskoi SSR v 1984 goda, 113; *Narodnoe khoziaistvo Kirgizskoi SSR v 1984 goda*, 129; *Narodnoe khoziaistvo Tadzhikskoi SSR v 1982 goda*, 170; *Narodnoe khoziaistvo Uzbekskoi SSR v 1984 goda*, 209; *Narodnoe khoziaistvo Gruzinskoi SSR v 1984 goda*, 149; *Narodnoe khoziaistvo Armianskoi SSR v 1984 goda*, 185; *Narodnoe khoziaistvo Azerbaidzhanskoi SSR v 1983 goda*, 104; *Narodnoe khoziaistvo Litovskoi SSR v 1980 goda*, 129; *Narodnoe khoziaistvo Litovskoi SSR v 1984 goda*, 124; *Narodnoe khoziaistvo Latviiskoi SSR v 1984 goda*, 186; *Narodnoe khoziaistvo Estonskoi SSR v 1984 goda*, 127; *Narodnoe khoziaistvo Belorusskoi SSR v 1984 goda*, 121; *Narodnoe khoziaistvo RSFSR v 1984 goda*, 222; *Narodnoe khoziaistvo SSSR v 1984 goda*, 378.

Some figures, for which direct data are unavailable, are based on the author's calculations.

In 1985 (the first year under Gorbachev's leadership) investment in Uzbekistan fell by 4 percent (from 7.145 to 6.811 billion rubles).[8] And for Central Asia as a whole, investment dropped by 1.5 percent. For the USSR as a whole, investment that year rose by 3 percent.[9] Hence, the end of the preceding five-year plan heralded a worsening of the investment situation for the Central Asian economy. Seen against the general background of investment in the USSR, Central Asia's situation has deteriorated.

No less important than aggregate investment is its distribution among sectors of the economy. The data in Table 2.8 show the breakdown for Central Asia and compare that region with other areas of the USSR. The table shows that Central Asia is distinguished by a most unusual type of investment policy: (1) the investment share for industry is the lowest and that for agriculture the highest, thus perpetuating the bias toward the region's agricultural sector; (2) the share allocated for transportation has declined substantially; (3) the quota for construction is less than that for the RSFSR, the Transcaucasus, and the Baltic regions; and (4) allocations for the social sphere are exceedingly low.

In short, investment allocations within the region continue to subordinate economic development to one overarching goal—cotton. All other areas of the economy are sacrificed to increase the cotton output. No other region of the USSR is bound so completely to a one-sided strategy of economic development. Further, Central Asia has the lowest (and declining!) investment quotient for the social sphere, although it has the highest rate of population growth in the USSR.

Peculiarities of the Economic Structure of Central Asia

Published statistics provide only one basis for analyzing the structure of the Central Asian economy: fixed capital. Table 2.9 compares the distribution of fixed capital among economic sectors in Central Asia with the distributions in the USSR as a whole and in the Baltic and Transcaucasus

Table 2.9 Distribution of Fixed Capital by Economic Sector (as a Percentage of Total Fixed Capital)

Sector	Year	USSR	Baltics	Transcaucasus	Central Asia
Industry	1970	29.6	24.0	29.5	22.6
	1975	30.6	25.1	29.5	23.6
	1980	31.8	26.0	31.0	24.8
	1984	32.2	26.0	30.7	25.1
Agriculture	1970	12.3	18.3	14.3	21.8
	1975	13.3	19.6	14.6	22.8
	1980	13.7	20.2	15.1	23.2
	1984	13.8	20.3	15.5	23.5
Transportation	1970	13.6	14.5	13.4	11.5
and	1975	13.6	14.0	14.3	12.4
Communication	1980	13.6	13.4	14.0	12.7
	1984	13.6	13.3	13.9	12.6
Construction	1970	2.6	2.0	3.0	4.7
	1975	2.8	2.1	3.2	4.5
	1980	3.2	2.3	3.5	4.3
	1984	3.4	2.5	3.8	4.4
Social	1970	42.0	41.0	39.4	39.3
Sphere	1975	39.6	39.2	39.1	36.4
	1980	37.8	39.1	36.5	34.9
	1984	37.0	37.8	35.8	34.3

Note:Data based on comparable prices from 1973.

Sources: Narodnoe khoziaistvo SSSR v 1970 godu, 58, 60, 61; Narodnoe khoziaistvo RSFSR v 1960 godu, 18; Narodnoe khoziaistvo RSFSR v 1965 godu, 38; Narodnoe khoziaistvo RSFSR v 1975 godu, 27; Narodnoe khoziaistvo RSFSR v 1980 godu, 27; Naronoe khoziaistvo RSFSR v 1983 godu, 27; Narodnoe khoziaistvo Ukrainskoi SSR v 1980 godu, 29; Narodnoe khoziaitsvo Ukrainskoi SSR v 1983 godu, 20, 21; Narodnoe khoziaistvo Litovskoi SSR v 1980 godu, 25, 39; Narodnoe khoziaistvo Litovskoi SSR v 1983 godu, 32; Narodnoe khoziaistvo Litovskoi SSR 1984 godu, 20; Narodnoe khoziaistvo Latviiskoi SSR v 1980 godu, 39; Narodnoe khoziaistvo Latviiskoi SSR v 1983 godu, 32; Narodnoe khoziaistvo Latviiskoi SSR v 1984 godu, 35; Narodnoe khoziaistvo Gruzinskoi SSR v 1975 godu, 26; Narodnoe khoziaistvo Gruzinskoi SSR v 1981 godu, 26; Narodnoe khoziaistvo Gruzinskoi SSR v 1984 godu, 22; Narodnoe khoziaistvo Azerbaidzhanskoi SSR v 1983 godu, 13, 14; Narodnoe khoziaistbo Azerbaidzhanskoi SSR v 1984 godu, 25, 26; Narodnoe khoziaistvo Armianskoi SSR v 1975 godu, 25; Narodnoe

regions. The data reveal clearly that the share devoted to industry, transportation, and communication in Central Asia is small, whereas that in agriculture is large. This distribution reflects, of course, Central Asia's concentration on the production and processing of cotton.

In addition, these data demonstrate that Central Asia has a remarkably low share of fixed capital in the social sphere—housing, culture, education, trade, science, recreation, and services. Indeed, this share has undergone a significant decline. Even though the reduced share of capital in the social sphere is characteristic of the entire Soviet economy, its effect is disproportionately greater in Central Asia, whose population is growing so much faster than that in other areas of the USSR. Between 1970 and 1984, the Central Asian population grew by 44 percent, while its share of fixed capital in the social sphere shrank from 39.3 to 34.3 percent.

In short, the "productive" sphere of the economy (industry, agriculture, transportation and communications, construction), has registered a modest increase, but these gains have come at the expense of a reduced investment quotient for the social sphere. Given Central Asia's demographic explosion, that policy can only be fraught with serious social consequences.

---

khoziaistvo Armianskoi SSR v 1980 godu, 29; Narodnoe khoziaistvo Armianskoi SSR v 1984 godu, 36; Narodnoe khoziaistvo Uzbekskoi SSR v 1980 godu, 22; Narodnoe khoziaistvo Uzbekskoi SSR v 1982 godu, 19; Narodnoe khoziaistvo Uzbekskoi SSR v 1984 godu, 28; Narodnoe khoziaistvo Tadzhikskoi SSR v 1975 godu, 20; Narodnoe khoziaistvo Tadzhikskoi SSR v 1976 godu, 20; Narodnoe khoziaistvo Tadzhikskoi SSR v 1981 godu, 25, 26; Narodnoe khoziaistvo Tadzhikskoi SSR v 1982 godu, 28; Narodnoe khoziaistvo Kirgizskoi SSR v 1975 godu, 17; Narodnoe khoziaistvo Turkmenskoi SSR v 1976 godu, 30; Narodnoe khoziaistvo Turkmenskoi SSR v 1980 godu, 44; Narodnoe khoziaistvo Turkmenskoi SSR v 1982 godu, 18; Narodnoe khoziaistvo Turkmenskoi SSR v 1984 godu, 24.

CHAPTER 3

Problems of Industrialization

Industrial development in Central Asia has lagged noticeably behind that in other parts of the USSR. Approximately 80 percent of the national industrial production and energy consumption is located in the European zone, although this area is poorly supplied with resources (energy, minerals, and raw materials). Conversely, Soviet Asia has the bulk of resources, but only a small share of industrial production. Data in Table 3.1 show how production in some basic

Table 3.1 Territorial Proportions of Industrial Production in the USSR and the Role of Central Asia (1975)

Industrial Sector	European Zone	Asian Zone	Central Asia**
Electrical Energy	75%	25%	4.1%
Fuels*	40	60	4.5
Ferrous Metallurgy	70	30	0.2
Chemicals and Petrochemicals	87	13	2.0
Machine Building	86	14	2.4
Timber and Woodworking	72	28	1.2
Construction Materials	75	25	5.4
Light Industry	82	18	9.0
Food Processing	81	19	3.7
Other Sectors	86	14	4.1

*Figures on the fuel industry can be given only as approximations, based on indirect data for the first half of the 1980s.
**The figures for Central Asia comprise part of the data for the entire Asian Zone.
Source: R. Rakhimov, *Problemy razvitiya*, 75.

industrial sectors is distributed between the European and Asian zones of the USSR, as well as the role that Central Asia plays in the Asian zone. These regional disparities constitute one of the chief problems in the Soviet economy.

The Structure of Industry

Let us examine the distinctive features of the structure of industrial production in Central Asia. Unfortunately, because the pertinent statistical data are not available for all the Central Asian republics, it is necessary to focus on Uzbekistan, with the assumption that this republic is broadly representative of the region as a whole. Uzbekistan does have approximately 60 percent of the region's fixed industrial capital.[1]

As Table 3.2 indicates, the industrial structure of Uzbekistan differs from that of the USSR in two respects: the high share concentrated in electrical energy and light industry, and the low share in machine building, fuel, and food processing. These data reveal several key characteristics of the Central Asian industrial sector.

(1) The proportion of fixed capital allocated to the generation of electrical energy has declined sharply and output has risen only modestly. These patterns are also characteristic of the USSR as a whole, but are more pronounced in Central Asia. Greater use of existing capacity has sustained old production levels, but the growth of new capacity has evidently been sharply curtailed. The share of electricity in fixed capital in Central Asia and the USSR exceeds its share in gross industrial output, but the gap in Central Asia is larger. This may reflect the higher ratio of hydroelectric stations in the production of electricity in Central Asia generally, but fixed capital per unit of production is higher for hydroelectric stations than for thermal power stations.

(2) A comparison of shares of the fuel industry in Central Asia and the USSR (in fixed capital and gross output) shows that this sector is much less capital-intensive in Central Asia. That apparently explains the insignificant share of coal in the production of fuels in the region.

(3) Light industry's higher share of gross output than of fixed capital, both in Central Asia and in the USSR, is explained by the addition of the turnover tax to this sector's output. The same holds true for the food-processing industry.

(4) The share of machine building (in both fixed capital and gross output) has remained strikingly stable in Central Asia. By contrast, the USSR as a whole shows substantial increases for both indices.

In sum, Central Asia has experienced a significant decrease in its energy-producing sector, minimal change in its production of consumer goods, and—of particular moment—no change in the small role accorded to machine building.

Table 3.2 Structure of Industry in Uzbekistan and the USSR

	Uzbekistan			USSR		
	1970	1975	1982	1970	1975	1982
*As Share of Fixed Capital**						
Electricity	21.8	20.6	17.1	17.4	16.8	15.4
Fuels	5.1	3.1	2.2	13.1	12.6	13.7
Machine Building	14.5	14.7	14.9	20.0	21.5	24.1
Light Industry	10.0	10.2	10.5	4.6	4.4	4.2
Food Processing	6.0	7.2	6.7	8.0	8.2	7.4
*Share in Total Volume of Production***						
Electricity	3.4	3.8	3.7	2.9	2.8	3.9
Fuels	4.8	4.7	4.6	6.2	5.7	8.0
Machine Building	15.9	15.2	15.2	23.2	27.8	25.4
Light Industry	40.7	39.8	39.2	17.0	14.9	15.7
Food Processing	17.3	17.7	17.8	21.0	19.0	18.2

*in comparable prices
**in actual prices of corresponding years
Sources: *Narodnoe khoziaistvo SSSR v 1975 godu*, 197, 223; *Narodnoe khoziaistvo SSSR v 1982 godu*, 118, 134; *Narodnoe khoziaistvo Uzbekskoi SSR v 1975 godu*, 29, 72, 73; *Narodnoe khoziaistvo Uzbekskoi SSR v 1982 godu*, 19, 44.

ENERGY SECTOR

Central Asia's fuel industry consists of gas, petroleum and petroleum refining, and coal. The high rate of development in gas and petroleum has turned this region, which was once energy-poor, into one of the primary energy bases of the USSR, helping to compensate for the rising fuel shortages in the European zone.

The main role in Central Asia's fuel sector belongs to the gas industry. The large-scale development of natural gas production in the 1970s has had a major technological and social impact.

Richest in gas and oil is Turkmenistan, which has 80 percent of the region's oil reserves and 64 percent of its natural gas reserves. By contrast, Uzbekistan has 30 percent of the gas reserves and an inconsequential share of the petroleum. The main coal reserves are concentrated in Kirghizia (43 percent) and Tadjikistan (41 percent); much less coal is found in Uzbekistan (16 percent) and virtually none in Turkmenistan.[2] Most of the large oil reserves, however, are concentrated in western Turkmenistan, at a significant distance from potential consumers. Gas reserves are concentrated primarily within western Uzbekistan and eastern Turkmenistan, which means they are much more propitiously located for exploitation in the region itself. At present, 90 percent of the petroleum comes from western Turkmenistan and 80 percent of the gas from Uzbekistan. Most of the petroleum refining is done in Turkmenistan and Uzbekistan.[3]

Because of the accelerated development of gas extraction (along with more gradual development of petroleum production and coal mining), the fuel production potential of Central Asia rose rapidly in the 1960s and 1970s. It was then, too, that the fuel sector underwent a radical reconstruction and modernization, with natural gas playing an increasingly prominent role as efficient ways were found to tap the rich gas fields and process a host of valuable by-products.

The natural gas produced in Central Asia, however, does not remain there, but rather goes to satisfy the demands of other, fuel-deficient areas of the country. Similarly, natural gas from Iran and Afghanistan, which enters the USSR through Central Asia, is sent on to European Russia. This policy naturally provokes opposition among cadres of indigenous nationalities in Central Asia, especially in Uzbekistan. It is a widely shared opinion that the bulk of the natural gas should be used in the region itself: that it should provide raw material for the local chemical industry (which was established in the 1970s and which, in local opinion, should receive greater development).[4] There is no sign, however, that Gosplan is inclined to heed this position.

Another striking feature of the Central Asian economy is the intensive development of electrical energy. As Table 3.3 shows, electricity generation has grown much faster in Central Asia than in the USSR as a whole. Altogether, in the course of a quarter century (1960-1985), the production of electricity in Central Asia increased eight times, compared with five times for the USSR as a whole.[5]

Table 3.3 Annual Average Rate of Growth in the Production of Electrical Energy in the USSR and Central Asia

	1971–1975	1976–1980	1981–1985
USSR	7.0	4.5	3.6
Central Asia	12.0	6.0	6.0

Sources: *Narodnoe khoziaistvo SSSR v 1975 godu*, 236; *Narodnoe khoziaistvo SSR v 1985 godu*, 155.

Central Asia possesses significant hydroelectric potential. But despite the significant development of energy production in the region, electrical energy remains a major problem, for several reasons.

First, electricity in Central Asia is generated mainly by thermal stations (65 percent), the remainder (35 percent) coming from hydroelectric stations. The corresponding figures for Siberia are 53 percent thermal and 47 percent hydroelectric; for the USSR as a whole the ratio is 86 percent thermal, 14 percent hydroelectric. Central Asia's hydroelectric resources are exceptionally favorable for electricity generation, for they are located on waterways with enormous power and great drops. But hydroelectric stations must not only produce electricity, but also support the irrigation systems that are so vital to the region's cotton economy. To ensure large cotton yields and fulfillment of processing plans, resolution of other economic problems is invariably deferred. Thus, for a significant part of the year, minimal hydroelectric capacity is used to generate electric power. Reserves at thermal power plants, however, do not compensate for the loss of electrical energy during these low periods.[6]

Second, agriculture consumes a high proportion of electrical energy in Central Asia—three times the average in the USSR. Mechanized irrigation of cotton plantations is a major user. Moreover, the land area under mechanized irrigation has increased rapidly; in 1976–1980 alone it increased by 4 million hectares. As a result, the consumption of electricity for irrigation more than tripled during this five-year period.[7]

The only solution is to increase the output and capacity of thermal power stations. But because the thermal stations use mainly natural gas for fuel, their capacity can be expanded only if gas shipments to other regions are reduced and diverted to satisfy local needs. That, however, is possible only if demand in the European part of the country can be satisfied through the delivery of natural gas from Siberia. Development of Siberian reserves has encountered serious difficulties and appears unlikely to deliver a significant increase in gas or petroleum production. Hence, Central Asia will hardly be able to cut back its gas deliveries to European Russia.

In discussions of Central Asia's need for electrical energy, the possibility of constructing nuclear power stations is sometimes raised. That approach would keep gas deliveries flowing to the European part of the USSR at current rates; it would, simultaneously, meet Central Asia's own need for additional electric power. In fact, however, this is not a real option: Central Asia has a high rate of seismic activity and suffers from frequent, occasionally powerful earthquakes. That is why all plans envision the construction of nuclear power plants only in the European part of the country.[8] Moreover, the Chernobyl catastrophe has also caused plans to undergo careful review; the intent is to slow implementation in order to improve plant safety. All this has increased the cost of nuclear power and the scale of investment required, making it all the more unlikely that Moscow would consent to divert the resources needed to construct nuclear power plants in Central Asia, assuming the safety problems could be overcome.

MACHINE BUILDING

The manufacture of machine tools in Central Asia focuses primarily on agriculture and textiles. There are some exceptions—aviation (Uzbekistan), instruments (Kirghizia), transformers (Tadjikistan), and oil equipment (Turkmenistan) —but the production of agricultural machinery, primarily for the cotton-growing complex and secondarily for textile manufacturing, predominates.

The tempo and character of Central Asian machine building development are determined chiefly by the undeveloped state of ferrous metallurgy in the region. The sole plant with a full metallurgical production cycle is in Bekabad; with an annual output of one million tons of steel, it simply cannot satisfy demand. Hence, large quantities of steel must be shipped to Central Asia from other regions of the country, particularly from the Urals and Kazakhstan. The development of ferrous metallurgy (with the complete production cycle) is, however, not a real option, given the absence of iron ore (or at least its exploration) as well as an acute shortage of water. To be sure, the region does have significant resources in scrap metal, and if the electricity were available, it would be possible to create a recasting metallurgy by means of electrical steel furnaces. But given the current shortages of electrical energy, such projects are hardly feasible.

The large and underused labor resources, together with the

shortage of steel, impel Central Asia to develop those sectors of the machine-tool industry that are high in labor intensity and low in metal consumption, such as instruments and electronics. This development depends, of course, on Moscow's willingness to allot the necessary investments. It is highly doubtful, however, that this will occur in the foreseeable future. At present, the European part of the USSR produces approximately 90 percent of the country's total output of machinery and equipment; the share of Central Asia and Kazakhstan is just 4.1 percent.[9]

Despite the problems caused by the continued concentration of machine-building capacities in the old industrial centers, investment will continue to flow to the same regions of the country. This is precisely the policy adopted at the twenty-seventh party congress: with the goal of diverting capital resources toward the modernization of old capacity rather than the creation of new plants, this investment policy crushes any hope that Central Asia will be able to expand its local machine-tool industry and thereby meet local demand more fully. On the contrary, Central Asia's dependence on imports of machinery will probably increase.

The Case of the South Tadjik Territorial Production Complex

This picture of industrial development in Central Asia would be incomplete without attention to its largest industrial complex—the South Tadjik Territorial Production Complex (South Tadjik TPC). As noted in Chapter 1, territorial production complexes became exceedingly fashionable as an economic-geographic model, in both the theory and the practice of planning, in the 1970s. Plans were drawn up for such complexes in the Urals, Siberia, Moldavia, and a number of other regions, including the South Tadjik TPC in Central Asia. The South Tadjik complex is located in the southern part of Tadjikistan; until recently this area was characterized chiefly by the basic production and primary processing of cotton.

The main economic advantage for creating an industrial

center here was the hydroelectric potential of the area: it has approximately 50 percent of the hydroelectric resources in Central Asia and 8 percent of the total in the USSR. Another favorable factor was the presence of natural mineral deposits (sodium chloride, limestone, certain rare metals) useful for various industrial branches.[10]

The heart of the new industrial center is an energy-industrial complex, comprising hydroelectric stations and extremely energy-intensive nonferrous metals and chemical enterprises. The main enterprises of the complex are the Nurek hydroelectric station, the Tadjik aluminum plant, and the Iavan electrochemical plant. Development of the complex is to proceed over several stages. The first phase, consisting of the construction of these three enterprises and a railway line (Termez–Kurgan-Tiube–Iavan), is virtually complete. But the task of putting the three plants into full operation is far from resolved. Let us examine briefly the main enterprise—the Tadjik aluminum plant, which holds considerable significance for the USSR as a whole.

Construction of this plant in the city of Tursun-zade began in 1965 on the basis of a plan prepared by the Central Asian *sovnarkhoz*. But construction proceeded slowly for lack of investment capital. In theory, this was supposed to be one of the largest aluminum plants in the USSR, equipped with the most modern technology and capable of producing top-quality metal. The plant design assumed that raw materials would have to be shipped in, but that the abundance of cheap electrical energy would justify its location. So it seemed, at least, when the whole project was first drawn up on paper.

The plant was finally put into operation in 1984, but it proved an utter fiasco, and—at least in the foreseeable future—there is no hope that this will change substantially. The plant is constantly plagued by accidents; its grounds are splattered with hardened aluminum because the bottoms of the pot-liners have disintegrated. In 1984, the plant's losses amounted to 33 million rubles, and the next year they climbed to 48 million rubles. The best prognoses predict similar, if not greater, deficits in the future. People at the plant say that their aluminum costs more than the gold

51

extracted from the bottom of the Zeravshan River. Thus, just two years after start-up, the plant is already in urgent need of major overhaul and reconstruction. Ironically, until recently, this whole enterprise was proudly exalted in the Soviet press as the embodiment of "the aluminum industry of tomorrow" and was regarded as the most advanced industrial enterprise in Central Asia.[11]

The situation is not much better at another component of the South Tadjik TPC: the chemical plant at Iavan. Because of mistakes in the plant's design, it is operating at barely 40 percent of its planned capacity and, even though it has just begun to operate, reconstruction has already started.[12]

The construction of this and other enterprises has had a serious ecological impact on the contiguous territories. The Tadjik aluminum plant is located in one of the most beautiful settings in Central Asia, amid mountains whose snow-capped peaks (in the poetic description of one author) "exude freshness and serenity."[13] But the traveler begins to sense the plant's existence from afar: the outlines of the mountains fade behind a greenish haze caused by the plant: its exhaust fumes and gases (which contain extremely harmful substances) are not first purified in a cleaning and scrubbing system to remove pollutants, but instead pour straight into the atmosphere.

Apart from the question of the plan's implementation, does its very creation optimize the industrial structure of Central Asia? The share accorded to heavy industry will of course increase. But the creation of large complexes that are voracious consumers of electricity and water can only aggravate the existing deficiencies of natural resources. No less important, the final product is not manufactured in Central Asia, but in other regions of the USSR. For example, finished rolled aluminum is not produced at the Tadjik plant (where technologically and, presumably, economically, one would expect it); rather, the plant's aluminum ingots are shipped to European Russia for processing. The Tadjikistan Gosplan has for many years insisted that this final processing and rolling take place at its aluminum plant. It argues that this would "improve the supply of aluminum goods for Tadjikistan and all Central

52

Asia (where the demand for these goods is great) and permit the rapidly increasing labor force to be drawn into production."[14] But up to now the situation has remained unchanged.

Character and Rate of Industrial Development in Central Asia

The industrialization of Soviet Central Asia has been uneven, without any long-term strategy. It has indeed run contrary to "the law of planned, proportionate development" that Soviet ideologists and political economists claim is the foundation of planning in the Soviet economy.

The initial great leap came under the first two five-year plans. This was a time when industrialization encompassed the entire territory of the USSR. Moreover, it was precisely in this period that serious attention was given to the development of backward regions on the empire's periphery. The first plans (and, especially, the second five-year plan) built the initial plants for the cotton-processing industry and its infrastructure. A good example here is Uzbekistan: the most industrially developed republic in Central Asia, it bore the imprint of accelerated industrialization that was overtaking the USSR as a whole (see Table 3.4).

But in the years immediately preceding World War II, the pace of industrialization slowed markedly. The reasons for this downturn were many; apart from the higher diversion of resources for military purposes, the sluggish growth rate can be attributed to the production-branch planning and administration of industry and the concentration of resources on new construction programs (mainly in the old industrial centers of European Russia). The result was a sharp decline in the growth of industrial output at the end of the 1930s.

The second surge of industrialization in Central Asia occurred during World War II. In this period, the region acquired heavy industry through the evacuation (especially to Uzbekistan) of many industrial enterprises from the European part of the USSR. The equipment from more than 100 industrial plants (in toto or in part) was shipped to

Uzbekistan alone: metallurgy, coal industry, machine building and others. In Uzbekistan, this equipment provided the basis for 47 new industrial enterprises established during the war, more than half of which were located in Tashkent or its environs.[15] This development transformed Tashkent and the contiguous territory into the greatest industrial complex in Central Asia.

The magnitude of this forced relocation of heavy industry and its impact on the economy of Central Asia is reflected in the data on Uzbekistan: in the period 1940–1950 the output in machine building increased 653 percent—more than 6.5 times—while steel production increased from 11,000 to 119,000 tons, and coal output climbed from 3,000 to 1,500,000 tons. The output of electricity rose from 481 million to 2,679 million kilowatt-hours.[16]

Table 3.4 Growth in Industrial Production in Uzbekistan and the USSR (in Percent)

	USSR		Uzbekistan	
	Total Growth	Per Year	Total Growth	Per Year
1st five-yr plan (1928/1932)	202	15.0	157	9.4
2nd five-yr plan (1933/1937)	221	17.0	242	19.3
3rd five-yr plan (1938/1941)	145	13.2	131	9.4
4th five-yr plan (1946/1950)	189	13.6	171	11.4
5th five-yr plan (1951/1955)	185	13.0	161.5	10.0
6th five-yr plan (1956/1958)	134	10.2	119	6.0
7-year plan (1959/1965)	–	–	178	8.7
8th five-yr plan (1966/1970)	159	8.5	136	6.3
9th five-yr plan (1971/1975)	143	7.4	151	8.6
10th five-yr plan (1976/1980)	124	4.4	127	4.9
11th five-yr plan (1981/1985)	120	3.7	126	4.7

Sources: *Promyshlennost' SSSR* (Moscow, 1964), 34; *Narodnoe khoziaistvo Uzbekskoi SSR v 1970 godu*, 132; *Narodnoe khoziaistvo SSSR v 1970 godu*, 141; *Narodnoe khoziaistvo SSSR v 1975 godu*, 203; *Narodnoe khoziaistvo SSSR v 1980 godu*, 132; *Narodnoe khoziaistvo SSSR v 1985 godu*, p. 10.

In the first two five-year plans after World War II, Central Asia's growth rate in industrial production remained high, but lower than that in the USSR as a whole. Investment in the region's industries decreased, for almost all available resources were being concentrated on rebuilding industrial enterprises in European Russia that had been destroyed during the war. Still, the Central Asian capacity for heavy industry created during the war, the rising production of cotton, and the output in the food-processing industry combined to sustain a high rate of growth.

In the second half of the 1950s, however, Central Asia's industrial growth declined markedly. Several factors played a part. First, the war-time surge was so great that a certain fall-off was to be expected. Second, the industrial potential added during the war received too few funds for expansion or proper maintenance. The result was a rapid depletion of fixed capital, which was offset neither by replacement nor by repair, still less by upgrading.

Moreover, a significant portion of the equipment and machinery evacuated from the western regions was already badly deteriorated at the time of installation. The assembly, installation, and construction of necessary buildings, communications, and other components of the industrial infrastructure had to be completed under the acute pressure of the war, when every minute counted and no attention was given to durability. The result was such massive deviation from standards that, to maintain production in the postwar years at previous levels, very considerable resources would have been required. The upshot was that, a decade after the war had ended, capacity use in Central Asia's plants had declined substantially.

Finally, departmentalism and the central management of industry (and hence resources) dominated the first postwar plans. As a result, the interests of individual regions, especially those that had not suffered during the war, were relegated to secondary importance.

The third upsurge of industrialization in Central Asia came in the early 1960s. The primary impetus was Khrushchev's new system of *sovnarkhozy* for territorial economic administration (1957–1965). For the only time in

Soviet history, national regions were given a real opportunity to control their own economies. The ensuing "regional autarky" contributed mightily to the establishment of many new industrial enterprises, reinforcement of the infrastructure and construction industry, and expansion of the raw material and energy base.

Although initially each Central Asian republic had its own *sovnarkhoz*, in 1962 these were combined to form a single *sovnarkhoz* for the region. That made a major contribution to the integration of the republican economies into a unified economic system. The distribution of investments within this territory was now dictated not by Gosplan and ministries in Moscow, but predominantly by the Central Asian *sovnarkhoz*. Although Moscow still exercised oversight, the *sovnarkhoz* independently managed many spheres of economic activity and used its new authority to expand the region's industrial base.

These years, significantly, saw the creation of industrial enterprises unrelated to the processing of agricultural products or the exploitation of local minerals, raw materials, and energy resources. The *sovnarkhoz* laid the foundation for new branches of industry (for example, chemicals) and expanded industrial capacity for construction materials and machine building. The greatest attention was given to the chemical industry (on the basis of oil and gas treatment and processing)[17] and nonferrous metallurgy, which emerged as the dominant sectors of heavy industry in Central Asia. These branches began to play an ever greater role in the region's industrial production.

Although the *sovnarkhozy* could not overcome cotton's predominance, they did provide a base for accelerated industrial expansion in later years. This legacy included the exploration and technical and economic assessment of natural resources, the improvement of construction materials and equipment, the expansion of schools for training labor, and the development of a better transportation network. Consequently, the period of the *sovnarkhozy* formed an important stage in the industrial development of Central Asia, and the momentum gained in these years had an impact in later, post-*sovnarkhoz* years as well.

56

But the five-year plan that followed the abolition of the *sovnarkhozy* (1966–1970) dealt the region's economy a deep shock, as the organizational system that had been created during the preceding eight years was suddenly shattered. Moscow completely reversed policy, returned to centralized planning and management, and denounced the *sovnarkhozy* policy as narrow-minded localism (*mestnichestvo*). It also strengthened the production-branch system and promoted vertical integration in territorial industrial planning. All this was diametrically opposed to the decentralization under the *sovnarkhozy*.

The new policy, inevitably, had a negative effect on the industrial growth of Central Asia in the second half of the 1960s. But because construction and start-ups are a protracted process (normally from five to ten years), the full impact of *sovnarkhozy* investment programs did not come until the early 1970s. The post-*sovnarkhoz* period also marked the greatest cotton production since World War II, which further stimulated growth in the cotton-processing industry. As a result, the rate of industrial growth continued to rise until the mid-1970s and even surpassed the general rates for the USSR.

Thereafter, however, Central Asia (like the USSR as a whole) experienced a sharp slowdown in its industrial growth, for the earlier *sovnarkhozy* projects were not followed by new ones. Thus, industrial growth slumped sharply in the period of the tenth five-year plan (1976–1980); nor did the situation improve with the eleventh plan (1981–1985). The factors that caused this poor economic performance in the USSR generally apply as well to Central Asia; these have been amply discussed in both Soviet and foreign literature and do not require detailed elaboration here. Nevertheless, each region has its own unique problems, and it is important to identify those that were specific to Central Asia.

Although industrial growth in Central Asia continued at a significant pace for some time after the end of the *sovnarkhoz* period, it bore an entirely different character. Branch ministries, not regional planning organs, determined where and what kind of plants were to be built, giving scant regard to the need for complex, integrated development. The

57

central ministries increasingly tended to concentrate industrial production in areas with well-developed infrastructures, where capacity could be expanded more quickly and at less expense. This policy meant, however, a concentration of industrial complexes in previously developed centers and persisting neglect of sparsely settled territories.

This tendency was particularly salient in the most developed industrial zone of Central Asia, the area around Tashkent. During World War II this area received the greatest influx of evacuated capacity for heavy industry; later, as the capital of the Central Asian economic region in the *sovnarkhoz* period, Tashkent garnered a disproportionately large share of resources from the Central Asian *sovnarkhoz* for industrial development. Similarly, after severe earthquakes in 1966, Tashkent obtained enormous investment funds to create capacity for its construction industry. As a result, it acquired one of the largest construction bases in the USSR—a circumstance that proved highly alluring to the central production-branch ministries and encouraged them to concentrate investment for new industrial capacity in Tashkent. The following comment by a prominent Uzbek economist, Sh. Zakirov, is characteristic:

> The more rapid development of industry in the Tashkent zone, especially in recent years, derived from the fact that new plants were drawn toward a preexisting industrial base. The placement of firms in the Tashkent zone was motivated by the desire to cut expenditures, but also by *the interests of all-union [central] ministries, for whom Uzbekistan means a single point—Tashkent* [emphasis added].[18]

Thus, even when central departments do invest in the industrialization of Central Asia, it is for reasons largely extraneous to indigenous needs and potential.

Moreover, recent planning has failed to develop further areas of major achievement in the *sovnarkhoz* era. One such sector was the chemical industry, which received keen attention in the 1960s in order to exploit the abundant raw materials of the region. But since then the expansion of capacity has failed to keep pace with the growth in demand, so that production of fertilizers, pesticides, synthetic fibers, plastics, household chemical products, and the like does not satisfy local demand for these products. Hence, Central Asia still depends on the European regions for such goods and continues to ship its own raw materials to those regions for processing and manufacturing.

Nonferrous metallurgy, which can take advantage of rich deposits of ore and raw metals, is also one of Central Asia's main industrial sectors.[19] Several major enterprises have been built to tap these mineral resources—for instance, gold mines and a gigantic aluminum plant. But the peculiar trait of this nonferrous metallurgy is that it is confined to the extraction and enrichment of metals—that is, the production of ore concentrates. The final processing and rolling (the manufacture of finished products) is generally performed outside the region.

The Central Asian establishment, especially its indigenous elements, is sharply critical of Moscow's failure to develop the chemical and nonferrous metallurgical sectors and argues that this natural expansion has been thwarted by the central ministries in Moscow. The ministries pursue their own vested interests and find it more advantageous to expand production on the basis of existing enterprises. Indeed, in some writings of Central Asian scholars,[20] it is possible to read between the lines and find a much more important idea: that Moscow is in general not even interested in establishing industrial branches in Central Asia with a complete production cycle, from extraction of the raw material to manufacture of the finished product. No one yet dares to express such subversive ideas openly, but it appears that they are widespread among the local national cadres of Central Asia.

In all fairness, however, it is necessary to adduce other factors and considerations that have formed objective barriers to the placement of these industries in Central Asia. Nonferrous metallurgy, as well as the production of synthetic fibers and plastics, consumes vast quantities of energy and water, the two resources that are so scarce in this region.

Electric power growth, likewise, fell by more than half from the tenth to the eleventh (1981–1985) five-year plan.[21]

If the situation in electric power is no better in other regions of the USSR, then, in terms of the strains created by the water balance, none can compare with Central Asia. Herein lies the whole paradox of industrial development in the region: the predominant industries here are characterized by high water consumption. These include, besides chemicals and nonferrous metallurgy, cotton processing and silk production. If Central Asia is unique as a producer of cotton and silk, Moscow finds it expedient to shift the processing of nonferrous metals and chemical production to other regions, where the water shortage is less acute.

Central Asian planners, however, give insufficient attention to these difficulties in water supply when they design new industrial enterprises and select machinery and equipment. Even when it is feasible, they often fail to select a less water-intensive technology. An example of this is the cement plant in Akhangaran (near Tashkent), which is based on so-called wet technology, which uses large quantities of water; by making some additional expenditures, it would have been entirely possible to substitute a "dry" technology much more economic in its water consumption.

Another instructive case is the gigantic chemical plant built in the 1970s in Navoi, Uzbekistan. It was built to manufacture plastics and synthetic fibers and to use the natural gas from the deposits of Gazli as its raw material. This plant consumes 80 million cubic meters of water a year, of which one half is irretrievably lost and the other half emerges in the form of polluted drainage. Because the problem of purifying this drainage is not yet solved, all 80 million cubic meters of water that the plant takes from the Zerafshan River are in effect wholly lost.[22] To put the magnitude of the waste in perspective, the same volume of water could irrigate 6,000 hectares of cotton. What makes the situation so absurd is that the bulk of the production from this plant is shipped out of Central Asia to other regions, where the water problem is much less acute.

Do the inertia of the industrial structure and the priority given to extractive over manufacturing industries reflect a definite policy on Moscow's part to reinforce Central Asia's economic dependence and to pump out its raw materials and energy resources for the full-scale industrial development of the empire's European center? Many in the West hold that to be the case, but the question is in fact much more complex; nationality policy in the Soviet Union is shaped as well by economic calculations that take into account broader national interests. For the present, we shall defer a judgment on this issue and turn to the main sector of the Central Asian economy—cotton.

CHAPTER 4

Cotton

Central Asia is the cotton base of the USSR, and cotton development has always been given highest priority. In Uzbekistan the sector of the economy directly engaged in the cultivation and processing of cotton produces more than 65 percent of the republic's gross output, consumes 60 percent of all resources, and employs approximately 40 percent of the labor force. Altogether, the republic accounts for about two-thirds of all the cotton produced in the USSR.[1] The same picture is seen in the rest of Central Asia. Thus, cotton constitutes two-thirds of the region's total output and employs more than one million people. In the main cotton-growing areas[2] the share of the land sown with cotton exceeds 70 percent.[3]

The Decline of Soviet Cotton Exports

Cotton from Central Asia is one of the important exports of the USSR, which ranks among the world's leading exporters of this staple. In 1983 Uzbekistan alone produced almost as much cotton as the entire United States. And cotton exported from the USSR is sent to more than 30 countries. For the period 1965–1983, the Soviet share of the world's production of cotton fiber rose from 15 to 21 percent.[4] According to data for 1983, the largest producer in the world was China, followed by the USSR, with the United States in third place.

In the early 1980s, however, the volume of cotton exported by the USSR declined sharply: whereas cotton exports had risen by 55 percent in the 1970s, they fell 25 percent between 1980 and 1985.[5] Production, too, declined, but not so drastically; in Uzbekistan, for example, output fell by only 6 percent.[6] Given the Soviet Union's demand for hard currency (heightened by the reduced production of oil and its falling price on the world market), it is clear that the nation cut back its cotton exports—one of its most popular goods on the world market—only from dire necessity. Several factors help to account for the reduction in cotton exports.

First, in the mid-1980s the USSR suffered a fall in the production of raw textile materials generally—not just cotton, but also chemical fibers. As a result, it could not easily cut its domestic consumption of cotton and divert the difference to sustain its export level.

In recent decades, cotton's share of the textile market in Western countries has declined (with a concomitant increase in chemical fibers). But, significantly, in the early 1980s the pressure from synthetics abated slightly and the demand for cotton increased. That change was due to several factors, including an improvement in the quality of cotton, changes in the relative prices that favored cotton over synthetics, and recognition of the superior hygienic properties of cotton textiles.

The USSR ranks significantly below the world level in both the production and consumption of synthetic fibers, and hence cotton still dominates in its mix of raw materials for textiles. As a result, it could not compensate for the downturn in cotton production by increasing its output of chemical fibers. Indeed, growth rates in the production of the latter have been inconsequential and in 1985 actually declined.[7] In the mid-1980s, therefore, the only way that the USSR could sustain its old export level was by cutting domestic consumption. In recent years, the inability to satisfy domestic demand for cotton textiles has intensified sharply.

Second, conditions on the world market changed with China's rise to leadership. Beginning in the late 1970s China adopted a variety of measures to stimulate greater cotton production and an improvement in its quality. That country's enormous labor reserves, its abundant state subsidies, its favorable climatic conditions in a number of regions, and the strong material incentives to make quantitative and qualitative improvements put China in a separate class from the other competitors. China's entry into the world cotton market brought a sharp intensification of competition, for buyers soon began to show increasing interest in Chinese cotton. Demand for the inferior Soviet cotton fell accordingly. The results were a decline in the Soviet share of the world cotton fiber market and a reduced proportion of production for export (from 30 to 24 percent of total output in the 1980–1985 period).[8]

As the reverses on the world market suggest, the chief problem in Soviet cotton production is not so much quantitative as qualitative. The assortment of raw cotton has deteriorated, and the yield and quality have declined. Thus, the share of superior varieties in the total harvest declined from 77 percent in the early 1970s to 58 percent by the early 1980s. The share of the most inferior varieties, by contrast, rose from 14 to 29 percent.[9]

The Crisis in Cotton Production and Its Causes

Since the early 1980s, cotton—the backbone of the Central Asian economy—has been in the throes of crisis. The harvest of raw cotton in 1985 was 12 percent less than in 1980; yield (output per hectare) declined by 17 percent.[10] Such a downturn is utterly without precedent in the history of Soviet Central Asia.

The causes of this state of affairs are diverse, but one crucial nontechnological factor stands out: the producers have a personal interest in increasing the gross output of raw cotton, but not in improving its quality. Nor are there material incentives for the employees at cotton-processing plants to store the cotton properly and give it higher-quality processing. The entire system of material incentives is geared toward achieving the quantitative goals of production.

It is imperative to evaluate performance and establish remuneration according to qualitative indices, a change that should involve several measures. Most obvious, state procurement payments should shift from raw cotton to fibers and by-products, taking into account their quality. Moreover, the pricing of fibers and by-products should take into account the work of cotton-processing plants—their expenditures for the treatment of the raw cotton, the quality of the processed product, and the yield in fibers. Finally, procurement centers and cotton-cleaning plants must store and process raw cotton from each producer separately.

But other, more technical problems have also played a role in causing the current crisis in cotton production in Central Asia.

STAGE 1: SELECTION OF COTTON VARIETIES

To improve the quality of cotton, it is above all necessary to develop and introduce only high-yield, disease-resistant, and fast-growing varieties with a large fiber output. Until now, attention has focused on a single characteristic—high yield. By default, the other properties—in which the producers had no material interest—have been ignored. Hence, the tasks now are to develop new varieties with a superior combination of characteristics and to put them into production. It is particularly important to achieve maximum volume in the production of thin-fiber varieties.

STAGE 2: CULTIVATION AND HARVESTING

The cultivation and harvesting of the cotton plant is an extremely protracted and labor-intensive process. Cotton is, in general, one of the most labor-intensive of all agricultural crops. Thus, whereas the direct expenditure of labor for the production of one *centner* (100 kilos) of cereal is 1.6 man-hours, it requires 36 man-hours to produce one centner of cotton.[11] Despite the favorable demographic conditions in Central Asia, cotton production has encountered steadily mounting problems of insufficient labor. The primary reason is that the rural population in Central Asia has been migrating to the cities in recent years; secondarily, the population that remains prefers other employment to the cultivation of cotton. Hence, it has become routine for cotton farms to recruit auxiliary labor to work the cotton fields by mobilizing significant contingents of people from other sectors of the economy as well as school children and students—with prolonged diversion from their regular work and studies.

The only solution is to increase the level of mechanization in the production process. Approximately 1,000 man-hours are currently expended on each hectare, but mechanization could reduce this to 600 man-hours.[12] Not all kinds of mechanization, however, lead to an improvement in the quality of the cotton grown. The technology of the machines used for cotton cultivation lags behind contemporary requirements. As a result, mechanized harvesting under adverse weather conditions increases the humidity and impurities in the cotton.

Contemporary technology, however, makes it possible for machines to bring in up to 95 percent of the entire yield. But this is possible only if the harvesters make five or six passes, which causes considerable damage to the soil's fertility and, hence, the next harvest.[13] Consequently, the scale of mechanized harvesting can be expanded only (a) if a new cotton harvester is developed that minimizes the number of passes required; and (b) if new varieties of cotton are developed that simultaneously lend themselves to mechanized harvesting and preserve the desired biological characteristics of the cotton fiber.

Another important means to reduce the labor required is to mechanize the watering system. The transition from watering by hand (which is now widely practiced in Central Asia) to mechanized systems would eliminate the onerous work of the workers engaged in watering. But this requires the creation and production of watering machines of a new design.

STAGE 3: COTTON PROCESSING

Greater use of mechanized havesters will lead to a bottleneck at the next stage, when the cotton is cleaned and processed. Indeed, there is already an imbalance between the level of mechanized harvesting and the technical capacities of cotton-processing plants. The latter have proved unprepared to handle the massive volume of machine-harvested cotton, which contains more moisture and impurities than hand-harvested cotton.

To raise the quality of cotton processing (and hence fiber quality), two problems must first be solved. First, the difficulty in processing very moist and impure cotton can be overcome only by increasing the capacity of cotton-processing plants by 25 to 30 percent.[14] The increased capacity would reduce the processing periods and thereby limit spoilage and damage to fiber quality. The second task is to outfit procurement centers with additional machinery to dry the cotton and to construct additional closed drying platforms. But the main objective must be to raise the technological level of cotton-processing plants by creating more efficient machinery and by constructing larger enterprises that can quickly handle large volumes of cotton.

IRRIGATION

So far we have looked only at the machinery and equipment needed for cotton cultivation and harvesting. But irrigation presents another problem that must be solved if the cotton crisis in Central Asia is to be overcome.

This problem is not new but became more critical when Moscow tabled plans to divert rivers to serve water-deficient areas in this region. Now, more than ever, it is vital to increase the return and efficiency of existing irrigation systems and to put more effective methods of watering into operation. If these opportunities are exploited, they can substantially alleviate this region's water problem. But that requires, in addition to improved organization and administration, the outfitting of irrigation systems with modern watering equipment, which could substantially reduce the water consumption per unit of production. Hence, whereas Central Asia as a whole uses 570 cubic meters of water to produce one centner of cotton, and whereas Khorezm Oblast consumes water at the rate of 700 to 800 cubic meters (because of the high salinity of the soil), the picture is radically different in the Golodnaia Steppe. There, the irrigation system is much more technologically advanced, with the result that water consumption is only 400 cubic meters per centner of cotton.[15] Water conservation could be further achieved by expanding the use of modern sprinkler systems.

Problems in the Central Asian cotton sector cannot be corrected by mere "organizational measures"—a favorite Moscow panacea for fundamental economic problems. Rather, it is plainly necessary to make enormous investments and to optimize their distribution within the sector. But, to judge from the tendencies in investment policy, that kind of radical turnaround appears highly improbable. An increase in the investment quota for the cotton-growing complex depends on Moscow, not on the authorities in Central Asia; and Moscow has other priorities for its sectoral and regional allocation of resources.

The "Tragic Experiment" of Cotton

This chapter has briefly reviewed the technological problems associated with the production of cotton. It is important to realize, moreover, that this "white gold"—as it is often labeled in the Soviet mass media—plays an exceptionally important role not only in Central Asia's economy, but also in its entire social sphere.

Soviet writers, with an eye to the Third World and especially Islamic countries, reject the claims that cotton in fact plays such a role. In the countless Soviet publications aiming to smash "bourgeois conceptions of the economic development of Central Asia," one major thrust has been directed at the proposition—widely shared in Western scholarly studies—that the Central Asian economy should be analyzed in terms of an agrarian-colonial model. Soviet propagandists are especially sensitive to this accusation and express the greatest indignation over the thesis of a "superspecialization in cotton" in Central Asia. Outraged by the injustice of such an accusation, Professor Akhmed Ulmasov at the Tashkent Institute of Economics wrote in 1985 that the proposition of "a superspecialization in cotton-growing" in Central Asia is "a method of falsification by Sovietologists." He asserts that cotton growing in Central Asia is "a contemporary, dynamic branch of production, based on a constantly expanding application of the achievements in science and technology." "How can one speak of superspecialization in cotton," exclaims Ulmasov emotionally, and he goes on to accuse "bourgeois theoreticians" of resorting to "fabrications and inventions at any price."[16]

However, Ulmasov should now direct his rage at the Moscow weekly *Literaturnaia gazeta*, which carried this blunt statement in early 1987:

> Specialization should be reasonable. In Uzbekistan it has degenerated into the dictatorship of a single crop, indeed one so highly specific as cotton. It first became a monoculture in a psychological sense, when it drove all the other needs of the region from the minds of certain leaders. Then it crowded the normal crop rotation from the fields and pushed everything else out of the plan. By being transformed into virtually one great cotton plantation, Uzbekistan embarked on a long, tragic experiment—to determine the capacity of a monoculture to corrode not only agriculture, but also industry, education, health, and finally public morality.[17]

One has to wonder whether Akhmed Ulmasov should not accuse the chief paper of the Soviet intelligentsia of falsification for describing the condition of the Central Asian economy in such extreme terms. Indeed, no "bourgeois Sovietologist" has gone so far!

A profound crisis has clearly descended on the cotton economy, with profound repercussions for the entire social system, as a close examination of Uzbekistan makes abundantly clear.[18] Data on the production crisis are particularly impressive. Thus, between 1975 and 1980 the harvest of raw cotton increased by 25 percent and yield (output per hectare) by 17 percent, but the output of cotton fiber increased by only 5 percent.[19] For many years, to judge from statistical data, the harvest of raw cotton and yield substantially exceeded the production of cotton fibers. And this gap is steadily widening. Obviously, the end product is the cotton fiber, not raw cotton. But for the cotton-growing *kolkhozy* (collective farms) and *sovkhozy* (state farms), the final product is precisely the raw cotton that they deliver to state procurement centers. All that matters is sheer quantity.

Plan fulfillment, similarly, is judged according to the total quantity of raw cotton delivered. But Soviet statistics consign the production of cotton fiber to another sector of the economy, light industry. It would be analogous if farmers sold wheat in its husks, not just the grain itself, and the production of wheat were treated as in the domain of agriculture, and the production of bread in the domain of bakeries.

Such cleavages in a single technological process have led to statistical falsification. One type of falsification occurs when the raw cotton is delivered to the procurement centers: the heads of *kolkhozy* and *sovkhozy* simply bribe the procurement inspectors to inflate the amount delivered, both on the delivery receipts and in reports to their superiors. Another type of deception is to expand the area under cultivation and then to conceal this from both the planning and statistical offices. The result is an inflated index. Both of these practices occur on a massive scale.

Fraud has proliferated because producers now find it virtually impossible to fulfill the plan by honest means—expanding the sown areas, raising the yield ratio, or other means. It was still possible to keep pace with plan targets in the 1960s and, apparently, even in the first half of the 1970s. But not thereafter: excessive exploitation of the soil—by ignoring proper crop rotations, by making excessive use of harvesters, and by overusing pesticides—finally began to take its toll.

In the opinion of a leading expert (academician Mirza ali Mukhamedzhanov), the condition of the soil in Uzbekistan is comparable to that of a gravely ill person. The cause, according to Mukhamedzhanov, is the transformation of cotton into a monoculture. Thus, cotton has been cultivated on many fields, without interruption, for some 50 years; that has exhausted the nutrients in the soil. Tractors cross a field up to 30 times a year. Cotton machines mercilessly compress the soil, destroying its microorganisms. And because cotton has a low immunity to disease and infestation, massive quantities of pesticides are used, killing every living thing in the fields. Norms for crop rotation have also been violated; cotton's share of sown acreage reaches 85 percent, whereas it normally should compose only 50 to 60 percent.[20]

From earliest times, Uzbek peasants rotated alfalfa with cotton cultivation. Alfalfa improves the structure of the soil and enriches it with nitrogen, thereby creating favorable conditions for high yields of cotton. Alfalfa made it possible to keep livestock, which, in turn, provided organic fertilizer for the cotton fields. But under constant pressure from Moscow to increase production at any price, it was impossible to let the soil rest. The classic cycle—cotton, alfalfa, manure, cotton—was broken. According to another Uzbek scholar, Favaris Kaiumov, in 1940, when the crop rotation was still practiced, alfalfa was planted in almost half of all land sown to cotton. But now alfalfa sowing is insignificant, and fertile soils are being exhausted.

The sowing of cotton also pushed out the other agricultural crops traditional to Central Asia, including fruits and vegetables, and pasturelands for livestock were cut back. Even the trees around peasants' houses were cut down to make way for cotton—and that amidst the scorching sun of Central Asia.

Fertile soils have been depleted, and the acreage under cultivation has reached its absolute outer limits, given available water supplies. Yet Moscow, operating as ever on the principle that one must surpass the "attained level," constantly raises the plan targets. There remains but one alternative: inflation of the data. After the death of the Uzbek "grand vizer," Sharif Rashidov, when first Andropov and then Gorbachev launched purges of cadres, the terrible consequences of the grandiose cotton affair came to light. Virtually the entire *nomenklatura* (power elite) of Uzbekistan was involved. To cite *Literaturnaia gazeta* again:

Cotton, to which everything was sacrificed (including the normal life of townspeople, who were incessantly dispatched to work on cotton), had the same harvest in 1984 as in 1969. Only the production costs had increased. And how they had increased, warping the economy of the entire republic! To this very day the return on capital continues to decline; the construction of new housing is being cut back. After beginning with cotton, the leprosy of inflated reports permeated the entire republic, spread to the social sphere, and did not pass by culture

71

and law enforcement organs. It is said: Make no idols. But they made one here: cotton, and cotton alone. It degenerated into a deception of society and themselves, into false honors, into bribery.[21]

After 1983 Uzbekistan was swept by a massive wave of arrests. Hundreds of leaders in *kolkhozy* and *sovkhozy*, ordinary employees as well as top figures in the economy (including ministers) and in the party apparatus—all were put in the dock and brought to justice. And the majority of cadres were ethnic Uzbeks. Most of those affected, however, found that the only way to protect their positions and careers was to collaborate in the deception, the cheating, the violation of laws that had taken hold in the republic. This has now become a major catastrophe for the republic, involving not only the elite *nomenklatura*, but also entire strata of the population. But the root cause was not the Uzbeks' cupidity; it was Moscow's economic policy.

Central Asia's Exclusion from Textile Manufacturing

Central Asia is the cotton base of the USSR, but it has only a minor role in the manufacture of cotton textiles. Uzbekistan produces some 70 percent of the nation's cotton fiber, but it has a negligible share in textile output—just 2.7 percent in 1940, 3.7 percent in 1960, 2.8 percent in 1970, 2.7 percent in 1980, and approximately 4 percent in 1984.[22] Only 4 to 5 percent of the region's cotton production remains there;[23] the rest is shipped to the European part of the country, where more than 70 percent of the USSR's output of cotton textiles is produced.[24]

For more than a half century, the Central Asian planners have attempted, in vain, to lessen this disproportion. Opponents of such demands argue it is more advantageous to ship cotton fiber than textiles. A typical expression of this view was advanced in the 1960s by E. Pospelova and E. Slastenko:

The basic principle that should determine the placement and distribution of textile production is its proximity to the consumer. Proximity to the source of the raw material does not have the significance for the textile industry that it does for machine building or metallurgy. It has been well known for a long time that *the shipment of raw cotton is more economic than the shipment of textiles* [emphasis added]. Therefore, based on the opportunities [offered by] a high concentration, *it is far from expedient to create everywhere new districts of textile industry* [emphasis added].[25]

Obviously, this passage refers to Central Asia, since no other regions in the USSR have the raw material to create such textile centers.

The above assertions are not, however, supported by any concrete calculation. The purported advantage in transporting cotton fiber rather than finished textiles is based merely on the lower rail tariffs set for the shipment of fiber. But the difference is not great and in any event simply reflects state tariff policy, which reflects not economic reality but the state's policies to regulate the development of various regions. Indeed, the shipment of cotton fiber over such immense distances is very costly and compounds the acute difficulties that already beset the creaking and overloaded railway system. If to that are added the costs of reshipping textiles back to Central Asia and Kazakhstan to clothe the population there (approximately 50 million inhabitants), the entire Moscow argument proves specious.

Moreover, the largest textile factories in Central Asia (in Tashkent and Fergana) have significantly better economic indices than analogous plants in the Moscow, Ivanovo, and Vladimir oblasts of European Russia. Central Asia's abundance of labor, increased by the large number of people outside the official labor force (especially among the female population), constitute an important argument in favor of establishing textile mills in the region. Indeed, providing employment opportunities (especially for the population of small towns, where industry is completely absent) is a critical economic and social desideratum for the region. According to data compiled by Nikolai Bedrintsev, a member of the Uzbek

Academy of Sciences, in the 1970s the work force of Uzbekistan grew by 250,000 persons a year, whereas the number of jobs (outside of *kolkhozy* and *sovkhozy*) increased by only 100,000 a year (of which only 25,000 were in industry).[26] Under the circumstances, it would seem expedient to expand the most labor-intensive production, which includes the textile industry. Although this industry seems ideally suited for Central Asia, Moscow has refused to modify its policy and expand that sector.

The indignation of the Central Asian establishment sometimes comes through on the pages of the local press. Here, for example, is the statement by one of the leading Central Asian economists, I. Iskanderov:

> Is it not clear that the majority of enterprises manufacturing cotton in this country are detached from both the sources of raw material and the consumer? Most distressing of all is the fact that central planning organs [Gosplan in Moscow] have become inured to this situation and do not notice the disproportions in the distribution of production in cotton textiles. *Moreover, economists have come forward to try to legitimize the existing territorial structure of production of raw materials and finished products* [emphasis added]. In my view it is unwise to ignore any longer the exceptionally favorable conditions in Central Asia, especially in Uzbekistan, that would permit the manufacture of cotton textiles with the lowest production costs. Is it not time to reconsider the long-range plans with an eye toward increasing Central Asia's share in the national production of cotton textiles with the calculation that they might completely satisfy all its own needs as well as those of Kazakhstan, Siberia, and the Far East?[27]

Those lines appeared in 1966. But policy has not changed in the interim, and in 1986 Iskanderov was still trying to persuade Moscow to alter its policy:

> It is urgently necessary to prepare concrete proposals to create a gigantic center of textile industry in Uzbekistan, based on the favorable economic and natural conditions at hand, and also on the surfeit of labor resources. At the present time approximately

74

94 percent of the cotton fiber is exported out of the Uzbek SSR at the cost of great transportation expenditures. Part of this raw material is then returned to the republic in the form of finished cloth. This two-way shipping wreaks enormous economic harm on the economy of the country. Hence the creation of a large center of textile industry in Uzbekistan (to provide for the needs of the republic and eastern regions of the country for the basic types of textile products) is economically advantageous in every sense.[28]

But at least for now, there is no evidence that such appeals will impel Moscow to revise the pattern of one-sided regional specialization that it has so systematically developed over several decades.

In declining to allocate investment to develop another labor-intensive branch of industry, machine building, Moscow cites the absence of a sufficient metallurgical base. But what kind of objective arguments can be adduced to explain the stubborn refusal to develop the textile industry in Central Asia?

CHAPTER 5

Water

Central Asia constitutes one of the arid zones of the planet. Resolution of the region's water problem is the most important factor shaping its economic development. The Soviet government cannot be accused of having paid too little attention to this problem: from the first five-year plans it has made major efforts to deal with the water shortage, allocating significant investment to create irrigation systems, to build a system of canals, and to regulate the flow of rivers. Nevertheless, these efforts have not gone far enough, and now, more than ever, the region faces an acute shortage of water for consumption by agriculture, industry, and the population.

Moreover, Central Asia's water resources are unevenly distributed. Most of the water supply is concentrated in mountainous areas, from which all the major and lesser rivers emanate to form a rather well developed river network. After leaving the mountains, these rivers enter desert areas, provide water for oases of land, and lose much water through filtration and evaporation. Four-fifths of this water network is located in Kirghizia and Tadjikistan, which have a small land area; Uzbekistan and Turkmenistan, which occupy approximately three-fourths of the region's land area and most of its arable land, have only one-fifth of the water network.[1] The water level of the largest river in Central Asia, the Amu Darya, falls perilously at critical times of the year, because so much water is diverted from its tributaries for irrigation.

Central Asia is well endowed with underground waters, however. The conditions for their formation are exceptionally favorable here: the mountain massifs feed not only rivers but also subterranean water. Moreover, the region's plains (which are most suitable for agriculture) have few rivers, but rains do lead to the formation of temporary, local surface water, called *takyry*, in many areas. In prerevolutionary times both the *takyry* and underground water were used extensively for agriculture and day-to-day needs. At present, however, these sources of water are given very little attention, and their role in solving the water shortage is considerably less than they merit.

The water supply has been a major issue in Central Asia's economic development. The intensive development of irrigated agriculture, the growing needs of industry, the demands of hydroelectric power systems, the growth of cities—all mean that water flows must be carefully ordered and regulated. For this purpose the Soviet Union has constructed a number of reservoirs, but their total capacity is not great enough to satisfy the demand. A peculiar feature of Central Asia is the dominance of reservoirs intended for use by hydroelectric power generation (and whose use is therefore controlled by the demand schedule for energy). Reservoirs for irrigation canals, in general, are relatively small and serve only local needs. The result is an incessant conflict between the hydroelectric and agricultural sectors, each of which makes demands on the reservoirs—demands that for the most part are utterly contradictory and irreconcilable. Given cotton's predominance in the regional economy, irrigation usually takes precedence, which in turn leads to underuse of hydroelectric capacities and, consequently, shortages of electrical power.

The continuing construction of water reservoirs for hydroelectric stations raises the possibility that the water from the two main rivers in Central Asia, the Amu Darya and the Syr Darya, will be wholly diverted, thereby shutting off their flow into the Aral Sea. Excessive use of these rivers, at both the current and projected levels, will speed contraction of the Aral Sea and eventually cause it to evaporate entirely. And that will create a whole complex of economic and ecological problems of cardinal importance to Central Asia and Kazakhstan.

The Controversy over a "Water Shortage"

The problem of supplying Central Asia with water is now a subject of acrimonious polemics that has divided specialists and the general public into two irreconcilable camps. One side believes that the region's water resources are nearly exhausted and therefore that supplementary water from other areas is urgently needed. Without this, an ecological catastrophe and economic crisis are inevitable. The other side holds that Central Asia is quite capable of solving its own water problems, for it still possesses substantial resources. It is simply a matter of using them rationally, economically, and in a technologically sensible fashion.

To put the debate into perspective, it should be pointed out that most of the Soviet Union's water resources (84 percent) are concentrated in sparsely settled eastern regions of the country. The southern zones, which have 80 percent of the population, have only the remaining 16 percent of the water resources. Yet demand in those southern areas is steadily rising. In Kazakhstan, for example, the land area under irrigation has expanded from 2.9 million hectares (1950) to 7.2 million (1980). Water consumption for that land has risen threefold.[2] However, such consumption has its limits—specifically, those dictated by the capacity of the Syr Darya and the Amu Darya rivers. And riverway reserves are such that, if the growth in water use continues at the current pace, by the 1990s the rivers' potential will have been completely exhausted.[3]

Yet it seems hardly possible to slow the expansion of newly irrigated land. According to current estimates, the population of Central Asia will increase another 16 million by the year 2000, thereby rising to some 50 million people. How is this massive populace to be fed—indeed, in a region where even now observers report "the lowest actual norms for the consumption of meat and other food products"?[4] Thus it seems reasonable to argue that "it would be not only uneconomic, but even incomprehensible and senseless to import (as is now the case) agricultural products to this region, whose bioclimatic indices demonstrate that it should provide its own food and fill the state granary as well—if only it were not for the lack of water."[5]

According to this argument, the land area under irrigation should be increased. It should be noted that the growth proponents say nothing about reducing cotton fields or replacing cotton with the cultivation of grains and vegetable crops. At any rate, such is the viewpoint of the Central Asians, the Ministry of Waterways, and its allied institutes.

Their critics assert that the "theory of a water shortage" is the mere fabrication of the ministry and its allies, who are simply interested in expanding irrigation projects and receiving the appropriate investments. The ministry's opponents hold that the water-shortage proposition is based on two unproven assumptions: (1) that the South has too little water and the North too much and (2) that economic development inevitably entails increased water consumption.

As for the volume of water, critics argue that the water flows really favor the South. Thus, in European Russia, rivers flowing northward carry 31 percent of the water, those flowing westward 12 percent, and those moving southward 57 percent. And, according to their calculations for Central Asia, the water reserves are twice as large as reported by the proponents of the water-shortage theory.[6] In addition, critics contend that more effective use should be made of underground water supplies and soil moisture created through precipitation.

Critics likewise reject the assumption that development means increased water consumption. They note the world-wide tendency to exercise greater economy in the use of water; the problem in Central Asia, they argue, is simply that their opponents do not use methods that would reduce water consumption. Indeed, water usage in Central Asia is significantly—60 to 70 percent—higher than the modest norms that now exist. Losses through irrigation run to 60 percent. Nor will the current population growth rate necessarily persist. As P. Khabibullaev, the president of the Uzbek Academy of Sciences, wrote:

> Is it really necessary to agree with the tendency for a 50 percent increase in the population by the year 2000? Is it not time to

give serious thought to this whole demographic problem? The world has already amassed considerable experience in dealing with this problem. Why should we perceive an unrestrained demographic explosion as something given and something beyond our control?[7]

This declaration has distinct elements of demagoguery: implementation of measures to reduce fertility, as experience everywhere demonstrates, is complicated and time-consuming. And realization of such steps among a Moslem population has still less chance for success.

To support their position, the critics of the water-shortage theory cite the experience of the United States and other Western countries:

In the United States the demand for fresh water declined between 1975 and 1985 by 55 cubic meters. In recent years demand has been stabilized by a significant increase in the use of sea water, which is virtually untapped in the USSR. All developed countries have reduced not only the relative water demand (that is mandatory!), but also the absolute volume of water consumed.[8]

By implication the Soviet Union can—and should—take similar steps to economize on water consumption.

In recent years this discussion has lost its academic character and turned into an acrimonious fight with mutual insults. Here, for instance, is the rhetoric used by the proponents of the water-shortage thesis in describing their opponents:

It seems to us that a number of members of the Writers' Union per hectare of irrigated land on earth must be sharply reduced. On the one hand, this should be achieved by an increase in the irrigated lands, and on the other, by expelling from the Writers' Union those writers who have slid into the dissident, demagogic and categorical reflections of ignoramuses and opportunists exploiting a fashionable theme.[9]

The most powerful weapon in these debates is the

accusation that one's opponents are providing materials for anti-Soviet propagandists. As one participant wrote:

> Enemies are always to be found abroad that are eager for any provocation in nationality questions and to inflame these for their own benefit. And you, instead of serious criticism, have permitted abusive language and insinuations, aroused distrust, and failed to consider that all this is grist for our enemies' mill. And by drawing false conclusions, you have given grounds for discontent, for agitation among the peoples of Central Asia about the fate of their children and grandchildren—as remaining without water.[10]

Equally serious accusations are made by the opposing camp. Supporters of the water-shortage thesis are accused of corruption, of a criminal attitude toward nature, of destroying the historic values of Russian national culture, and of many other sins, the likes of which, in Stalin's time, would have earned them the label "saboteur."

A discussion on such a low plane does not reflect a desire on either side for objectivity. More important motives are material and corporate interest, nationalism, and personal prestige.

The Aral Sea Problem and Alternative Solutions

The smooth waters of the Aral Sea spread out over an area of almost 64,000 square kilometers. A white, smokelike haze of evaporating water rises almost constantly from its surface. The Amu Darya and Syr Darya have been replacing the lost water for 3,500 years. But this source is now drying up and the Aral has been put on starvation rations. The result is dramatically described by the president of the Uzbek Academy of Sciences:

> The history of mankind knows no other example where, before the eyes of a single generation of people, an entire sea disappears from the face of the earth. And in its place will spread out a new sand and salt desert occupying six million hectares. Alas, precisely this is the sad fate that threatens the Aral Sea.[11]

If water delivery ceases completely (and this will occur soon if the current tendencies persist), then the rapid rate of evaporation will cause the entire Aral Sea to dry up in 25 to 30 years.[12]

From 1965 to 1984 the water level in the Aral Sea fell by seven meters.[13] This sharp decline, caused primarily by the diversion of rivers for irrigation, has led to a degradation of the ecological system in immense territories. According to prognoses of possible changes in natural conditions in the event the Aral Sea disappears (based on many years of geological and archeological research), the flourishing territory of Central Asia and southern Kazakhstan will be replaced by a desert.

It is difficult to exaggerate the dramatic consequences for the population of Central Asia that would ensue from an ecologic catastrophe like the evaporation of the Aral Sea. On its beds the Kyzylkum and Karakum deserts would be joined. Saline sand would invade the once-fertile delta of the Amu Darya, causing the loss of more than a million hectares of land. Winds that once brought rain from the Aral would now carry blasts of salt, poisoning the soil and air ever further to the south, finally reaching the oases of Karakalpakiia, Khorezm, and eastern Turkmenia. The salt content in the milk of nursing mothers who live in the territories around the Aral already exceeds the norm severalfold.[14]

Strictly speaking, there is nothing unexpected in what has been transpiring in the Aral Sea. It was consciously seen as a sacrifice to the unlimited expansion of cotton growing. As early as 1968 the head of the Soviet Union's Hydro-Technical Institute (Gidroproekt) declared, "It is obvious to everyone that evaporation of the Aral Sea is inevitable."[15] To justify this sacrifice, several rationalizations have been adduced.

Because of the conditions for raising cotton and other agricultural products, Central Asia and the contiguous areas form a unique zone in the USSR. Here are found highly fertile soils, enormous untapped rural labor resources, and centuries of experience with irrigated agriculture. The land areas of this zone, however, significantly surpass the irrigation potential of the Amu Darya and Syr Darya rivers.

The land areas suitable for irrigation comprise more than 26 million hectares, of which only 8.5 million can be irrigated by the water resources found in the region.[16]

To exploit this land fully, the central institutes have worked out elaborate irrigation plans. Aware that these schemes endanger the Aral Sea, some planners in the 1960s waxed eloquent about the positive results from their water-development projects:

> The introduction of new land areas in the Aral basin into agriculture will not cease in the future. The total land area will be doubled. The fields will be watered by more than 70 cubic kilometers of water instead of the current 40. The increase of irrigated land promises not only to double the output of cotton and rice, but also to increase fourfold the production of meat and to increase the harvest of vegetables, fruits and grapes.[17]

Two decades have since elapsed, but not one of these optimistic predictions has come true. The harvest of cotton and rice has not been doubled. As for the other food products, Central Asia now produces a share in several categories that falls below medical norms for adequate nutrition—26 percent of its meat, 42 percent of its milk, and 53 percent of its fruit. Only the use of chemical fertilizers has increased dramatically. The cotton plantations now use pesticides and mineral fertilizers at several times the average rate in the USSR or the United States. Water consumption has likewise increased sharply; cotton plantations now use not 70 cubic kilometers (as promised), but 90.[18] In addition, the area of irrigated land has by no means doubled. In short, the multibillion ruble investment to expand irrigated land has not brought Central Asia the promised prosperity. But it has enormously aggravated the economic, ecological, and social problems of the region.

It is difficult to find in Central Asia anyone who would agree with Gidroproekt's view regarding the fate of the Aral Sea. The idea that the Aral is doomed has always been anathema to public opinion in Central Asia. Rather, there are two main views on how the Aral is to be saved, how the coming ecologic catastrophe is to be avoided, how the water crisis is to be resolved.

One viewpoint emphasizes a restructuring of the economy and application of water-conservation policies. That means a restriction on cotton production (because of its high consumption of water) and even some reduction in the land area under cultivation; the freed resources should be redirected to restore the soil and increase food production. Indeed, the goal of "cotton self-sufficiency of the USSR" is a crude archaism, inherited from Stalinist times. It would make much more sense to purchase the shortfall of cotton from Third World countries, where its production requires far smaller outlays. It is, in short, time to abandon the view of Central Asia as an agrarian region, as the cotton base of the USSR. Strict economies in water consumption must become the key to the region's economic development.

This school of thought, moreover, urges a broad program of water-conservation methods. Khabibullaev, for example, actively furthers the idea of providing Central Asia with water resources by using the water efficiently: "Local water reserves are quite sufficient to sustain the [Aral] Sea and vital activity in its basin. That is really the whole paradox of the Aral problem: the reservoir is evaporating, but the moisture for its support is more than sufficient. It is merely necessary to use it sensibly."[19] The assertions of this leading Uzbek scholar are based on analyses of effectiveness in the use of the region's water.

According to studies conducted in the 1970s, in a ten-year period the Aral basin provided 85 billion cubic meters of water for effective irrigation, while another 100 billion cubic meters were lost through evaporation, diversion to canals, and the like. In short, most of the water drawn off for irrigation is simply lost. The introduction of newly irrigated lands on cotton plantations will perpetuate this ratio of loss, and the water used will not return to the Amu Darya and subsequently reach the Aral Sea. The irrigation inundates agricultural areas, turns them into swamps, spoils the arable land, ruins fertility, and destroys buildings. According to the most conservative estimates, at least 10 cubic kilometers could be returned to the Aral if the water were used efficiently.[20] This program demands, of course, large-scale projects with corresponding investment. The Uzbek Academy of Sciences prepared a multiyear program for regulating river flows, reconstructing irrigation systems, establishing stricter norms for land use, and introducing water-conservation technologies.

In contrast to this first school, which seeks to restore and support the existing land and water potential, the second school seeks to supplement the Central Asian water with resources from other regions. To be sure, this school supports water conservation and higher efficiency but regards these measures as palliatives rather than as a real solution to the region's enormous needs. In this view, the solution, quite simply, is to go beyond the Amu Darya and Syr Darya basins by constructing a canal to deliver water to the region. This idea was realized in a plan that acquired enormous importance in public life in the 1970s and 1980s, not only in Central Asia, but also in the USSR as a whole. It is worthwhile to stop for a moment and examine this matter more closely.

The Project of the Century

The phrase "project of the century" is used often by the Soviet press—which is much given to hyperbole—to describe the plans to divert the Siberian rivers to Central Asia.[21] In its general contours, the project consisted of the following. The water was to come from the Ob River (from the point at which it is joined by the Irtysh River) and be directed over a canal through the Turan Lowlands to the Amu Darya. The main canal for water diversion (2,200 kilometers in length) would bisect the arid lands of the semidesert and desert areas of Kazakhstan and Central Asia, permitting irrigation.[22]

The peculiarity of the project is that water is taken from a northern zone for diversion to a southern one. Consequently, if even a small volume of water is diverted, the impact can be felt as far as the Kara Sea. Hence, the main question is whether the harm inflicted on northern areas will be outweighed by the gains achieved by supplying additional water to the southern region. In addition, this water diversion is portrayed as more cost-effective than better use of water resources already at the disposal of the region.

Proponents of the project defend it as follows:

1. Even if various steps are taken to increase the use of regional water resources (including reconstruction of the existing irrigation system), by 1995 (or by 2000, according to other estimates) the water resources of the Aral Sea basin will nevertheless be exhausted. Thus, any further expansion of irrigated land would be impossible and the construction of a canal is absolutely necessary.[23]

2. The moderate diversion of water from Siberian rivers (somewhat more than 6 percent of the waterflow in West Siberian rivers) will not have any appreciable influence on the environment of Siberia or the ice flows of the Arctic Ocean, or on agricultural conditions in the southern areas of Western Siberia, but will yield an enormous profit in the form of an upsurge in agricultural production in Central Asia. According to such calculations, the construction of the canal will be extremely profitable, paying back its investment in ten years.[24]

Opponents of the project offer a radically different perspective. They explain the optimism of its protagonists by citing their inadequate research on the ecological consequences and by noting the egotistical, vested interests of the Ministry of Reclamation and Water Management (which seeks to obtain investment capital as quickly as possible and to expand work on a scale that will expand its role and prestige). According to critics, the water resources of Central Asia are used with such extraordinary inefficiency that the irrigated lands do not yield the appropriate return; hence, the enormous investments for the project would not pay off in the foreseeable future. Indeed, the evaporation loss through the movement of water across an open canal (together with its absorption into the soil) would be extraordinarily great. And so forth.[25]

This project has given rise to an unprecedented battle of ideas, of national and economic interests, of personal pride and individual careers, of ministerial ambitions, and of scientific conceptions. I am no specialist in these matters and cannot attempt to untangle all these convoluted polemics and present an objective, scientific evaluation. Nevertheless, the project for the Siberian-Aral Canal ("Sibaral") has played so significant a role for several decades in all of the plans for the economic and social development of Central Asia, the hopes placed on this plan were so great, the determination of Moscow to implement this scheme was so unqualified, and the abandonment of the plan in August 1986 was so unexpected that I believe it is essential to examine this development more closely. In doing so, however, I must digress from a strictly economic approach.

THE BACKGROUND OF THE SIBARAL PROJECT

The project to construct a canal from Siberia to Central Asia and Kazakhstan already has a 100-year history. In the 1870s a professor at Kiev University, I. Demchenko, published a book entitled *On the Flooding of the Aral and Caspian Lowlands for the Improvement of the Climate in Surrounding Areas*, proposing the diversion of Siberian waterways to Central Asia. Even at that time the author foresaw the possibility that water from the Amu Darya and Syr Darya would not suffice to irrigate the millions of hectares of fertile lands in Turkestan (as the territories of Central Asia and Kazakhstan were then called) that, for lack of water, would otherwise remain useless.

Interest in this scheme intensified after the Bolshevik Revolution. Proposals to redirect Siberian rivers toward Central Asia were put forward by D. Bukinich in 1920, N. Botvinkin in 1924, V. Monastyrev and Z. Kirilets in 1927, and others. All of these proposals suggested damming the Irtysh and Enisei Rivers and then directing the water (through the force of gravity) over the Turan Lowland to Central Asia. Of a fundamentally different character was the proposal offered in 1938 by A. Miller-Shulga, who sought to overcome the watershed through the use of pumping stations at a height of 30 to 50 meters.[26]

In the late 1940s Gidroproekt, the leading Soviet research and design center for hydroelectric construction, conducted economic research on the problem and concluded that the construction of a canal would bring extraordinary economic advantages. Concretely, Gidroproekt proposed to construct an artificial waterway that would redirect one-sixth to one-third of the waterflow of the Ob, Irtysh, and Enisei rivers to the arid territories of Central Asia and Kazakhstan.

There were two basic concepts for effecting the water diversion: by means of gravity over a natural incline and by means of pumping stations. The latter method required immense expenditures of electrical energy, roughly equal to the capacity of the Krasnoiarsk hydroelectric power station, the most powerful hydroelectric station in the USSR and one of the most powerful in the world. The gravity approach did not require any significant consumption of energy, but its realization required the creation of water reservoirs of such magnitude (to create the requisite downward pressure) that vast areas of Western Siberia would be under water—along with oil and gas deposits, the majority of population points, industrial enterprises, agricultural resources, and railways. The gravity approach was rejected on these grounds, and all further research pursued some kind of mixed variant, partly involving the use of the natural relief and partly relying on the use of pumping stations.

In the postwar era, interest in the project and work on its development periodically flared and died. But activity was particularly apparent after Soviet leadership decisions to intensify research on the problem. Over the last several decades three main initiatives have been brought forward.

1. *The Khrushchev Plan* At a plenum of the Central Committee in January 1961, Nikita Khrushchev advanced the idea of irrigating the arid lands of the South both to solve the food problem and to increase cotton production. Khrushchev, characteristically, envisioned irrigation as a panacea for all the failures of Soviet agriculture, as "the most reliable means to obtain guaranteed harvests."[27]

At the time Khrushchev was enthralled by the idea of irrigation, which "will permit us to exploit the rich lands of the South, where there is much sunshine but not enough water."[28] To his mind, expanding the amount of land under cultivation was the most effective way to increase agricultural output.

Even as Khrushchev spoke, the Soviet Union was engaged in another enormous undertaking (in terms of both scale and investment): the conquest and development of the virgin lands. Nevertheless, he insisted on giving attention to the next gigantic project of irrigating the lands in the South (above all, in Central Asia), with the argument that realization of the project would permit the USSR "to satisfy 30 to 40 percent of the country's need for guaranteed grain" and "always to obtain the required amount of such valuable agriculture products as cotton, rice, corn, etc."[29] Khrushchev became positively exuberant over these plans and exclaimed to the participants of the Central Committee plenum, "You can imagine what it means in Turkmenistan, Tadjikistan, and Uzbekistan to have such a quantity of irrigated land!" To carry out this program, he proposed to rechannel the rivers from the Arctic Ocean to the South, particularly to Central Asia.

But the imagination of the Soviet leader was not limited to the irrigation of land. He was fascinated by the idea of river diversion because "We will obtain a new economically advantageous path from the north of the country to the south" and hence "our southern seas will be linked with the Arctic Ocean."[30] Khrushchev drew a picture of spectacular prospects for an unprecedented leap in the production of cotton and concluded his speech with the following slogan: "Full steam ahead in the production of cotton!"[31]

Khrushchev assured his listeners that, although this proposal would demand no less effort and investment than development of virgin lands in Kazakhstan and Western Siberia, this undertaking nevertheless "is entirely within our capacity."[32]

No one made an open rejoinder to Khrushchev. However, his ideas were not—and indeed could not be—implemented, for valid economic reasons. And Khrushchev himself did not return to these ideas. Other experiments and events distracted his attention from the grandiose scheme to redirect the flow of Siberian rivers.

2. The Brezhnev Proposal In 1971, Brezhnev directed the Ministry of Reclamation and Water Management to organize research and exploratory work on the diversion of Siberian rivers to the Amu Darya and Syr Darya basins.[33] In 1976 the twenty-fifth party congress adopted a resolution "to conduct scientific research and, on the basis of this, to carry out project studies connected with the problem of diverting part of the flow of northern and Siberian rivers to Central Asia, Kazakhstan, and the Volga River basin."[34]

This formulation—reflecting the ambivalence of the leadership toward the feasibility of the whole scheme—was quite cautious in several respects. First, it shows a lack of certainty about the economic feasibility of the undertaking. Second, initiative, enthusiasm, and "gigantomania" in economic policy were not among Brezhnev's main traits, in contrast to those of his predecessor. Accordingly, the Brezhnev leadership also evaded a definitive decision on the question at the twenty-sixth party congress in 1981, and, in effect, simply reiterated its previous decision "to continue scientific and planning studies on the diversion of part of the water of Siberian rivers to Central Asia and Kazakhstan."

3. The Chernenko Proposal In this phase important decisions were finally taken to complete the research and preparatory work for the diversion project. To be sure, Chernenko's name is used here as a kind of political shorthand, since this expiring figurehead was hardly capable of dynamic initiatives. But a group of highly placed figures, with strong vested interests in the project, became exceedingly active. They include N. Vasil'ev (the minister of Reclamation and Water Management), G. Voropaev (director of the Institute of Water Problems at the Academy of Sciences), and I. Gerardi (the ranking executive behind the whole project). Reacting to pressure from this group, the Central Committee resolved in October 1984 "to complete preparation of the plan to construct a canal from Siberia to Central Asia."[35] In accordance with this resolution, the Ministry of Reclamation and Water Management was to undertake planning of the main canal and to complete all exploratory and planning work by 1986. Thus, the whole matter suddenly acquired a completely concrete character. This exploratory and planning work, conducted across the enormous length of the project, was an extremely costly operation; the command to begin signified an end to lingering doubts and the intention to construct the canal. And precisely at this point passions became inflamed.

THE GREAT RIVER PROJECT AS A FOCUS OF THE RUSSIAN NATIONALIST MOVEMENT

At this point there occurred an incident without precedent in Soviet history: a decision taken by top authorities in Moscow encountered active resistance from the Russian intelligentsia. To be sure, one must take into account the special dynamics of the period. Under Khrushchev and Brezhnev, the plans for the diversion project evoked mute dissatisfaction among the Russian nationalist elite, but overt opposition was out of the question. The most that could be expected was an occasional article in *Literaturnaia gazeta* raising doubts about the feasibility and expediency of the policy.[36]

This time it was different. In 1985 an assault was launched on the project and its proponents—or *perebroschiki* (diversionists), as the "village writer" Vasilii Belov deftly labeled them. In an interview with the West German journal *Der Spiegel* in April 1985, Valentin Rasputin, the most prominent village writer and voice of the nostalgia theme so popular among the ethnic Russian population, gave this description of the relationship between the people and the party on the issue:

Rasputin: "The population has been constantly resisting this. Thank God that this is the case."
Spiegel: "Why does the party fear a discussion [of the issue]?"
Rasputin: "First, to create the impression that there is only one opinion and that there can be no other solution to the problem. . . . Second, they avoid a discussion—probably—so that the West does not know that there are disagreements among us. . . ."
Spiegel: "What have you done [to resist] this project?"
Rasputin: "I have signed many letters against the diversion of the northern rivers."

Spiegel: "And what was the reaction to this?"

Rasputin: "They summoned many of the letters' authors and scholars to the Central Committee in Moscow for a discussion. However, this discussion did not bring any results; each side stubbornly defended its own position."

Spiegel: "Do Soviet citizens have any other means to thwart this project? Can they appeal to the courts?"

Rasputin: "No. A court will not intervene in this matter."

In Rasputin's opinion, the sole possibility for achieving anything—as was done to defend Lake Baikal—was to open a public discussion of the project.

By this time, the Soviet Union had already accumulated considerable bitter experience from the creation of canals and water reservoirs that were economically unjustified and ecologically catastrophic. The White Sea–Baltic and Volga–Don canals; the Rybinsk, Tsimliansk, and Krasnoiarsk reservoirs (which inundated vast areas of fertile soil); the diversion of water from Lake Sevan, regarded by Armenians as a holy national shrine—all these gave ample cause for alarm at the prospect of rerouting Siberia's rivers southward. And, with uneven success, the village writers had battled the bureaucracy to stop the flow of industrial waste that had been poisoning Lake Baikal.

In general, by the late 1970s and early 1980s ecology had become both a popular and a permissible subject of debate. Environmentalists were not punished for attacks on local authorities and ministerial officials for their criminal behavior toward nature. Indeed, it even became rather fashionable in the press to demonstrate a concern for nature. But all this was for writers and journalists; it was by no means possible for ordinary citizens. And the writers knew the limits of criticism: they never criticized the highest levels of leadership and avoided generalizations. Manifesting concern about "the natural environment of our homeland" gave an outlet for nationalist feelings and established a reputation of civic courage for the nationalists eager to express public opinion. It was also important, from the regime's point of view, to sustain the illusion of a "public discussion."

Gorbachev's accession to power inaugurated an unusually

vigorous movement to defend the Russian environment and Russian culture—by a group that, for convenience, can be called the Russian party. Indeed, defense of the Russian national idea began to acquire an increasingly aggressive, even chauvinistic, character. This is hardly the first efflorescence of such phenomena in Soviet history. But if this previously took the form of anti-Semitism, it has now spread to other non-Slavic populations—in particular, the Moslems of Central Asia and Kazakhstan.[37] It is to be found not only in the writings of the village writers, but also in the nationalist policy of the new leadership.

As always, a policy shift in this sensitive area immediately sent shock waves through the ideological machine. The Russian party sensed that the winds were now favorable and launched a vigorous offense on all fronts. But the primary objective was to kill the project for diverting Siberian rivers to the South.

In the first few months of Gorbachev's rule, the Russian party assumed a wait-and-see position. But as the new leader's intentions remained obscure and the state and party apparatus treated the question as already decided, the opponents of the river-diversion project took action. Apparently, it came as a shock when the project surfaced in the draft version of *The Basic Directions of Social and Economic Development in the USSR* (published on November 9, 1985). This public reaffirmation of the intent to carry out the project unleashed a wave of criticism in the press. It was all the more easy to raise the issue because the draft for *The Basic Directions* offered a contradictory formulation of the project. Thus, on the one hand, it vowed "to improve the scientific foundations" of the plan, but on the other it hastily sought "to expand the work related to the diversion" of the rivers.

Criticism was not long in coming. In December 1985 *Sovetskaia Rossiia* published an article by a United Nations expert on environmental affairs, Dr. M. Lemeshev, who warned of the dangerous consequences that could ensue if the project were actually carried out.[38] The same month *Pravda* published an article on the same subject.[39] Leading writers from the Russian party (Viktor Astaf'ev, Vasilii

Belov, Iurii Bondarev, Sergei Zalygin, Valentin Rasputin, and the spiritual head of the movement, academician Dmitrii Likhachev) published a collective letter in *Sovetskaia Rossiia* under the title, "It Causes Concern."[40] An article like that must have unleashed a flood of letters from ordinary citizens voicing their opposition to the project. Thus the project provoked widespread indignation in the Russian population—an intense outburst of popular sentiment that the leadership evidently could not ignore.

The arguments against the project also changed. If earlier critics relied on ecological arguments and appeals to patriotic feelings, beginning in late 1985 they aimed another lethal weapon: that the project was economically unsound. Thus *Literaturnaia gazeta* published a series of articles on the subject of "The Price of Water."[41] initiated by an open letter from the writer Sergei Zalygin to the minister of Reclamation and Water Management, N. Vasil'ev, the highest placed proponent of the water-diversion project. Summing up this series of articles in January 1986, Zalygin raised this rhetorical question about the diversion plan: "What is the economic significance if one does not calculate the price of the water?"[42] Here Zalygin was referring to the fact that the state would spend billions of rubles on the project, yet in calculating its economic effectiveness for irrigated agriculture, it treated water as a free good!

The project's antagonists also stressed the harm from relying solely on increasing the water supply to boost agricultural production in the South, and the need to use other methods. The latter included soil improvement and enrichment (including crop rotation), since these are much less costly, save on water consumption, and do not lead to irreversible ecological consequences. One of the many publications on this problem stands out—an essay in *Pravda* in February 1986, two days before the twenty-seventh party congress, bearing the title "Land Is the Primary Wealth." It carried the signatures of leading scholars and scientists, including the economist A. Aganbegian, the geologist A. Ianshin, and the agronomist V. Tikhonov.[43] Publication of the article at that critical juncture was an unmistakable sign that the Russian party was close to victory.

Events surrounding the project took a truly dramatic turn. At the twenty-seventh party congress, the first secretary of the Uzbek Party Central Committee, I. Usmankhodzhaev, declared that "the potential of the Amu Darya and Syr Darya is exhausted" and then launched a direct assault on the procrastinating politicians: "These problems have been fruitlessly discussed for a long time in the Academy of Sciences of the USSR, but a concrete decision has still not been reached. We need—at long last—an answer: what is to be done?"[44] In this form the Central Asian leader expressed unambiguously the indignation of his region's nationalist cadres at the procrastination in realizing the diversion project.

Gorbachev, who remained silent on this issue even at the Central Committee plenum in October 1984, and who (as overseer of agriculture in the Central Committee) should have taken a position on this question, came under mounting pressure from the Russian party. Although he was evidently sympathetic to the Russian party (to judge from indirect evidence), for political reasons he could not come out openly in its favor. The general secretary's ambivalence and indecisiveness were reflected in the formulation that the congress finally adopted on the whole controversy, whereby it resolved "to advance the work on problems pertaining to the rational redistribution of water resources."[45] In a word, the whole issue—yet again—hung in abeyance, without a definitive resolution.

The struggle of the Russian party against the proposal reached its culmination at the Writers' Congress in July 1986. Passions became highly inflamed. All the civic emotion that for years had been denied any kind of expression suddenly came out into the open, in the public statements of Russian writers. Realizing that one would not be punished for this and that indeed such declarations could solidify one's reputation as a Russian patriot, writers attacked the river-diversion project and its proponents with furious denunciations. To quote Iurii Bondarev, "Even as the limits of publicity are being expanded, is it not too early to speak of its triumph if the Ministry of Reclamation and Water Management—the most serious criticism at its expense on the eve of the twenty-seventh party congress—continues undeviatingly, but clandestinely, to follow the same course— that is, to move toward the realization of the ill-starred project."[46] As Vasilii Belov remonstrated, "Supporters of the water-diversion project are continuing their activities. In our region they are already constructing moorings and shipping machinery."

The most popular contemporary Russian writer, Valentin Rasputin, in the name of all the writers opposed to the river-diversion scheme, demanded that a decision finally be taken on the issue: "We, a group of Russian writers . . . who (we hope) will be joined by writers of other republics, appeal to the Politburo and personally to Mikhail Sergeevich Gorbachev to authorize once again an investigation of the situation that has developed with respect to the northern rivers and Lake Baikal and to make a decision in the interests of the entire people—and not specific administrative organs"[47] [the Ministry of Reclamation and Water Management].

The Writers' Congress was preceded by a meeting of Gorbachev and various writers, including Bondarev and Rasputin. Apparently, at this point Gorbachev voiced his own support for their opposition to the water project; otherwise, it is most unlikely that any of the above would have dared, even in the era of glasnost, to have made such audacious speeches at the congress.

Finally, on August 16, 1986, came the announcement that the Politburo "has deemed it expedient to cease work" on the project of the century. Four days later the Central Committee and the Council of Ministers published a resolution on "the cessation of work to divert part of the water from the northern and Siberian rivers," with a specific instruction that "Gosplan and the Ministry of Reclamation and Water Management eliminate from the plan for 1986–1990 the assignment to complete the aforementioned work."[48]

This triumph significantly strengthened the hand of the Russian party, demonstrated its influence, and augmented its self-confidence. At the same time, its success reinforced the repression against manifestations of national self-consciousness by other, non-Slavic (especially Moslem) peoples. Censorship, that watchdog of ideology and conformity, pretends not to notice the unrestrained praise of the Russian spirit, Russian traditions, Russian ancestors, and even Russian saints, but refuses to tolerate similar tendencies among Uzbeks, Kazakhs, or Tadjiks.

Rasputin, for example, is permitted—on the pages of a weekly (*Ogonek*), with a circulation of 1.5 million—to appeal for a "return to the age-old traditions and fundamental rules of our people."[50] The journal *Nash sovremennik*, a veritable organ of the Russian party, can glorify the Russian religious fanatic Avvakum and sermonize about the "powerful spiritual forces of Russia."[50] Ideological authorities pay no attention to all this. That contrasts with the vicious attack in *Pravda* against a Kazakh paper that had published a letter proposing that the republic establish more nurseries and schools using the Kazakh language. The following passage in the letter provoked the special ire of ideological guardians in Moscow:

> To be proud of one's mother tongue, to be concerned about its purity, to promote its development—constitute one of the main duties of every Kazakh, every Kazakh family, and everyone who deems himself a Kazakh. We must transform the Kazakh tongue into one of the most literate and richest languages.[51]

If the same passage had appeared in Russian, it would have been entirely commonplace. But for making this appeal to preserve the Kazakh language, *Pravda* vilified the paper for propagating "national egoism."

Thus repudiation of the "project of the century" should be seen in the context of the Great-Russian, anti-Moslem tendencies in Soviet nationality policy that have intensified significantly since Gorbachev's accession to power.

The dramatic picture sketched above acquires various colorations, depending on how one views it. From the perspective of the Russian party, the refusal to divert the rivers is well founded, and the surging waves of Russian national enthusiasm are entirely justified. A. Solzhenitsyn is doubtless correct in arguing that the Russian population has suffered more, spiritually and physically, from communist rule than any other nationality in the USSR. As is well known, writers in Russia have traditionally performed the function of preachers and prophets (Tolstoi, Dostoevskii, Solzhenitsyn). The precursor, mentor, and professional master of the current leadership in the Russian nationalist movement of village writers is Aleksandr Solzhenitsyn. However, whereas Solzhenitsyn sees the entire evil resting with the communist regime and its ideology (and accordingly directs all his attacks at the Bolsheviks, beginning with Lenin), the village writers seek a compromise with the regime and do not dare make such inflammatory accusations. Rather, they seek to blame the national degradation either on some anonymous evil force or (heeding tradition) the Jews. Thus wrote one of the most influential of these writers, Viktor Astaf'ev:

What happened to us? Who hurled us into the depths of evil and misfortune and why? Who extinguished the light of goodness in our soul? Who extinguished the lamp of our conscience, toppled it into a dark, deep pit in which we are groping, trying to find the bottom, a support and some kind of guiding light to the future? What use have we for the light which leads to the fires of hell? . . .

We lived with a light in our soul, acquired long before us by the creators of heroic feats and lighted for us so that we would not wander in the darkness, run into trees, or into one another in the world, scratch out each other's eyes, or break our neighbor's bones. . . .

They stole it from us and did not give anything in return, giving rise to unbelief, an all-encompassing unbelief . . . . To whom should we pray? From whom should we ask for forgiveness?[52]

Astaf'ev begins one letter circulating in *samizdat* (addressed to Natan Eidelman in October 1986) as follows: "Everywhere people are talking and writing about the national renaissance of the Russian people." He ends the letter thus:

I wish for you the same thing that the daughter of our last tsar wished, the lines of which were put in the Gospels: "Lord!

Forgive our enemies. Lord! Embrace them!" And she, her sister, her brother (who finally lost the use of his legs during the exile), her mother and father were all shot—incidentally, by Jews and Latvians, who were headed by the inveterate, arrant Zionist Iurkovskii. As you see, we Russians have not yet lost our memory, and we are still a great people.[53]

As the above text makes clear, the Weltanschauung of this typical village writer represents a mixture of Christianity, nationalism, monarchism, and anti-Semitism.

Even if the issue of nationalism is left aside, there are good reasons not to trust the judgment of designers and officials of the Ministry of Reclamation and Water Management who compose the main core of protagonists for the project and who lobby on its behalf in Moscow. Many prominent Soviet scholars argue that the project lacks a sound scientific basis, that many fundamental questions have not been sufficiently studied, and that serious hydrologic, ecological, and economic questions will arise. It is not clear, in particular, what share of the water diverted from the Ob will actually reach its destination, how many minerals this water will contain, how the flora and fauna of cold Siberian waters will react to the hot climate of the desert, or what the construction of the canal will cost.

There is no doubt that Central Asia does not try to economize in its water consumption, that it uses water inefficiently, and that it does not maintain its irrigation system properly. But that is hardly surprising: water is free to its users. An experiment undertaken in Kirghizia demonstrated that, when a fee was charged to *sovkhozy* and *kolkhozy* for the use of water, their consumption fell significantly.[54]

According to a prominent Soviet expert, A. Nekrasov, data showing growth in Soviet water consumption are greatly exaggerated, for they are based on agricultural use that exceeds official norms by 30 to 50 percent and disregard methods for economizing on water consumption. Since agriculture accounts for 55 percent of Soviet water consumption, the uneconomic use in this sector has a considerable impact on the total water usage.[55] Nekrasov contends that these exaggerated figures on water consumption (artificially inflated by various government organizations with a vested interest) justify the need to plan and construct waterworks projects "never before seen in the world and global" in their massive dimensions. Nekrasov obviously has in mind the "project of the century" when he asserts that, in the work to establish the desirability of the project, "alternative variants for satisfying the water need by using local sources were not prepared and taken into account."[56]

On the total cost of the project, the difference of opinion is exceedingly great. There is little point in reviewing the disagreements between the project's advocates (who give low cost estimates) and its adversaries (who give high estimates). But it is worthwhile to cite the authoritative estimate of an expert commission from Gosplan, which set the construction costs at 14 billion rubles.[57] Can the Soviet leadership at the present time (or in the foreseeable future) afford such gigantic investments to construct Sibaral? It seems certain that investment capital must have been as important as the nationalism of the Russian party in persuading the leadership to shelve the project.

But let us consider this decision from the viewpoint of Central Asians. Their water problem is becoming ever more acute. The shortage grows steadily and has an impact on the daily lives of the population; between 1975 and 1985 the region suffered four times from catastrophic drought, causing enormous losses to its economy.[58] Over recent decades, the expansion of cultivated land on cotton plantations—under pressure from Moscow, year after year, to increase the production of cotton—has led to incessant expansion of irrigated land. For example, between 1966 and 1985, the area of artificially watered land in Uzbekistan increased from 2.6 to 3.7 million hectares.[59] And the rate of increase in water consumption was still higher. A freeze on new irrigation, with the aim of stabilizing the water consumption, will lead (according to estimates by Central Asian specialists) to an annual loss of 3.5 billion rubles in national income, even if the productivity of existing irrigated land is raised to the optimum levels.[60]

At the same time that Moscow drove Central Asians to abuse their natural environment and to upset the region's water balance, it promised to compensate for the exhaustion of local resources by diverting water from Siberia. For more than 25 years Moscow vowed to construct the canal; meanwhile, all the plans for Central Asia's social and economic development assumed that this would happen. Confident about the delivery of Siberian waters, reassured that Central Asia's own water resources could in the interim be exhausted, the region built industrial complexes and expanded cities. And all the while Central Asians became accustomed to the wasteful use of water. Then suddenly, the linchpin of this whole system—the presumption of water diversion from the North—was abruptly removed.

It is hardly surprising that one finds no expression of disgruntlement in the local press. But it is doubtless safe to assume that abandonment of the canal project provoked profound disillusionment among national cadres as well as among the general population in Central Asia.

Stalemate

The acrimonious discussion in the Soviet press—about the river diversion project, about saving the Aral Sea—shows no sign of abating. Why not? Should not the whole controversy have been settled, once and for all, by the August 1986 resolution "On Termination of Work on the Diversion of Part of the Northern and Siberian Rivers"?

So far as the project's adversaries are concerned, the issue has been conclusively and permanently settled. Academician Aganbegian made this unambiguous declaration: "The project to divert the water of European northern rivers to the South, and Siberian rivers to Central Asia, is not [merely] *halted, but is terminated and closed.*"[61]

That view is most definitely not shared by project supporters. They point out two articles in the resolution to prove the contrary: the article referring to "a continuation of research on scientific problems associated with the regional redistribution of water resources," and another article recommending that Gosplan (together with other agencies) prepare and present by the first quarter of 1987 a report on the economic development of Central Asia by the year 2010, "with a calculation of developments in the water and demographic situation."[62] Relying on these instructions, the proponents of the river-diversion project interpret the resolution to mean that "the idea of diversion is not categorically rejected, but only temporarily deferred."[63]

The ambiguity in the resolution was hardly accidental. Apart from reflecting indecision or factionalism in Moscow, the text served as a tranquilizer for Central Asians and, no less important, left the door open for subsequent reconsideration. Perhaps most important, the resolution was a statement of procrastination: to anyone familiar with Soviet bureaucratic language, the formula "prepare a report" meant that the Gorbachev leadership is not now willing to take concrete steps to alleviate the Central Asian water crisis.

Nor have the Central Asians—the tranquilizer notwithstanding—failed to grasp the real import of the resolution. The results have been considerable agitation among the local intelligentsia and a public campaign to defend the Aral Sea. That movement has been particularly active in Uzbekistan. Following the example of Russian writers, who had defended their rivers from diversion to the South, Uzbek writers assumed leadership in the nationalist-ecological movement. They founded a new public organization (the Committee to Save the Aral Sea) and a monetary fund; the Aral Sea became a central theme of the Uzbek intelligentsia, a symbol of their determination to defend national interests. As Khabibullaev has written, "The heat of passions is truly Shakespearean: to be or not to be?"[64] The Uzbek media are permeated with dramatic descriptions of the Aral's evaporation, the transformation of the land into a desert, the inundation of Uzbek land and water with salt from the dried-out basin of the Aral, and a sharp rise in illness and infant mortality. High-ranking figures from the local nationalities have joined this campaign to avert an ecological catastrophe. Typical is the description of the dire consequences—salinification of land and water, grave health hazards for the population—offered by D. Iadgarov, chairman of the Council of Ministers of Karakalpakiia.[65]

Under the aegis of three organizations (the USSR

Academy of Sciences, the Uzbek Academy of Sciences, and the State Committee on Melioration and Conservation), in October 1987 an all-union conference was held in Tashkent on the problems of ecology and water resources in the Aral basin. The conference decided that the first priorities were to provide water for the population in territories contiguous to the Aral (through construction of reservoirs and desalinizing plants) and to ban the use of dangerous chemicals in fertilizers. The conference further recommended a reevaluation of the agricultural system in Uzbekistan so as to reduce the scale of cotton cultivation and to increase the production of food.[66]

The conference represented one of the most substantial, authoritative discussions of the Aral problem in recent years. But it left a number of important questions unanswered. First, it is not altogether clear whether the ministries in Moscow and Central Asia are actually obliged to implement its resolutions. Second, the published documents say nothing about the allocation of requisite resources to realize the resolutions. That omission leaves the impression that the conference expressed pious wishes only. Third, and most important, the conference failed to construct a program to save the Aral Sea or to rehabilitate the region's ecology. It seems that Moscow has once again pacified public opinion in Central Asia by creating the illusion of concrete measures; that may well have been the true function of the Tashkent conference.

How does one account for the indecisiveness of Soviet leaders in addressing a question that is obviously of such importance for the people of Central Asia? The heart of the issue is simply investment resources: no matter what scheme is adopted to resolve the Central Asian water crisis, it invariably requires the allocation of enormous quantities of funds. But that kind of capital diversion simply does not fit within the current priorities of the Gorbachev leadership. Is it not, however, politically dangerous to ignore the water problem, which has created a complex social-economic crisis and generated widespread discontent in the local intelligentsia? After all, Central Asians could not fail to notice that the very resolution shelving their project included a provision to use the freed investment capital "for the melioration of land in the non-black-soil zone of the RSFSR and to expand work on the reconstruction of the irrigation system in the Volga basin."[67] It is quite fair for Central Asians to conclude that the regime prefers to save the declining, sparsely populated historical center of old Russia (Novgorod, Pskov, Vologda) at the expense of the historical national center of the Uzbeks (Khorezm, Urgench, Bukhara).

The social and economic problems that have emerged in Nagornyi Karabakh concerned the regime least of all. But the nationality conflicts that erupted there in early 1988 were an entirely different matter and compelled Moscow to admit "shortcomings in social-economic development" of the region and to take steps to bolster its economy (through allocation of significant material resources and investments).[68] The events in the Transcaucasus, like those a year earlier in Kazakhstan, should have served the Gorbachev leadership warning that it cannot afford to relegate the problems of national regions to the periphery of its interests. Moscow's refusal to tackle the water crisis in Central Asia is becoming ever more dangerous.

CHAPTER 6

Labor and Employment

The relationship between labor resources and the investment capital allocated by Moscow is a key determinant of economic development in Central Asia. The growing disparity between these two components, the divergence between this region's increasing share of the Soviet population and its share of the investment pie, evokes dissatisfaction within the Central Asian establishment, which regards Moscow's policy as outright discrimination. There are many dimensions to this problem, and the more important of these will be examined here.

The Central Asian Labor Surplus

Since the 1970s Soviet economists have made extensive use of the terms "with surplus labor" and "with sufficient labor" to describe the Central Asian economic region. As the potential for tapping additional labor resources shrank in most parts of the country, Central Asia—with its high rate of natural population growth—emerged as the main reservoir of the labor force. The phrase "with sufficient labor" means that the region has an adequate supply, whereas the term "with surplus labor" denotes an excessive supply that, implicitly, could be diverted to labor-deficient regions. The term used is therefore of considerable importance, for it alters the conception of—and approach to—the problem. In Central Asia itself the term "with sufficient labor" is preferred, whereas Moscow describes the region chiefly as being endowed "with surplus labor." Behind this difference in terminology lies a profound conflict.

Economists and sociologists in Central Asia flatly deny the existence of any surplus labor forces in the region. In their view, the high rate of labor not officially employed is explained not by objective factors, but by misguided planning, insufficient investment, and the discrepancy between the region's economic (above all, industrial) structure and its labor resources.

When speaking of labor resources, Central Asian economists emphasize that the labor force is a *potential* one and that its realization requires organizational efforts and capital investment.[1] They distinguish between the ideas of "labor resources" and "labor force"; it is by no means an abstract exercise in theoretical hair-splitting.

The term "labor resources" was first used by academician Stanislav Strumilin in 1922. Previously, the specialized literature as well as government and party documents had used the term "labor force."[2] One of the earliest official documents to use "labor resources" was the first five-year plan (1928–1932). Thereafter "labor resources" and "labor force" received broad currency and appeared in all official planning documents, with no attempt made to distinguish between the two terms.

In recent years, some effort has been made to give "labor resources" a more specific meaning. Nonetheless, according to M. Sonin and E. Kotliar, "labor resources" and "labor force" are virtually identical. A somewhat different view is expressed by N. Kistanov and P. Kosiakov, who argue that "labor resources" is broader than "labor force." By contrast, Professor Evgenii Kasimovskii argues that "labor force" is broader than "labor resources."[3]

Without examining in detail the contradictory views of Soviet specialists in labor economics, I would like to point out that the methodological literature on planning fails to define these terms. The main difficulty may be that neither Marx nor Lenin used the term "labor resources" or, more important, gave it a specific definition. To surmount that hurdle, the Central Asian economist N. Khonaliev used this passage from *Das Kapital*: "Under labor force, or capacity for labor, we understand the sum of physical and spiritual capacities that are possessed by an organism or a living person. . . ."[4] Khonaliev interpreted this passage to mean that labor force conveys the idea of potential; consequently, the transformation of this potential into a real labor force requires both effort and investments.

In any event, the Central Asian cadres assert that the surfeit of labor in the region arose because Moscow's investment policy ignored the demographic situation. Many also believe that the economic development of a labor-rich region should be a top priority, to assure employment for the labor force. They hold that the foundation of economic planning for Central Asia at the present time should,

> above all, be the presence of labor resources and level of life of the population in *various regions* [emphasis added], while the economic effectiveness of using natural and material resources should stand as a secondary factor. . . . In republics with a high birthrate, one of the main thrusts of social-economic policy must be to *guarantee in those very areas* [emphasis added] the highest possible employment rate for the labor force by means of accelerated development of the labor-intensive branches of the manufacturing, agricultural, and service sectors.[5]

From this it follows that the rate of social-economic development of a region should be determined "primarily on the basis of the rate of growth of the population and labor force."[6]

The quotation above comes from the vice director of the Institute of Economics of the Uzbekistan Academy of Sciences and was published in 1983 in the chief organ of the Central Committee of the Uzbekistan Communist Party (the journal, *Kommunist Uzbekistana*). But the author goes still further to assert that:

* only this kind of methodological approach will make it possible to raise Central Asia to the same economic level as other regions of the USSR.
* labor-rich regions "require a special approach to the problem of [evaluating] the significance of labor resources, not only as the main producer, but also the consumer force of society."[7]
* from this follows the necessity of accelerated development of the consumption sphere, since in this aspect the

region "lags considerably behind the average index for the entire USSR."[8]

Such is the view of Central Asian specialists on the special role of their region and the corresponding approach required for its economic development.

This proposal to replace the criterion of economic efficiency in regional economic planning with the goal of guaranteeing full employment is a direct challenge to the centralized, production-branch system of economic planning and management that has ignored the special economic problems of Central Asia. In the broadest terms, the statement above juxtaposes the regional-national interests of Central Asia with the economic policy of Moscow, which pursues the interests of a larger, all-union integrated economy (as defined by the political goals of the regime).

From the Central Asian perspective, however, the industrial structure should accord with the goal of increasing employment for a rapidly expanding population. Concretely, that means steps to promote labor-intensive branches of industry in Central Asia. Significantly, the proponents of this view stress intensified growth of the machine-building sector—a proposal that elicits little enthusiasm from Gosplan in Moscow. It is characteristic that the author cited above asserts that the region has all the conditions and, above all, "sufficient labor resources for the creation of such complex sectors of production as machine building and the manufacture of instruments, radios, and electrical products—i.e., advanced contemporary branches, which require larger expenditures of labor." For this it is "necessary to implement measures for accelerated training of qualified workers and specialists *from the ranks of the local youth*" [emphasis added]. The author asserts that "the recommendation to develop light and food industries in the region has aroused objections from certain scholars."[9] This group evidently includes the vice director of the All-Union Research Institute of Gosplan, Vladimir Kostakov, who has declared:

It is important to surmount the existing tendency to copy the structure of industrial production of the entire USSR or particular republics which are at a higher level of development. Local leaders endeavor, at any price, to construct "prestige" lines of production with technologically complex forms of products, even though it is extremely difficult at present to supply their own qualified cadres for them.[10]

This clash of opinion is exceedingly important for understanding the conflict between Moscow and the ethnic establishment in Central Asia over the character of the region's economy.

Nor is this simply a debate of cloistered academics. The first author—R. Ubaidullaeva—is vice director of the leading economic research center of Central Asia; her ideas on economic development in the region have been published in the local party journal, *Kommunist Uzbekistana*. The second author—V. Kostakov—is vice director of the leading brain trust for the All-Union Gosplan; his position has been published in the leading theoretical journal of the Central Committee of the CPSU, *Kommunist*.

The disagreements embrace not only questions of industrial structure, but also investment policy in the region. The key aspects of investment strategy—for both the Brezhnev and the Gorbachev leadership—are a maximum increase in the share of investments to renovate and reconstruct existing enterprises, and a smaller allocation for new production capacity. This investment policy was formally announced and approved by the twenty-fourth, twenty-fifth, twenty-sixth and twenty-seventh party congresses. Central Asian specialists, however, continue to insist that, in their region, just the opposite policy should be pursued—that preference should be given to the construction of new capacity, for only this approach can assure an increase in the number of jobs and development of the productive and social infrastructure of the region. That view of investment policy was explicitly stated by the director of the Institute of Economics of the Tadjikistan Academy of Sciences, Rashid Rakhimov, and it has drawn the support of other Central Asian economists.[11]

These economists stress the exceptional character of their region and the necessity and legitimacy of developing its economy in ways contrary to Moscow's current economic

109

program. If the main thrust of Gorbachev's economic policy is summed up in the word "intensification" (that is, the renunciation of an extensive, expansionist path of economic growth), the Central Asian economists want precisely that "extensive" model, which alone can create new jobs for the region's growing labor force.[12] Contrary to Moscow's goal of reducing the capital coefficient in the investment process, Central Asian economists want an increase in capital intensity in order to create new jobs and the requisite infrastructure. In a word, the policy applied to the rest of the country should not be extended to Central Asia, above all because it possesses "a sufficient labor supply."[13]

While denying a surplus of labor resources, Central Asian economists insist, paradoxically, that this region with sufficient labor resources nonetheless has a shortage of labor. To sustain this seemingly paradoxical thesis, they note the uneven distribution of population. In Uzbekistan, for instance, two-thirds of the population lives on 15 percent of the land, the remainder of the area being very sparsely populated. Consequently, the unemployed in areas of high population density should be shifted to the sparsely inhabited areas. But that means creating jobs and an attendant infrastructure, all of which requires additional capital investment.

The second argument runs as follows. The notion of a "surplus" labor force connotes a low proportion of qualified labor, which essentially is caused by weak development of the system of professional preparation. In other words, occupational mobility in Central Asia is retarded by insufficient investment in professional education and training. Given the demographic conditions of the region, it is essential to create an appropriate system for vocational and professional education.

The education question is also important because low occupational mobility retards the transfer of the work force from agriculture to industry and other sectors of the economy. More than one-third of the population is employed in agriculture. Indeed, the demographic dynamics of Central Asia run contrary to national patterns: its rural population is steadily increasing, while elsewhere in the USSR the villages are inexorably being emptied.

110

The Demographic Dimension of Agriculture

According to data for 1986, rural inhabitants composed approximately 60 percent of the population in Central Asia, compared with just 34 percent for the USSR as a whole (and 34 percent for the RSFSR). Arable land is just 4 hectares per capita in Central Asia (even less in Uzbekistan [2.6 hectares] and Tadjikistan [1.4 hectares]), much less than the average for the entire USSR (5.8 hectares). By modern standards, it is normal, with adequate mechanization, to have a ration of eight to ten hectares per worker; in Western countries, especially the United States, this ratio is significantly higher.[14]

An important peculiarity of the demographic situation in rural areas of Central Asia is a broad-based "demographic pyramid"—that is, a population with a high proportion of potential and actual parents, with a rough balance of men and women. The result is high reproductive potential. To this characteristic must be added the low migratory rate of this region's rural population.

These factors determine the high share of manual labor in agriculture, the low level of mechanical power employed, and (compared with other regions) the much smaller amount of fixed capital per worker. Thus, the average horsepower per worker is 14 to 15 in Central Asia, compared with 32.6 in the USSR at large, 42.6 in the RSFSR, and over 50 in the Baltics. The share of manual labor in agriculture is 2.5 times higher in Central Asia than, for example, in Western Siberia and Kazakhstan, and fixed capital is 3.5 times less.[15]

There are no grounds to conclude that Central Asia is the victim of discrimination in Moscow's efforts to supply the rural population with machinery and equipment. Rather, it is simply a matter of surplus agricultural labor. Whereas most of the USSR has a dearth of labor and a need to bind people to the village, Central Asia faces just the reverse problem: it must find sufficient employment for its population.

The use of a large contingent of manual labor in agriculture in Central Asia leads to a low index of labor productivity. The Central Asian index is half the average for the USSR, one-third of the index in the Baltics. This meager rate for labor productivity in agriculture causes the index for the Central Asian economy overall to be accordingly low.

The output per agricultural worker in Central Asia, measured in gross product, is about half that for the USSR. Per-capita output in the USSR exceeds that in Central Asia for a range of items—meat (2.2 times), milk (2.4 times), eggs (2.4 times), grain (6.5 times), vegetables (1.9 times).[16] The food produced in Central Asia goes to feed the rural population, and a much smaller share is left to satisfy demand from the local urban population or other regions of the USSR. Hence, Central Asia belongs to the category of areas in the USSR that are least prepared to provide their own foodstuffs. As an agroindustrial (not industrialized agrarian!) region, Central Asia is one of the largest consumers of food produced in other parts of the USSR.

Lack of Job Opportunities in Agriculture

Rural under- and unemployment in Central Asia are becoming more critical and demand that the surplus labor be shifted either to cities or to small towns with industrial production. The birthrate in Central Asian villages is 36 to 42 per thousand (compared with only 23 per thousand for the USSR as a whole), and the best prognoses envision no reduction. The high fertility rate has caused rising population density in rural areas (500 or more persons per square kilometer in the zone of irrigated vegetation). The resulting population pressure has caused the amount of arable land to decline from 0.59 hectares per capita in 1959 to 0.27 hectares in 1984.[17]

Rural overpopulation in cotton-growing areas has reached a critical level and triggered a spontaneous relocation of population to the sparsely settled and economically under-developed territories. These new settlements, especially those in mountainous areas, remain outside the field of vision of the authorities, planners, and statistical census-takers. Nor is it easy to control such developments; many even lack electrification and road connections with more developed settlements.

The gap between Central Asia's unskilled and its trained or educated stata in the rural population is growing steadily. Although the standard of general education here is hardly inferior to that in the USSR as a whole, the proportion of those who have some form of advanced vocational training is considerably smaller than in other regions of the country.

The inhabitants of Central Asian villages, moreover, have a low rate of geographic mobility. According to sociological studies, in Dushanbe (the capital of Tadjikistan) only 8.2 percent of its youth have come from rural areas; in other large cities of the republic the corresponding figure is still lower (6.7 percent).[18]

The overpopulation of Central Asian villages, the spheres of employment opportunity, the lack of stable income for a significant part of the rural population—all have led to an expansion of private agriculture, excessive exploitation of available land, and onerous and exhaustive toil to secure maximum production from minuscule plots. In Tadjikistan, 25 percent of the labor force is employed in this private, auxiliary agriculture.[19] Significantly, the scale of private agricultural production is substantially larger than these data suggest, for by no means all of this production comes to the attention of government statisticians.

Private agricultural activity—so intensive, unregulated, and unplanned—has significant consequences for the local ecology. One obtains some sense of this from the case of the *kishlak* (village) Dar-Dar in Tadjikistan. For lack of jobs in this village (which has only 0.7 hectares, or 2 acres, of arable land per capita), the population supports itself by raising sheep and, naturally, strives constantly to increase the number of livestock. As a consequence, the mountain pastures adjacent to the village have been unduly trampled and thereby suffered significant erosion; in many areas this process has become irreversible.[20] This is true of most of the summer pastures in Tadjikistan, where research has shown that despoliation of the mountains is due to overpopulation in the villages and widespread unemployment.[21] Mountain pastures make up 93 percent of the territory of Tadjikistan,

113

and sheep raising on these pastures is one of the main forms of agricultural activity in the area. The difficulty of finding legal employment has spawned various illegal means of earning money: corruption, thievery, cultivation of drug crops, and the like.

An analysis of the job shortage must also take into account the region's demographic peculiarities, especially those so starkly evident in rural areas, such as the high proportion of children and large family size (tending toward clannishness and extended families). Data for 1985 (averages per 1,000 families) show the following breakdown:

1. Families with five or more children under 18 years of age: 254 in Uzbekistan, 311 in Tadjikistan, 9 in the RSFSR. For rural families, the corresponding figures are 341, 422, and 25.
2. Families with six or more members: 485 in Tadjikistan and Uzbekistan, 9 in the RSFSR.
3. Families with parents, with two or more married couples: 175 in Uzbekistan, 195 in Tadjikistan, 44 in the RSFSR. For rural areas, the corresponding figures are 215, 262, and 31.

There is no reason to assume that these demographic patterns will change significantly in the foreseeable future. Research conducted in 1985 showed that, of every 1,000 married women between the ages of 18 and 44, the following number expected to have six or more children: 437 Uzbeks, 510 Tadjiks, 593 Turkmen, and 3 Russians.[22]

This demographic picture suggests two observations. On the one hand, a large number of children with limited employment opportunities leads to increasing pauperization of the region's rural population. On the other hand, large extended families with a common household economy temper the severity of this problem. Nevertheless, in the final analysis the rural populace in Central Asia (60 percent of the region's inhabitants) is poor, not only by Western, but also by Soviet, standards.

The demographic conditions of the region, which sustain the traditional family order, hinder the social-cultural, geographic, and professional mobility of youth, and contribute to the preservation, reinforcement, and dissemination of Moslem customs and Islamic beliefs and practices.

The demographic situation in Central Asia's rural areas underlies the impetus to create employment in the villages, rather than to relocate people to the cities. Central Asian specialists have their own scenario for the development and territorial distribution of industry in the region: a strict limitation on the creation of new enterprises and the expansion of existing ones in large cities, in densely populated rural areas, or in territories that have been recently settled and developed. This proposal aims to transform large villages into "settlements of an urban type," which will thus lead to urbanization of the rural population.

Some circumstances in the region—the presence of an oasis type of settlement and a high concentration of inhabitants in large villages—favor such a line of development. It completely contradicts the policy of the central ministries and Gosplan, however, which, in planning the creation of new productive facilities or the expansion of old ones, make economies in investment their guiding principle. And that, in turn, means a preference for the development of industrial capacity where the infrastructure already exists and where the appropriate cadres are already available. There is not the slightest indication that Moscow, when deciding how to distribute industrial capacity, pays any attention to the ideas of the local patriots of Central Asia.

The Problem of Vocational Training

Under existing conditions, it is hardly surprising that many branches of the Central Asian economy lack sufficient labor. In Tadjikistan, for example, it was reported in 1986 that approximately 60,000 skilled workers were needed—that is, about 10 percent of the republic's labor force.[23] Hence resolving the problem of employment and full use of local labor resources requires not only the creation of new jobs but also expansion of the system of vocational training. Although this situation has improved somewhat in recent years, Central Asia still lags behind other regions of the country (see Table 6.1).

Table 6.1 Graduation of Skilled Workers from Vocational and Technical Schools (per 1,000 Inhabitants)

Area	1970	1985
USSR	6.7	9.2
Ukraine	5.7	8.4
Belorussia	6.4	8.8
Baltics	5.2	7.5
Transcaucasus	5.2	9.5
Central Asia	3.8	8.4

Narodnoe khoziaistvo SSSR v 1970 godu, p. 5; *Narodnoe khoziaistvo SSSR v 1985 godu,* p. 405

As these data indicate, the gap in education between Central Asia and the USSR as a whole has narrowed substantially. Indeed, the index for Central Asia is markedly higher than for the Baltic republics and has reached the Ukrainian level. Nevertheless, when one takes into account that Central Asia's population growth far exceeds that in other areas, that the share of the young cohort is substantially higher here, that the proportion of unemployed rural inhabitants is substantially higher, and that hitherto the education gap was substantially greater, the training of skilled labor should be substantially higher than what Table 6.1 indicates.

Tadjikistan, which has the highest rate of natural population growth and the lowest employment level of all the Central Asian republics (and, by extension, of all republics in the USSR), offers the following picture on the preparation of trained, skilled labor. In the 1975–1982 period, approximately 30,000 new workers entered the labor force each year, of which only 66 percent had received specialized training. Whereas in the USSR as a whole in the 1970–1982 period the rate of growth in preparing skilled labor exceeded the increase in the labor force by 30 percent, in Tadjikistan the comparable figure fell short by 10 percent.[24]

According to data compiled by the State Committee on Professional and Technical Education in Tadjikistan, in the early 1980s the training of workers in the system of vocational schools satisfied only 30 percent of the republic's needs.[25] The committee concluded that the number of vocational schools should be doubled.

But it is not only a matter of expanding the network of vocational-technical schools. A further problem is that the indigenous nationalities are significantly underrepresented among the students. This is especially evident in the training of workers for the industrial sector, which requires more highly skilled labor. That is why, in the machine-building sector of Kirghizia in 1983, Kirghiz nationals accounted for only 12.5 percent of the labor force, as opposed to 31 percent in the food-processing industry and 31.5 percent in light industry.[26]

The situation is similar in the other republics of Central Asia. As a whole, the indigenous nationalities receive less training than do other nationalities in the region. This difference is illuminated by data for Tadjikistan in the early 1980s (see Table 6.2). Although the indigenous share of more highly skilled workers is increasing in particular branches of industry (electrical energy, nonferrous metallurgy), overall it fell between 1965 and 1985 (with a corresponding increase in the proportion of unskilled and untrained labor).

Table 6.2 National Composition of Workers in Tadjikistan (Share of Industrial Workers with Highest Level of Training)

	Indigenous Nationalities (Tadjiks, Uzbeks)	Others
Basic Production	25%	34%
Auxiliary Production	22	40

Source: E. Nasyrov, "Professional'naia podgotovka rabochikh kadrov Tadjikistana," *Sotsiologicheskie isssledovaniia,* 1986, no. 4: 29.

It follows that the quality of the labor force in the republic is deteriorating even as it grows in size.

Tadjikistan exemplifies the anomalies in the vocational training of the indigenous nationalities of Central Asia. In 1984 students from these nationalities (Tadjiks and Uzbeks) were only 19.7 percent of all those studying in PTUs (professional-technical schools), although some 85 to 90 percent of the population in the republic is Tadjik or Uzbek.[27] At the same time, more and more Tadjiks and Uzbeks are being sent to study in PTUs elsewhere in the USSR. Only youth from indigenous nationalities, not Russians, are dispatched to study in other regions of the USSR, although it would be incomparably easier for ethnic Russians to adapt to Russian cities than it would be for Tadjiks and Uzbeks. Russian youths make up the main contingent of pupils in the PTUs of Tadjikistan.[28]

Despite these organized efforts, despite propaganda about the advantages of obtaining training in the large industrial centers of Russia, so far not much has been achieved in enticing the Central Asian youth to these areas. For example, Tadjikistan sends only about 2,500 to 3,000 people each year to study outside the region.[29] Moscow's aim is, of course, to provide training for Central Asian youths, but on the condition that they remain and work in the labor-deficient areas of the European part of the country and in Siberia. Yet some 70 to 75 percent of these people nonetheless return to Central Asia, because of limited capacity to adapt to an alien ethnic environment, because of language barriers (that is, a weak knowledge of Russian), and generally because of the alien social-psychological climate.[30] As was demonstrated by a survey of parents whose children were candidates for study in PTUs elsewhere in the USSR, only 13 percent had a favorable attitude toward the idea.[31] That attitude is important, given the authority of parental opinion in the Moslem families of Central Asia.

What is the fate of young people who obtain professional and vocational training in Russian schools and return to Central Asia? Are they in fact employed in the specialities for which they were trained? Typical is the case of the Tadjik Iso Dzhumaev, who had been sent to a PTU in Gorky, where for two years he was trained to operate a numerically controlled machine tool. Workers in this speciality are acutely needed in the country's machine-building plants. But Iso Dzhumaev did not remain in Gorky. Instead, he returned home, where he could not find a job in his speciality and instead began working on the local cotton plantations.

This case belies the assertions of Central Asian planners that qualified workers are in very short supply. Thousands of truckdrivers, lathe operators, milling-machine operators, repairmen of various specialities, gas and electric welders, and people in various other occupations (who have all completed a PTU) cannot find work in Central Asia. In Tadjikistan alone, 4,215 PTU graduates were unable to find work in 1987. The main reason for the growing unemployment among skilled workers is the sheer lack of jobs, which in turn is caused by the inadequate investment and structural change in the local economy.[32]

Whereas Moscow's aim is to tap the Central Asian labor force for use elsewhere in the USSR, the leadership of the Central Asian republics has just the opposite goal: to have this labor return home. It is clear that the Moslems of Central Asia resist the extraction and Russification of their youth, and that Moscow's policy evokes considerable discontent among the indigenous population of Central Asia.

But the policy of diverting labor from Central Asia to other republics also arouses opposition in Moscow. Those opposed include, among others, Vladimir Kostakov, director of the Research Institute of Gosplan, who wrote the following in *Kommunist* in 1986:

> Skepticism is evoked by proposals, for purposes of employment, to transfer the "surplus" [the quotation marks are Kostakov's] of workers to other regions of the country that have an acute need for labor. People are not raw materials or equipment, which one can arbitrarily shunt from one place to the next. The freedom for maneuvering with respect to human resources is severely limited by the peculiarities in life style, which are determined by national tradition. These are the causes of a persisting

inadequacy in mobility and the inability to adapt to unfamiliar conditions. The indigenous rural population is not eager to move to the city, even within the confines of their own republic. Hence a mass relocation is not something achievable in the near future.[33]

An analysis of conditions in labor resources and their use permits one to conclude that a hidden conflict exists between the decision makers in Moscow and the Central Asian republics. The Central Asians believe that the concept of a surfeit of labor resources in their region is "artificial."[34] Their increasing unemployment, they contend, stems from underinvestment and from Moscow's disregard for the demographic situation as it shapes the development of the economic structure in Central Asia.

But the interests of the production-branch ministries (whose viewpoint is shared by Gosplan) dictate quite different policies: (1) to develop not the labor-intensive branches of manufacturing, but the capital-intensive extractive and primary industries, which will lead to only a small increase in jobs; (2) to expand production not in small and medium-sized cities and rural areas, but rather to concentrate plants in large cities, where construction is easier and cheaper and where it is also easier to staff the new facilities with a trained labor force; (3) not to disperse industry, but to concentrate it to the maximum extent possible.

With the lowest employment rate in the USSR, Central Asia receives the lowest per-capita allocation of capital investment. To raise the level of employment, it is necessary to create new jobs—that is, to allocate additional investment. But the investment policy of the Gorbachev leadership leaves no hope for an increase in the capital allocated to Central Asia. It is hard to imagine that Central Asian economists, planners, and managers have any illusions about that.

The Plight of Women

The status of women in Central Asia is particularly unenviable, even by the modest standards of the USSR.

Women must perform the most onerous work of all—harvesting the cotton crops. When one reads about the exploitation of female labor on the cotton plantations of Central Asia today, it is difficult not to think of the slave economy in the antebellum American South. Central Asian women toil under exceedingly difficult conditions, under the burning rays of the sun, from dawn to dusk, without a chance to wash and cool off. Mothers with babies leave the fields to nurse the infants, and then go back to work. It is not uncommon for them to give birth in the fields, for they work up to the last minute of pregnancy.[35]

Our stereotypes of Eastern traditions notwithstanding, maltreatment of women is by no means characteristic of Uzbeks, Tadjiks, Turkmens, and Kirghiz. However poorly the peasant *dekhkanin* may have lived in prerevolutionary times, he never forced his wife to toil in the fields.[36] Her duties were limited to the household and child care. To those duties, however, have now been added an exhausting regime of field labor. And one must keep in mind the magnitude of chores at home, where the family often consists of six to eight children and the most rudimentary amenities (plumbing, running water, etc.) are lacking. An Uzbek writer has recounted the scene he witnessed at a cotton plantation when a group of women implored the brigade foreman to let them go home for two or three hours to do the laundry and look after the children. The foreman refused, even though it was Sunday and the women had been working without interruption for several days.[37]

The status of women in Central Asia has deteriorated substantially in the Soviet era. The curtain of lies and hypocrisy that conceals the plight of women in Central Asia has finally been lifted in the era of glasnost. To quote one commentary on this open discussion in the press:

> The truth has finally come out about the rural women in Uzbekistan, upon whose shoulders rests the entire burden of the millions of tons of "white gold" [cotton]. Our poor women! Submissive, silent, complaisant. Officials with any kind of "authority" from above had the right to scream at her, to threaten her with prison [for failing to fulfill the plan for cotton

harvesting]. And she cried, remained silent, worked ceaselessly, and also requested forgiveness for overlooking a boll [of cotton] on the bush.[38]

Thus, on top of the Moslem enslavement of women within the family, the Soviet model of "equal rights for women" has meant their subjection to the most onerous forms of physical labor. Great numbers of Soviet women work in heavy construction, in the laying and repair of railway lines, and in the most exhausting forms of hard labor. It is not only Uzbek or Turkmen women who toil under conditions that ruin their health; very much the same kind of exploitation grinds down Russian women employed in the antiquated textile plants of Ivanovo in central Russia.[39] The tragic consequences of this "emancipation" are manifold and extend to all spheres of social life and public health.

Nevertheless, the highest infant mortality rate is in Central Asia. Not in European Russia, but in Central Asia have young women begun to immolate themselves in the most horrifying manner. During a two-year period (1986–1987), Uzbekistan alone recorded 270 cases of self-immolation by women seeking to protest their reduction to mere chattel.[40] If the labor question involves many complex forms of injustice, of tensions between local needs and central planning, hardly any more tragic dimension can be found than the plight of women in Central Asia.

CHAPTER 7

The Standard of Living

Publications by Central Asian economists often assert that the general living standard in this region is the lowest in the USSR. Indeed, they treat this as self-evident and incontrovertible. The following statement by the Tadjik economist M. Makhshulov is typical:

> As is well known, the Central Asian republics at the present time lag somewhat behind the general indices for the average living standard in the country as a whole and also in other republics of the USSR. Of course, this is a direct consequence of the relatively low level of economic development in these republics [of Central Asia]. It should also be said that it may affect the potential for social-economic development of the region in the immediate future.[1]

All that seems clear enough. But why does Makhshulov say that "it may affect"? The lag in the living standard and the general economic backwardness of the region must unavoidably affect social development and indeed have already done so. This chapter examines the basic indices of the living standard in Central Asia to determine how much they "lag behind the general indices of the average living standard in the country as a whole as well as in other republics of the USSR".

Income of the Population

Within the limits of published statistical information, only two indices give a more or less reliable picture of the population's income: (1) the average monthly wages and salaries of workers and employees; and (2) the average amount of money in savings accounts. The problem with the first indicator is that it excludes a significant segment of the rural population: those people on collective farms. Unfortunately, we do not have any hard data on earned income from activities that lie outside the official statistical reports (that is, from the "second economy," or private agriculture). Although the data are too incomplete to characterize the population's living standard fully, the two available indices (Tables 7.1 and 7.2) nevertheless offer an adequate basis to address the comparative assessment offered by Makhshulov's statement above.

As Table 7.1 and Figure 7.1 demonstrate, the income in Central Asia throughout the period examined here was lower than in the USSR generally and in the two other national regions considered for comparative purposes. Data on savings in Table 7.2, similarly, demonstrate that Central Asia has consistently ranked below the average in the USSR and the two other regions. Only in Turkmenia was the index substantially higher, but in 1984 this republic's share of savings was only 20 percent of the savings for the entire Central Asian region.

It is of course possible that a larger proportion of the population in Central Asia (especially in rural areas) prefers not to use savings banks. Further, income from private

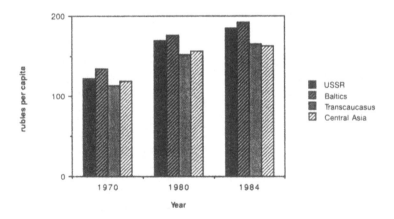

Figure 7.1   Average Monthly Wage of White- and Blue-Collar Workers

124

Table 7.1   Average Monthly Earnings per Employee (Rubles)

	1970	1980	1984
USSR	122	169	185
Baltic Region	134	176	192
Transcaucasus Region	113	152	165
Central Asia	119	156	163

Sources: *Narodnoe khoziaistvo SSSR v 1970 godu*, 519; *Narodnoe khoziaistvo SSSR v 1980 godu*, 364; *Narodnoe khoziaistvo SSSR v 1984 godu*, 417; *Narodnoe khoziaistvo Uzbekskoi SSR v 1984 godu*, 226; *Narodnoe khoziaistvo Kirgizskoi SSR v 1975 godu*, 251; *Narodnoe khoziaistvo Kirgizskoi SSR v 1984 godu*, 144; *Narodnoe khoziaistvo Tadzhikskoi SSR v 1982 godu*, 185; *Narodnoe khoziaistvo Turkmenskoi SSR v 1984 godu*, 145; *Narodnoe khoziaistvo Gruzinskoi SSR v 1984 godu*, 167; *Narodnoe khoziaistvo Azerbaidzhanskoi SSR v 1984 godu*, 146; *Narodnoe knoziaistvo Armianskoi SSR v 1984 godu*, 214; *Narodnoe khoziaistvo Litovskoi SSR v 1984 godu*, 146; *Narodnoe khoziaistvo Latviiskoi SSR v 1984 godu*, 211; *Narodnoe khoziaistvo Estonskoi SSR v 1984 godu*, 145; *Narodnoe khoziaistvo RSFSR v 1984 godu*, 243; *Narodnoe khoziaistvo Ukrainskoi SSR v 1983 godu*, 230.

agriculture, although not included in official statistics, is undoubtedly a major supplement to rural income. It is difficult, however, to gauge how much this factor increases the incomes of Uzbek and Tadjik peasants or of the sheep growers of Kirghizia and Turkmenia, especially in comparison with the Transcaucasus, Baltic, and other regions. In any event it is clear that private agriculture provides indispensable support for Central Asia's rural inhabitants, and that without this they could hardly manage to survive.

Private Farming

A major role in feeding the population is played by private farming, which is much more important in Central Asia than elsewhere in the USSR. According to figures for Uzbekistan in 1982, private farming occupied 0.6 to 0.7 percent of cultivated land area, yet it held 55 percent of the

Table 7.2   Average Amount in Savings Accounts (Rubles)

	1970	1980	1984
USSR	581	1102	1232
Baltic Region			
Lithuania	964	1781	1973
Latvia	647	1218	1384
Estonia	806	1361	1550
Transcaucasus Region			
Georgia	1016	1729	1824
Azerbaijan	672	1183	1191
Armenia	980	1636	1737
Central Asia			
Uzbekistan	541	1044	1149
Kirghizia	519	989	1054
Tadjikistan	551	959	1039
Turkmenia	688	1407	1488

Sources: *Narodnoe khoziaistvo SSSR v 1970 godu*, 564; *Narodnoe khoziaistvo SSSR v 1980 godu*, 408; *Narodnoe khoziaistvo SSSR v 1984 godu*, 462.

republic's cattle and produced 46 percent of its meat, 40 percent of its milk, and 40 percent of its vegetables. In Tadjikistan private farming accounted for 0.5 percent of agricultural land; nevertheless, this sector claimed much of the republic's livestock (53 percent of the cattle, 37 percent of the sheep) and produced a significant share of the foodstuffs (37 percent of the meat and approximately 50 percent of the milk). A similar picture emerges in Kirghizia, where the private sector produces 57 percent of the potatoes, 50 percent of the vegetables, 28 percent of the meat, 32 percent of the milk, and 42 percent of the eggs.

Moreover, in Central Asia the output of the private sector as a whole has been expanding more rapidly than that of the collective and state farm sectors. For example, from 1970 to 1982 product value in the state and collective farm sector in Uzbekistan rose by 51 percent, whereas that in the private sector increased by 72 percent. In Kirghizia the corresponding figures were 11 and 67 percent.

That stands in marked contrast to the development of private agricultural production in the RSFSR. According to data for the RSFSR in 1982, the private sector's share in the production of meat was 28 percent, vegetables 31 percent, and milk 27 percent; similarly, only 16.7 percent of cattle and 21 percent of sheep were in private hands. Unlike in Central Asia, growth in the private sector lagged behind that of the state and collective farms.[2]

The achievements of the private sector in Central Asia are astonishing if one takes into account that the state does not provide any equipment, fodder, fertilizer, or irrigation assistance and that, consequently, the population is left to till the soil by the most primitive methods. Leaving considerations of motivation aside, the high level of private production in Central Asia can be explained by the following three factors.

First, both Moscow and local authorities take a more liberal attitude toward private agriculture in Central Asia than in Russia proper. The bazaar has traditionally played a more important and legitimate role in providing food for the populace. In general, the behavior of the regime in Central Asia is more careful, more cautious. Moscow prefers to avoid actions that appear likely to provoke dissatisfaction gratu-itously among the Moslem populace of the USSR. It is largely for this reason that the regime, historically so hostile to private agriculture, has willfully closed its eyes to the intensive development of private agriculture in Central Asia.

The second factor is the availability of labor for private farming—a direct result of the rapid population growth and the large share of the population living in rural areas. Much of this population, moreover, is contained within traditional family structures, enabling the abundant labor to be used to cultivate private family plots.

Third (and in my view most important): Stalinist collectivization and agricultural policies did not wreak the havoc in Central Asia that they did in other regions of the country. In contrast to what happened in European Russia and the Ukraine, the most productive stratum of the Central

127

Asian peasantry was not eliminated, nor were love of the land and centuries-old experience eradicated among those who work the soil. The village community stayed intact. And the reason is simply that collectivization did not assume the extreme forms that it did in Russia.

Moscow, apart from its desire to avoid provocative behavior, focused its attention narrowly on cotton production, 100 percent of which is produced on state and collective farms, and which receives the lion's share of the agricultural resources devoted to the region. In no other region of the USSR has the development of agriculture been so concentrated on a single crop, nor has so much care been taken to avoid any disruption in output. Moscow closes its eyes to the intensive cultivation of food products by private farmers on the grounds that its decline would lead to a serious worsening of the food supply in the region, which is still far from abundant.

Nevertheless, private farming faces serious threats of its own: the land area available for this activity shrinks with each passing year because of the expanding cultivation of cotton. The rapid increase in population (due to the high fertility and to the low migration to urban areas), when combined with a reduction in private land plots, increasingly pauperizes the Central Asian peasantry. In the words of Vladimir Sokolov, an expert on rural life in that region, "The rural inhabitant [of Central Asia] is getting poorer all the time—his total income (per capita), including that from private activities, is a third of the average for the entire Soviet Union."[3]

Housing Stock

The published statistical information permits a relatively reliable comparison of the housing available for rural and urban populations in the various republics and investment in housing construction. These data (in Tables 7.3 and 7.4 as well as Figures 7.2 and 7.3) show clearly that in housing the population of Central Asia—in both cities and rural areas—ranks last in the USSR. Only the Transcaucasus

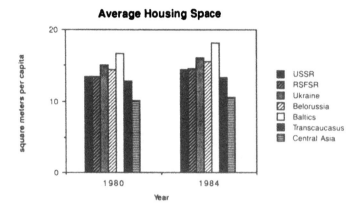

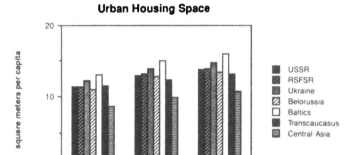

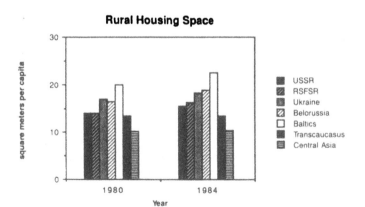

Figure 7.2   Housing Space

129

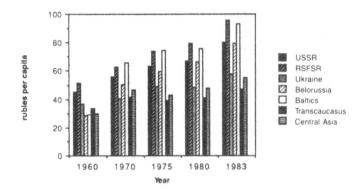

Figure 7.3   Capital Investment in Housing Construction (from all sources of financing)

region has received less investment per capita for housing construction. To be fair, the unusually large size of Central Asian families distorts these statistics. Nevertheless, this important index provokes considerable bitterness in Central Asia, where the population feels aggrieved and unjustly treated. Significantly, the gap between Central Asia and the USSR remained virtually unchanged for the period 1970–1984 (the difference declined by just 1 percent), and the gap between Central Asia and the RSFSR actually increased by 9 percent.

Too little housing (in square meters per capita) is only part of the issue: Central Asia also lags in the quality of housing. Sewage, an elementary requirement of modern housing, is indicative of the problem: only a fraction of the Central Asian urban population is provided with a sewage system. In Uzbekistan, for example, sewage systems exist for only 40 percent of the people in Urgench, 15 percent in Nukus, 14 percent in Kungrad, 10 percent in Takhiatash, and 17 percent in Druzhba. Likewise, running water is available in only a small proportion of urban housing. For example, in Karakalpakii, which has a population of more than one million, 73 percent of the inhabitants lack running water; in Khorezm oblast (population: 900,000), 71 percent

Table 7.3   Housing: Square Meters per Capita

	1970			1980			1984		
	Ave.	City	Rural	Ave.	City	Rural	Ave.	City	Rural
USSR	–	11.3	–	13.4	13.0	14.0	14.4	13.8	15.4
RSFSR	–	11.3	–	13.4	13.2	13.9	14.6	14.0	16.2
Ukraine	–	12.2	–	15.1	14.1	16.9	16.0	14.8	18.2
Belorussia	–	11.0	–	14.4	12.8	16.4	15.5	13.4	18.9
Baltics	–	13.1	–	16.7	15.0	20.0	18.2	16.0	22.6
Transcaucasus	–	11.5	–	12.9	12.4	13.4	13.3	13.2	13.4
Central Asia	–	8.7	–	10.1	9.9	10.3	10.6	10.8	10.4

Sources: *Narodnoe khoziaistvo SSSR v 1970 godu*, 541; *Narodnoe khoziaistvo SSSR v 1980 godu*, 390; *Narodnoe khoziaistvo SSSR v1984 godu*, 439.

lack running water.[4] Nor are sanitary conditions much better. Conditions are considerably worse in rural areas, which still hold 60 percent of the population.

Trade and Public Catering

As the available data (presented in Tables 7.5, 7.6, and 7.7, as well as in Figures 7.4, 7.5, and 7.6) illustrate, all three indices used to measure the commercial sector categorize Central Asia as the most backward region of the USSR. Again, it is only fair to point out mitigating factors: the population relies more on the bazaars, and the high proportion of rural inhabitants and large number of children in families help account for the small number of restaurants and cafeterias. In other words, the demographic and national peculiarities to some degree determine the comparatively smaller demand for commercial and public services.

The foregoing qualification appears logical when one is speaking of food products. But it can hardly explain why Central Asians have much less opportunity than do inhabitants of other regions to purchase durable goods. Data

Table 7.4 Capital Investment in Housing Construction (Rubles per Capita)

	1960	1970	1975	1980	1983	1983 as % of 1970
USSR	45.3	55.6	63.6	67.0	80.1	144.0
RSFSR	51.4	62.6	74.0	79.2	95.8	153.0
Ukraine	36.5	40.2	48.8	48.6	58.0	145.0
Belorussia	28.7	50.2	59.4	66.4	79.5	158.0
Baltics	29.5	65.7	74.5	76.0	92.9	141.0
Transcaucasus	33.6	41.6	39.2	41.2	47.2	112.0
Central Asia	29.7	46.8	43.0	47.8	55.0	118.0

Sources: *Narodnoe khoziaistvo SSSR v 1970 godu*, 541; *Narodnoe khoziaistvo SSSR v 1975 godu*, 572; *Narodnoe khoziaistvo SSSR v 1980 godu*, 389; *Narodnoe khoziaistvo SSSR v 1983 godu*, 420.

Table 7.5 State and Cooperative Retail Sales, Including Public Catering (in Rubles per Capita in Actual Prices of Given Year)

	1970	1980	1984	1980 as % of 1970
USSR	639	1019	1149	180
RSFSR	698	1114	1260	180
Ukraine	580	933	1056	182
Baltics	827	1405	1486	180
Transcaucasus	451	744	843	187
Central Asia	420	646	735	175

Sources: *Narodnoe khoziaistvo SSSR v 1980 godu*, 427–428; *Narodnoe khoziaistvo SSSR v 1984, godu*, 479.

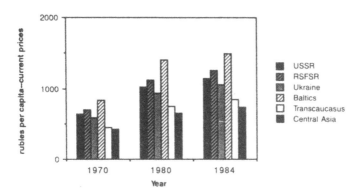

Figure 7.4 Turnover in State and Cooperative Retail Sales (Including Food Services)

portraying this sphere of trade, unfortunately, are incomplete and do not provide a comprehensive picture for entire national regions. Nevertheless, the differences (illustrated in Table 7.8 and Figure 7.7) are quite striking.

It is fair to assume that the per-capita demand for television sets is relatively smaller for the kinds of reasons cited above—the larger family size, the more conservative life-style, the small share of the population that speaks Russian (which is used in all national programming), the devotion to Islam (which discourages interest in television), and simply the onerous physical labor on cotton plantations or on private plots (leaving no energy and time for recreation). But it is much more difficult to find objective reasons why the demand for refrigerators is so low, especially considering the Central Asian climate.

Especially noteworthy is the difference in the sale of automobiles: demand in Central Asia is not less but even greater than in many cities and villages of Russia. It is well known that, among those seeking to purchase automobiles on the black market in Moscow, the highest proportion consists of Uzbeks, Tadjiks, and others from the Central Asian nationalities.

Despite all the extenuating circumstances based on the

133

Table 7.6 Commercial Space of State and Cooperative Stories (Square Meters per 10,000 Inhabitants)

	1970	1980	1984	1984 as % of 1970
USSR	129	173	185	143
RSFSR	132	183	196	148
Ukraine	135	182	196	145
Baltics	140	170	178	127
Transcaucasus	103	141	150	146
Central Asia	86	118	126	146

Sources: *Narodnoe khoziaistvo SSSR v 1980 godu*, 445; *Narodnoe khoziaistvo SSSR v 1984 godu*, 498.

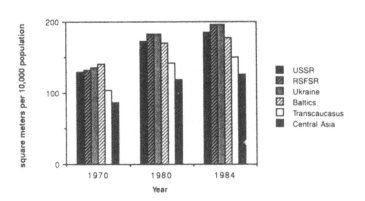

Figure 7.5 Trading Space of All Trade Enterprises (Food Stores, Department Stores, etc.)

Table 7.7 Restaurant and Cafeteria Seats per 10,000 Inhabitants

	1970	1980	1984	1984 as % of 1970
USSR	411	645	717	174
RSFSR	431	665	735	170
Ukraine	430	690	777	181
Baltics	567	851	934	165
Transcaucasus	418	625	716	171
Central Asia	294	461	505	172

Source: Narodnoe khoziaistvo SSSR v 1984 godu, 498.

Figure 7.6   Seats in Restaurants, Cafeterias, and so on

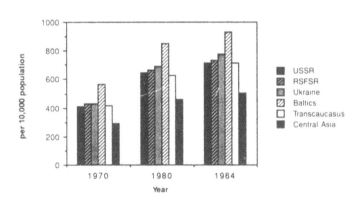

Figure 7.6   Seats in Restaurants, Cafeterias, and so on

135

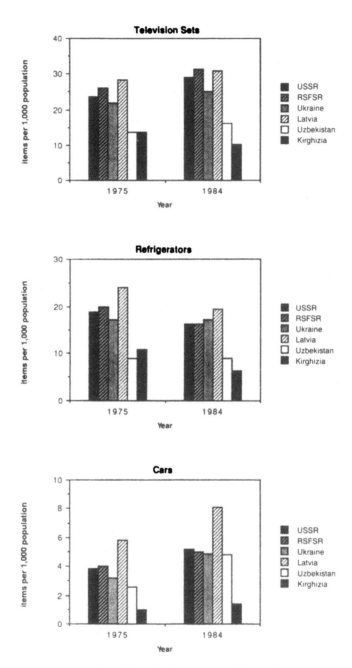

Figure 7.7 Sales of Selected Durable Goods

136

Table 7.8 Sale of Durable Goods (Units per 1,000 Inhabitants)

	Television Sets		Refrigerators		Automobiles	
	1975	1984	1975	1984	1975	1984
USSR	23.5	29.0	18.9	16.3	3.8	5.2
RSFSR	26.2	31.4	20.0	16.3	4.0	5.0
Ukraine	21.8	25.1	17.1	17.1	3.2	4.9
Latvia	28.2	30.7	24.0	19.4	5.8	8.1
Uzbekistan	13.6	16.1	9.0	8.9	2.6	4.8
Kirgizia	13.6	10.3	10.8	6.3	1.0	1.4

Sources: Narodnoe khoziaistvo SSSR v 1984 godu, 458; Narodnoe khoziaistvo RSFSR v 1980 godu, 245; Narodnoe khoziaistvo RSFSR v 1984 godu, 269; Narodnoe khoziaistvo Ukrainskoi SSR v 1983 godu, 273; Narodnoe khoziaistvo Uzbekskoi SSR v 1984 godu, 249; Narodnoe khoziaistvo Kirgizskoi SSR v 1980 godu, 226, 227; Narodnoe khoziaistvo Kirgizskoi SSR v 1984 godu, 163; Narodnoe khoziaistvo Latviiskoi SSR v 1984 godu, 245.

Table 7.9 Medical Care

	Number of Doctors of All Specialties			Number of Hospital Beds per 10,000 Inhabitants		
	1970	1980	1984	1970	1980	1984
USSR	27.4	37.5	41.2	109.4	124.9	128.7
RSFSR	29.0	40.3	44.1	112.5	129.5	133.9
Ukraine	27.7	36.5	40.5	107.9	125.4	130.4
Baltics	32.2	41.5	45.3	106.3	118.5	122.4
Transcaucasus	30.0	38.8	42.2	90.1	95.8	95.9
Central Asia	19.5	27.3	30.5	103.4	109.0	111.5

Source: Narodnoe khoziaistvo SSSR v 1984 godu, 554, 558.

national and demographic peculiarities of the region, one fact is incontrovertible: in supplying the population with food and durable goods, Central Asia lags considerably behind the average in the USSR and behind all other regions of the country.

Health Care

In examining the supply of consumer goods, the comparative lag in Central Asia was partly attributed to the demographic

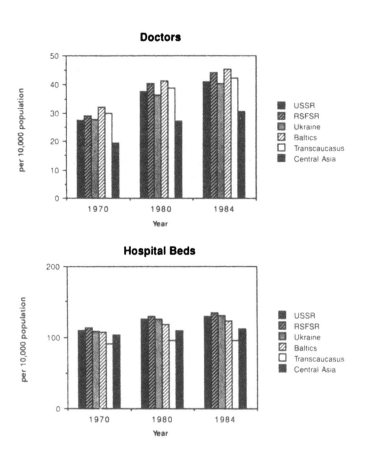

Figure 7.8 Health Services

Table 7.10 Availability of Sanatoria and Rest/Recuperation Facilities (Institutions per 10,000 Inhabitants)

	1975	1980	1984
USSR	70.2	80.2	85.2
RSFSR	72.1	81.5	85.0
Ukraine	94.0	112.0	123.8
Baltics	138.5	150.0	184.4
Transcaucasus	69.2	87.5	91.7
Central Asia	31.7	34.7	33.8

Sources: *Narodnoe khoziaistvo SSSR v 1975 godu*, 606; *Narodnoe khoziaistvo SSSR v 1980 godu*, 414; *Narodnoe khoziaistvo SSSR v 1984 godu*, 468.

factor. This factor must also be taken into consideration in assessing the health-care services available to the population. In this case the demographic peculiarity—the highest population growth rate in the USSR—objectively predetermines the high demand for doctors, hospital beds, and other forms of medical care. What is in fact the state of health care in Central Asia? As the data (Tables 7.9 and 7.10; Figures 7.8 and 7.9) demonstrate, Central Asia ranks last in medical care in the USSR; only in the category of hospital space does its position appear somewhat better (next to last).

In medical assistance for women, particularly during pregnancy and delivery, Soviet Central Asia is probably indistinguishable from Third World countries. Midwives handle an enormous number of births, the majority of which involve disease and various complications. This region with the highest birthrate has grossly inadequate provisions for assistance at birth and for infant hygiene:

More than half the pregnant women in rural areas have already given birth before. All of them belong to the "high-risk" group; they are ill with anemia. Many begin giving birth without ever having seen a doctor and indeed come with a "bouquet" of

139

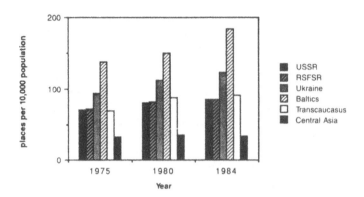

Figure 7.9 Sanatoria, Rest Homes, Resort Hotels, Medical Dispensaries, and so on.

various ailments. Rural districts, as a rule, have no provision for women's consultations. There are offices in the central district hospitals, where a doctor each day receives 60 to 80 women who are pregnant or who suffer from gynecological diseases. The equipment for these offices (which are pompously called "[Clinics for] Women's Consultations") consists of a tonometer and stethoscope. The quality of health service during pregnancy is very low.[5]

The result, predictably, is a very high mortality rate among mothers and babies.

A few years ago Moscow drafted a plan calling for the creation of 65,000 new beds in the maternity wards in two years to accommodate Central Asia's high birthrate. Instead only 6,000 new beds were installed.

The low quality of doctors and gynecologists contributes to the health problem. Poor food and inadequate water combine with lack of sanitation to make hospital conditions unbearable for these women.

A reporter who visited a maternity ward for ordinary people in Tashkent writes that for every 25 beds, 100 women were staying at the hospital. Not enough air was a big complaint, as the temperature was regularly 100 degrees F.

Twenty babies lay in a room designed for four babies. It was impossible to use the toilet. The journalist reported that these conditions were quite common.

In many districts bottle-fed babies receive only 7 percent of the milk they need to survive. The shortage of milk derives from the scarcity of land for grazing, since most of the land in Central Asia grows cotton. Many children in the area suffer from malnutrition, and die from pneumonia and infections.

Because of the shortage of labor during the cotton harvest season, children are forced to leave school and work in the fields alongside the women. The hundreds of thousands of children recruited would otherwise be in high schools and elementary schools. The pesticides often have an even worse

Table 7.11 Budgetary Expenditures for Social and Cultural Development, Health Care, and Social Security (Rubles per Capita)

	1970	1975	1980	1983
RSFSR	161	207	248	271
Ukraine	139	176	220	244
Belorussia	141	191	233	254
Baltics	170	224	284	312
Transcaucasus	149	182	215	235
Central Asia	129	157	182	196

Sources: Narodnoe khoziaistvo RSFSR v 1983 godu, 368; Narodnoe khoziaistvo Ukrainskoi SSR v 1984 godu, 389; Narodnoe khoziaistvo Belorusskoi SSR v 1984 godu, 227; Narodnoe khoziaistvo Litovskoi SSR v 1984 godu, 231; Narodnoe khoziaistvo Latviiskoi SSR v 1984 godu, 326; Narodnoe khoziaistvo Estonskoi SSR v 1984 godu, 251; Narodnoe khoziaistvo Gruzinskoi SSR v 1984 godu, 269; Narodnoe khoziaistvo Armianskoi SSR v 1984 godu, 336; Narodnoe khoziaistvo Azerbaidzhanskoi SSR v 1984 godu, 237; Narodnoe khoziaistvo Uzbekskoi SSR v 1984 godu, 346; Narodnoe khoziaistvo Turkmenskoi SSR v 1984 godu, 238; Narodnoe khoziaistvo Kirgizskoi SSR v 1984 godu, 226; Narodnoe khoziaistvo Tadzhikskoi SSR v 1982 godu, 274.

effect on the small children than on the adults. Children of party officials and other VIPs do not have to work on the cotton plantations.[6]

Development of the Social Sphere

The questions of how much attention Moscow gives to the social development of the backward periphery of the Soviet Empire, and what efforts it makes to ameliorate social and culture backwardness, can be objectively judged from expenditures for these purposes in republican budgets (see Tables 7.11 and 7.12 and Figure 7.10). The expenditures are largely determined by Moscow, not only at the all-union but also at the republican level.

The backwardness in consumer goods and the social-cultural sphere is essentially a consequence of Moscow's disregard of the special Central Asian demographic situation in its planning and distribution of resources. Here one sees clearly the negative effect of the centralized, production-branch system of economic management—the dominance of union republics, the priority of their interests, and the repression of the need for social development and consumer demands. This pattern is particularly apparent in Central Asia.

Table 7.12   Volume of per Capita Social Services in Rubles (Based on Comparable Prices in 1981)

	1975	1980	1984
USSR	21.5	29.6	35.6
RSFSR	23.0	31.4	37.0
Ukraine	21.8	30.4	37.0
Belorussia	22.8	33.7	45.0
Baltics	29.0	45.9	52.0
Transcaucasus	15.8	24.1	32.5
Central Asia	13.7	20.0	24.6

Source: *Narodnoe khoziaistvo SSSR v 1984 godu*, 507.

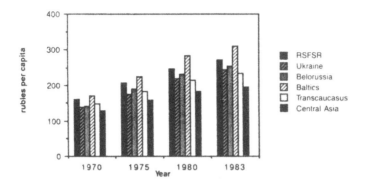

Figure 7.10 Republican Budget Expenditures for Social and Cultural Development, Health Care, and Social Security

CHAPTER 8

The Shadow Economy and Organized Crime

Thus far this analysis of the Central Asian economy has relied primarily on official statistics and the scholarly publications of Soviet economists. But these are inadequate if one wishes to reconstruct real life, to depict the actual living conditions of the population. A highly significant proportion of economic activity in Central Asia, just as in the USSR more generally, remains beyond the regulatory control of the state. The phenomenon of the shadow economy in the USSR is well known and has been the subject of detailed accounts in Western literature. More significant still, it has now become a subject of serious discussion in the Soviet press. In 1987 the popular journal *Ogonek* summed up the discussion in these terms:

> It is an open secret that for many years our economy has been directed not only by open means "from above," but also by clandestine mechanisms that are partly or completely illegal. To underscore the negative dimensions of this economic activity, it has become increasingly customary to use the term "shadow economy." However, a coherent explanation for the phenomena included under this term has not yet developed. As a rule, it tends to include those economic activities on "the other side" of the Criminal Code, that is, economic criminality.[1]

As the foregoing makes clear, the term "shadow economy" embraces a broad spectrum of illegal economic activity.

Some of these activities are more overtly illegal than others. Thus, one category—the extensive sphere of barter relations among economic enterprises, without which the

144

Soviet economy could not function—is in effect treated as lawful, as the following explanation by *Ogonek* shows:

> Behind the facade of a command economy were hidden a complex of informal methods of running the economy—quite independent of the administrative-directive methods that have been formally promulgated. These emerged as a method of adaptation to a controlled economy; although they often degenerated and acquired hideous forms, objectively they were the lubricant that permitted the rusty gear wheels to keep turning.[2]

The tolerance shown toward bartering does not, of course, extend to private entrepreneurship in the form of theft, underground businesses, speculation, and corruption. That form of economic crime is severely punished; even at the apogee of the Brezhnev era, when corruption was rampant, there were exposures and judicial proceedings that ended in severe sentences, including capital punishment.

The sheer scale of the shadow economy is evident from the involvement of tens of millions of people. Thus, according to rough estimates, some 20 million people are actively engaged in illegal services (auto repair, apartment renovation, minor construction jobs, etc.). Vladimir Treml has estimated that the shadow economy produces approximately one-third of the GNP of the USSR.[3]

The Brezhnev Era: Mafia Tendencies in the Shadow Economy

In the Brezhnev era, especially in its later years, the shadow economy blossomed as corruption permeated entire strata of the party and state apparatus, reaching epidemic proportions. The growth of that shadow economy can be partly attributed to a feeling of impunity: the entire vertical structure of authority was entangled in this illegal activity. People also came to believe that the theft of state property, or its use for private profit, was not amoral or contrary to generally accepted norms. It is not surprising that an aphorism by the satirist Mikhail Zhvanetskii became extremely popular in these years: "When citizens steal from the country, [the nation] gets rich!"

The world of shady operators is inextricably bound up with the corrupt system of *nomenklatura*: neither the black marketeers nor the party elite could get rich or satisfy their personal desires if they were not closely linked. Highly characteristic evidence of such connections was provided at the funeral of Budnitskii: head of the regional trade administration in Rostov, he had reigned as tsar of the local commercial mafia. After his crimes came to light in 1985, he was sentenced to 15 years but not long afterward died in prison. The solemn burial was attended by representatives of the local establishment and shady operators of underground businesses, who included directors of stores, lawyers, heads of enterprises, underground brokers, directors of vegetable warehouses, construction bosses, doctors who attend to the "beau monde" of Rostov, and also "corrupt officials from party and state organs." An elaborate funeral procession for Budnitskii went through the center of the city, concluding when this Rostov "godfather" was laid to rest at the "Pathway of Glory"—reserved for the burial of the most distinguished representatives of the Rostov elite.[4]

This transpired in 1986—that is, after Gorbachev's accession to power. It might be argued that the funeral was a flamboyant manifestation of opposition to attempts by the Gorbachev leadership to combat the organized crime and corruption that flourished in the Brezhnev years.

It seems that every city and region of the USSR has its own well-developed mafia structure, which controls the shadow economy. The post-Brezhnev era has witnessed the exposure and prosecution of mafias in Krasnodar, Rostov, Odessa, and many other cities of the RSFSR, Ukraine, and other republics. If the Gorbachev leadership does not retreat from its policy of glasnost, the itinerary of place-names for these criminal dramas will steadily grow. The dramas all tend to follow a similar scenario: first, a sensational exposé of the magnates and their illicit machinations in the shadow economy, followed by a wave of arrests and trials of leading figures from a corrupted local elite.

Peculiar Features of the Central Asian Mafia

Is the shadow economy particularly pervasive in Central Asia? Unfortunately, published data do not permit an unequivocal answer. If one considers income and wealth distribution, for example, the polarization and differentials in Central Asia are not greater than in other parts of the country; indeed, the concentration of wealth is possibly higher in the Baltic republics. Thus, a selective sampling of savings banks in Latvia (conducted in the mid-1970s) revealed 3 percent of the savings accounts contained more than half of the entire savings in the republic. One district of Leningrad, significantly, has more than six million savings deposits.[5] The presence of such wealth in the Soviet context points strongly to illicit economic activity. It is, of course, possible that Central Asians are more inclined to conceal money in mattresses than to place it in savings accounts. Still, it is quite conceivable that, in absolute terms, the shadow economy in Central Asia does not occupy the premier place in the country.

Nevertheless, the Central Asian system is deeply rooted, exercising a major influence on the region's politics and economy. In comparison with the general pattern of illegal business and corrupted elites elsewhere in the USSR, Central Asia has two distinctive characteristics that impart a special intensity and tenacity: a deeply rooted tribalism and the existence of a monoculture in both industrial and agricultural production.

The social-economic structure of Central Asia is extraordinarily complex, comprising a congeries of traditional and modern dynamics. It includes several key—and contradictory —elements. Some key traits are quintessentially Soviet: the monopolistic and absolute authority of the party elite over all spheres of public life, the absolute control exercised over the nationalized economy, the rigid centralization of authority, and the population's subjection to terror and political apathy. All these elements are endemic to the Soviet system, but in Central Asia they have fused with clan and Islamic traditions to produce a phenomenon peculiar to Central Asian society. Though one can find analogues for particular

147

aspects in the premodern and contemporary world, Central Asia nevertheless remains unique.

What is more, clan and tribal consciousness in Central Asia have not only survived, but have also become even stronger in the Soviet era. It is easy to see why: reinforcement and development of tribalism was a natural, spontaneous form of resistance to the assimilationist policies that Moscow pursued in an effort to divide national communities. Clan unity and solidarity make possible spiritual and material survival under the adverse conditions of Soviet life. A majority of the national cadres remain loyal to their clan and tribe.

Most striking, the traditional tribal structure has, in some bizarre fashion, fused with the party structure to form a single, indissoluble whole in contemporary Central Asia. Thus, local party leaders are considerably less worried that members of their own tribe will betray them. It was therefore only natural that the former party leader in Kazakhstan, Dinmukhamed Kunaev, surrounded himself with people from his own tribe, *uly zhuz*. Likewise, members of the *buga* clan predominated in the Central Committee of the Kirghiz party; in Turkmenia the *tekintsy* clan dominated the republic's Central Committee, Academy of Sciences, and Ashkhabad University. If the Soviet system gives rise to the phenomenon of "family relations" (*semeinnost*) among nonkinsmen (as a means of shielding themselves from Moscow's supervision and pressure), this tendency must understandably be much more pronounced in Central Asia, where political family relations have fused with blood ties.

Religion is a further distinctive factor in Central Asian politics. In contrast to Russian party members, the Central Asian party cadres and *nomenklatura* elite, though theoretically Marxists and hence atheists, have never sundered their ties with people from their tribe and clan who remain devoted to Islam. As a result, Central Asia has been marked by a solid unity of elites and masses, despite Moscow's efforts to weaken Islam's grip on the population. Those efforts have been unavailing; indeed, Islam has not only remained firmly rooted in the masses, but has even gained a new foothold in the national elites.

The clan structure, with extraordinarily high degrees of tribal fealty, has created especially propitious conditions for the development of illicit economic activity and its corollary, organized crime. The mafia-like clans form such resilient units that even tough *apparatchiki* from Moscow are at a loss to smash this sticky web of tribal connections.

Above all, outsiders find it exceedingly difficult to penetrate this local structure; their difficulty is all the more apparent when Central Asia is compared with other regions of the USSR. Consider the case of Taishet, a small town in Siberia: representatives from Moscow (dispatched to investigate reports of crime and corruption by the local elites) had no sooner arrived than local inhabitants inundated them with information about the transgressions of the town's fathers.[6] Nothing of the sort happens in Central Asia, where the native peoples rally around their bosses and refuse to let Moscow's emissaries sow division.

Moscow's powerlessness before Central Asian tribalism is abundantly evident in Uzbekistan. For a number of years now, Moscow's agents have labored to decapitate and decimate the system of organized crime, and between 1983 and 1987 they arrested and tried hundreds of leading party officials, including secretaries of the Uzbek Central Committee, first secretaries of oblast committees, the chairman of the republican Council of Ministers, the minister of internal affairs, and other high-ranking officials. A number of these people were shot or (as in the case of Ergashev, the minister of internal affairs) committed suicide. Thousands of people employed in the trade network, chairmen of *kolkhozes*, plant directors, officials in the judicial system, regular police, and judges have been convicted and sentenced to long prison sentences. Nevertheless, it is clear that Moscow's effort to clean up the republic has in fact only scraped off the upper crust of organized crime. Evidence for that assessment is provided by the trial testimony given by one of the accused:

Crimes like bribery, falsified and inflated production reports (*pripiski*), and theft have become the norm. There is really no serious attempt to combat these things. . . . Thus not a single question gets resolved without paying a bribe. The question is put thus: either you resign from your post, or you live according to the laws of criminals . . . [that fostered] the development of avarice, abuse of official positions, mutual coverups and graft, regional ties, and "family relations" [among responsible personnel]. The mafia stopped short of nothing, even giving tacit assent to the active growth of Islam, which (as is well known) preaches submission and humility before those who are senior in rank and age.[7]

All of Moscow's endeavors to establish control in the area have obviously gone for nought.

Immunity from Moscow's controls left local elites free to run their illicit operations. Cotton is the main source of enrichment for the shadow market and corrupted elite in Uzbekistan. For a number of years the local mafia systematically inflated reports on cotton production by one million tons; the profit for the nonexistent tons—amounting to billions of rubles—went directly to line the pockets of the cotton barons.[8] To this, one should add the untold millions of rubles that have been siphoned off through theft and otherwise amassed through a network of underground businesses, trade, and services; other profits come from private agriculture and the large-scale production of opium and other drugs.

Part of these illicit earnings went for personal consumption, but a significant share was also reinvested to expand the underground business. And a considerable part of the profits also had to be used to buy political protection—through bribes paid to the party-state apparatus, police, courts, and judicial system (not only local organs, but those in Moscow as well). As is typical in an elaborate network of organized crime, the Central Asian mafias created gangs of hoodlums to protect the leaders and became deeply enmeshed in a variety of rackets and illegal operations. Nor did Central Asia escape the violent side of organized crime: reprisals against competitors, torture, murder, drug trafficking. Thus, to judge from the Soviet press, the cities and towns of Uzbekistan have all the attributes of a mature system of organized crime.[9] Nor is the picture much different in the other republics of Central Asia.

Cotton Barons: The Adylov Case

Nothing better illustrates the magnitude of the problem than the case of Akhmadzhan Adylov—the quintessence of a "Central Asian variant" of Brezhnevism at its apogee. Adylov, director of the Papskii cotton combine, was one of Uzbekistan's top cotton barons, and until his arrest in 1984 he reigned for many years like a feudal lord over the town of Gurumsarai and surrounding settlements. Approximately 30,000 people were under his suzerainty. According to Vladimir Sokolov (who analyzed the case in a piece in *Literaturnaia gazeta*), Adylov "practically created his own small, sovereign state."[10] No one could enter his territory without permission; its borders were guarded by government militia, who were nominally under the jurisdiction of the Uzbek minister of interior (and, ultimately, the latter's superior in Moscow), but who in fact were in the service—and pay—of Adylov. This miniature state had its own system of investigation, police control, and underground prison, which was used to confine and torture residents who demonstrated the slightest independence. Adylov "had at his disposal colossal sums for any bribe. . . . Adylov's influence was so great that sometimes candidates for a ministerial post [in Uzbekistan] came to Gurumsarai for an interview, where they might hang around for days in [Adylov's] waiting room." A sketch of this lord's external attributes completes this picture:

The autocrat conducted himself with the dignity of a born sovereign. His favorite place was a granite podium alongside a fountain, beneath a shadow of a tree; there stood his desk with a multitude of phones (one of which was a direct line to Rashidov [the first secretary of the Uzbekistan Central Communist Party Committee]). Before the master's eyes was a pedestal, foreseen in good time as the resting place for his own bust (which was to be made after he received the second Gold Star [as Hero of Socialist Labor] which Rashidov had promised). Behind him was a statue of Lenin, whose right hand seemed to put a blessing on the master and his work. Adylov loved to hold meetings here in

151

the open air; it was here that he gave orders, issued reprimands, and, depending on his mood, scourged his subjects with the lash. It was also here that they brought outsiders who had been detained [for trespass on his territory]; and here, in the shadows of Lenin's right hand and before the eyes of the common people, they doused them with cold water in the winter (they called this method of interrogation *Karbyshevka*) until they confessed why they were there and who had sent them. . . . That is how the master governs a population of many thousands in the name of Soviet authority.[11]

The enterprise under Adylov received millions of investment rubles, of which about half were pilfered. Part of these stolen funds were spent to bribe the people "who gave Adylov resources and guaranteed his inviolability."[12] This statement, despite its careful formulation, makes clear that Adylov gave bribes not only to the top leaders in Uzbekistan, but also to their superiors in Moscow.

It is difficult to grasp some of the more exotic details from Adylov's personal life—his wealth, property, thoroughbred horses, and harem. The thumbnail sketch provided here can give only a rough idea of the deeds attributed to this "hero of socialist labor," deputy to the Uzbek Supreme Soviet, and member of the Uzbek Central Committee. What the case shows, more importantly, is the style of leadership and power of one of the leading cotton producers in Central Asia.

Such despotism was made possible in part by the submissiveness of the brutally oppressed population. One can judge the magnitude of this submissiveness from the way that the inhabitants of Gurumsarai endured the most fiendish brutality: Adylov cast them into an underground prison, tortured them with a red-hot iron, and beat pregnant women with a whip before the eyes of their husbands. And the populace tolerated all this! Old men bowed and scraped whenever they passed him, exclaiming, "Allah is Great!"[13] Such extremes would be impossible in Russia, the Ukraine, and the other national republics; only in Central Asia could such things have transpired.

Before Adylov was finally brought to justice in 1984, the press—not only in Uzbekistan, but also in Moscow—groveled in adulation of this Central Asian cotton baron. They sang his praises and imagined that the perfect, social agrarian-industrial enterprise was flourishing in the Fergan Valley, that it was "governed in a fatherly way by the wise, sensitive man Akhmadzhan Adylov," and that it offered ideal conditions of life. One publication that rejoices over Adylov bears the title, *Ladder of Bliss*.[14]

Is the Adylov "paradise" typical of Central Asia, especially the rural areas, where 60 percent of the populace lives? In broad outlines that is apparently so, to judge from recent publications. To be sure, the flamboyant personal traits of Adylov (who explained his brutality by his descent from Timur himself) may not be found in the other local lords. Moreover, not all attain such power and influence. Still, in general terms, the Adylov case is characteristic not only of Rashidov's Uzbekistan, but also of all of Central Asia in the Brezhnev era.

The wealth of the cotton barons and their entourages contrasts sharply with the destitution of a populace so mercilessly exploited for the harvesting and processing of cotton. Sokolov, who visited Adylov's domain, describes graphically the beggarly wages and acute poverty of its inhabitants. Alongside the poverty was paralyzing fear of the boss. Another journalist, who participated in a search for mafia treasures, offers this revealing sketch:

> We arrived at the village in the night, came to a halt by a semifinished house, and awoke its inhabitants—a young man and his pregnant wife. Three young children were sleeping in a pitiful semblance of a homemade bed. Cold and poverty filled the house. The family makes ends meet with bread cakes (*lepeshki*) and water, for they have heavy expenses: for two years they have been building the house they're living in, and the earnings at the *kolkhoz* are small. It seemed so strange: why did we come here, what kind of wealth can one find here? The head of the house, like a trapped animal, kept repeating: "No! Nothing at all [is here]! No! . . ."
>
> But out of some closet came two sealed suitcases containing dozens of leather coats (with and without fur), rolls of imported cloth, money, parcels with rings, precious stones. The wife's

eyes opened wide in astonishment: she had never seen such things before. But the most terrible thing for me was not her amazement at the sight of such wealth and [the realization] that someone could afford to let all this go to rot; rather, the most terrible thing was the slavish fright in the eyes of these young Uzbeks: how are they to account for this to the "boss"? It was like the terror of a rabbit being swallowed by a boa constrictor.[15]

Organized Crime

But who runs the shadow economy? As might be expected, this criminal netherworld has its own hierarchy, which ranges from the official *nomenklatura* elites (cotton barons, directors of trade administration, store managers, heads of industrial enterprises, and the like) to the small fry, the petty speculators at the base of the pyramid. The latter swarm like flies in the commercial districts of a major city:

Stroll a bit through Tashkent, go to the old part of town, visit the numerous bazaars, drop in at the commercial shops, and you will immediately notice how many shops, stores, workshops, shashlik restaurants, and cafes abound here. Here you will be offered black coffee and a tea bowl (called *piala* in Central Asia) of green tea, fashionable shoes and superfashionable pants, cosmetics, jewelry, sunglasses. . . . In a word, whatever you want is for sale here.[16]

All this came long before Moscow authorities passed a decree permitting "individual commercial activity." Indeed, Central Asia long ago developed a peculiar economic system, one that included firms that in theory belonged to the state but in fact were small private enterprises: shops for the production of various goods in short supply, cafes and restaurants, and repair shops.

These underground businesses bear no resemblance to the cooperatives legalized by recent laws. Illustrative is a shop for the production of jeans. It employs ten workers and, in theory, is a state enterprise with a plan of, say, 1,000 pairs of jeans per month. The shop, however, produces 1,500 pairs of jeans: 1,000 of these serve to fulfill the plan, another 100 are recorded for overfulfilling the plan, and 400 go to the private market, with the profit shared proportionately by the manager and workers. Naturally, a certain percentage of this profit must also be kicked upstairs to those who tolerate and conceal this private business.

Such activities have become exceedingly widespread, not only in Central Asia, but also in the Caucasus. The operators who run such businesses are known as shopmen (*tsekhovniki*), and they became particularly active beginning in the late 1970s.

It was, significantly, precisely from this point that organized crime became so prevalent, as Soviet-style gangsters extracted capital from the shopmen and other types of underground operators. The result was a sharp proliferation of racketeering and gangsterism—Central Asia was swept in the 1980s by a wave of armed robberies, homicides, and kidnappings. All this sounds incredible, especially for Westerners inured to the stereotype of ruthless law-and-order totalitarianism; nevertheless, even the Soviet press has finally raised the curtain on this macabre scene. Thus, one journalist, who has studied the criminal world of Uzbekistan, offered this sketch of Soviet gangsterism: "In 1984 the shopmen of Uzbekistan experienced hard times, for they personally had to endure the full burden and horrors of terror at the hands of criminal bands. In the overwhelming majority of cases, the objects of attack were criminals and white-collar employees."[17]

In the late 1970s the chieftains of gangster mobs in Central Asia held a meeting in Krasnodar and agreed to levy a 15 percent "tax" on the illicit income of the shopmen. The hapless objects of the new "tax" learned of the assessment in the following manner:

One fine day (or one wretched day), a group of people suddenly appeared on the doorsteps of a shop under one Said Akhmetovich specializing in the production of shoes for the black market. Without waiting for an invitation, they sat down in chairs, lit up cigarettes and started a conversation. All this they did as if to

155

say: "We have long been keeping an eye on you, our dear Said Akhmetovich, and we know perfectly well what you are doing. Why cover up, dear friend; you're just a godsend for OBKhSS [the criminal investigation bureau for theft of state property]. Therefore we propose the following: work as you please and don't be afraid, just be sure to put X percent on the table each month. If in fact the police suddenly take an interest in you, don't worry—we'll take care of it; if they should put you behind bars, you'll live in a splendid camp and in excellent barracks. And that will just last until the next [general] amnesty. If you, sir, should reject our offer, you can expect a lot of trouble: very soon you will become the object of attention by the authorities, and you'll get a sentence that's "to the hilt." Incidentally, don't you have a wife and children? We cannot guarantee their safety. So, make up your mind, most honorable Said.

After that kind of conversation, any black-market operator (even of the toughest mettle) will normally accept the gangster's terms. Perhaps, not immediately, but in any case sometime thereafter—after he has seen with his own eyes that the gangsters mean business, that they really have powerful and wide-ranging connections.

Soon the most experienced and clever shopmen understood that one should not foul one's relationship with the gangsters, but should involve them in the business—to protect oneself and one's business from attacks by other gangsters, to put pressure on intractable debtors and competitors. This opportunity was first grasped by the magnates of white-collar crime, for only they had sufficient means to hire a murderer and to employ bodyguards.[18]

That kind of shocking reportage comes not from journalistic phantasmagoria, but from a stream of trials after the mid-1980s. The following case is typical:

Azimov, the director of the *sovkoz* Pakhtakor in Kashkadar'inskaia oblast, for 60,000 rubles hired the brothers Azizovy and Tslani as murderers to settle scores with the former bookkeeper Saidov and others who had testified against Azimov for embezzling more than a half million rubles, On April 1, 1985, after receiving an advance of 20,000 rubles, the hired murderers threw a grenade into an automobile that contained Saidov and Babaev; when they saw that the grenade failed to explode, they opened fire from sawed-off shotguns.

After receiving 30,000 rubles from the director of public catering in Tashkent oblast (Radzhapov), a gang member (Boloshin) and two others murdered a citizen named Mirdadaev, set fire to the home of an OBKhSS employee, and prepared to disfigure the face of the deputy minister of trade. Radzhapov himself was later slain by hired murderers.[19]

The brazen scale of gangland-style crime hardly conforms to the usual image of an efficient, repressive police state in the USSR.

Moreover, law enforcement officials have been deeply enmeshed in organized crime. Illustrative is the case of the Iun gang, which controlled the production and sale of narcotics in four districts of Uzbekistan. The band included four police officers, whose duty consisted of frightening and "officially" confiscating concealed drugs from traffickers. Many other such examples could be offered. In some cases police officers even acted as hired killers.

Some sense of how deeply law-enforcement agencies were entangled in organized crime is evident from the fact that criminal investigations between 1984 and 1987 led to the arrest and conviction of virtually the entire top staff in the Uzbekistan Ministry of Internal Affairs and 98 percent of the heads of oblast offices in that ministry.[20] In the early 1980s Uzbekistan had been divided into the territories of various mafia clans; Tashkent, for instance, was divided into the territories of 20 clans, who controlled virtually all spheres of illegal economic activity, the production and sale of opium, prostitution, and so forth. The entire experience of mafia organization and operation in the West was duplicated by imitators in Uzbekistan.[21] Nor do the other Central Asian republics lag behind Uzbekistan in their scale of criminal activity, gangsterism, and involvement of law-enforcement agencies in organized crime.[22]

Moscow's Weakness in the Face of
Organized Crime

This chapter has sketched some fragments from the mosaic of a shadow economy in Central Asia—admittedly, its more extreme manifestations. But it is precisely these extreme manifestations, and the resultant crime, that were so characteristic of late Brezhnivism. It is clear that the efforts of the Gorbachev leadership to resuscitate the economy cannot succeed in Central Asia as long as this cancerous tumor remains in the economic organism.

No less important is that Moscow has lost a firm grip not only over the economy of the Moslem periphery, but also over other spheres of life in this region, which is geographically contiguous to Iran and Afghanistan and has strong ethnic and cultural ties to both. This situation is laden with danger and volatility, especially at present, when nationalistic movements have become so vibrant and explosive in the USSR.

Furthermore, every nationalist slogan in the USSR is invariably linked to some demand for economic autarky. From Moscow's perspective, the excesses of the shadow economy are not so dangerous as long as they are in a Rostov or Volgograd, because there they are devoid of a nationalistic tone. Matters are quite different in Central Asia. Here, Moscow's attempts to break up the mafia infrastructure evoke the most embittered resistance from various strata of the population, which unite on the basis of nationalistic demands and interests. The catalyst to a nationalistic backlash is Moscow's appointment of its own agents, who do not belong to the indigenous nationalities. Adherence to Islam has also played an important role. Hostility toward local oppressors has, consequently, receded into the background; indeed, these exploiters even elicit support and defense from their fellow nationalists. Nationalism, in a word, proves more powerful than class consciousness, as has been demonstrated in various parts of the world.

The transformation of the Soviet regime in Central Asia into some kind of "mafia-clan" structure may already be

158

irreversible. In any event, Moscow's efforts to restore order have been signally unsuccessful here during the last few years; none can gainsay that Moscow's special task force, dispatched to this eastern periphery to eradicate the rampant corruption, theft, and blackmail, has utterly failed to overcome the resistance of the indigenous infrastructure. On the contrary, Moscow's emissaries have been stymied by opposition from the general population, even to the point at which they have had to take to their heels to survive.

Nor does the mere replacement of one set of national cadres with another have much effect. Moscow dispatched thousands to prison and removed the entire native elite, but the successors were no different from their predecessors. A good illustration is afforded by the Adylov case: a tried and trusted party functionary replaced Adylov, but within a year and a half he too was incarcerated for abusing his authority, for beating subordinates, and for falsifying reports on cotton production. And this happened right after the shocking news about Adylov had reverberated around the USSR!

The Central Asian party elite simply lacks the cold fear that it once felt toward Moscow. The new attitude is apparent in such cases as that of Kirghizia, where a special commission from the Central Committee in Moscow unearthed blatant corruption and lawlessness in one oblast. The commission thereupon delivered a severe rebuke to the Kirghiz party leadership. The most significant fact about this case is the result: the report and reprimand failed to trigger any changes. The central leadership of Kirghizia coolly left all the local bosses in place and covered up the whole affair, contrary to Moscow's instructions.[23]

Such is the final testimony to Moscow's inability to penetrate and override national party infrastructures in the Gorbachev era. As long as Moscow lacks effective control over the periphery, as long as rampant lawlessness and organized crime dominate republic economies, the prospects for a fundamental turnaround—either in the USSR as a whole or in Central Asia—appear exceedingly dim.

159

CHAPTER 9

The Impact of the Gorbachev Reforms on Central Asia

Constitution, Planning, and Reality in Regional Economies

Gosplan and the Moscow ministries that conduct branch planning for the Soviet economy also prepare the main indices for regional economic development. But the primary reference is the nationwide development of a production branch—that is, total output for such sectors as ferrous metallurgy, machine building, and food processing. That dynamic also affects planning at the republic level, where primary attention is again given to the goals and interests of the production branch. The difficulty is that social-economic problems, especially in Central Asia, are virtually ignored.

If the planning system is examined closely, it turns out that Gosplan and the central ministries have only slight contact with the republic Gosplans. As a result, the central Gosplan mechanically takes the base figures on production and distributes all-union goals across the USSR, without giving serious attention to the conditions of a specific locale, the needs of its population, or its demographic and ecological peculiarities. For planners in Moscow, the borders between republics are a vague abstraction, the republican governments an irksome hindrance that threatens to lodge complaints about Gosplan or the ministry at the Central Committee if they commit a particularly outrageous·transgression against the interests of a republic. But such complaints are usually decided in favor of the central agencies, even if all this causes some discomfort and temporary headaches for the *apparatchiki* in Moscow. The latter are particularly inclined to flout the rights and interests of a republic when its head, the first secretary, is not a member of the Politburo, as is true in Central Asia.

Leaving aside the economic consequences of absolute dominance by production-branch administration and economic planning in so immense a country, I will examine here one important phenomenon—the confrontation between Moscow and the national republics over the latter's participation in decision making for their own economies. This confrontation has had a significant legal foundation since the adoption of the new Soviet constitution in 1977.

Like the dissident movement of the 1960s, which was born amid demands that constitutional guarantees of civil rights be strictly observed, the current movement by national cadres in the republics to assert their own right to regulate economic development in their republics relies on articles in the new constitution for justification. In my judgment, the cadres' audacity derives from Gorbachev's own criticism of Gosplan and the union ministries. It must be assumed that the statement by Sergei Maniakin at the twenty-seventh party congress ("History will not forgive the ministries for the stagnation that they have allowed in the rates of economic development of the country"),[1] together with Gorbachev's approving response, evoked enthusiam among the leaders of the national republics. Especially animated was the response from the predominantly Moslem republics, where lawyers and the economists have used the pages of the local press to insist that the constitution ensures their independence in the formulation of economic strategy. They have concentrated on article 77, which—for the first time in the history of Soviet constitutions—included a formula on the "complex economic and social development" of union republics. The article itself reads as follows:

The union republics provide for the complex economic and social development in their territories, assist in the realization of all-union directives in their territories, and implement the decisions of the higher organs of state authority and administration

161

of the USSR. With respect to questions in its purview, the union republic coordinates and supervises the activity of enterprises, institutions and organizations subordinate to the union.[2]

This text is rich in ambiguity. On the one hand, it holds that republican governments have the prerogative of higher authority in economic and social life. On the other hand, they are charged with implementing the decisions of Moscow. But what if the republic's interests in economic development diverge from those of Moscow (as happens constantly)? Moreover, the constitution declares that a republic's authority over "all-union enterprises" (that is, those directly subordinate to Moscow) is restricted to the sphere pertinent to their competence. But just what their competence encompasses is unclear.

These ambiguities are not the result of shoddy work by lawmakers in Moscow. On the contrary: they were deliberately manufactured, reflecting the indecision endemic to the Soviet economic system about conflicts between the republics and Moscow apparatus, between localism and central departmentalism. The formulation in article 77 allows each side in the conflict to interpret the passage as it sees fit. Thus, it leaves enough room for Gosplan and the union ministries to maintain their former command position over the republics' economies and yet remain within the formal limits of the law. But it also provides legal grounds for republican activists to defend local interests.

In the 11 years since the new constitution was adopted, Gosplan and production-branch union ministries have retained their primacy in preparing plans and exercising control over republic economies. As earlier, the only obligatory plans are those worked out by union ministries for production branches. To be sure, the preparation of complex plans for the development of republics is a matter of local initiative, but most such plans are neither examined nor endorsed by Gosplan.[3]

The key is that no one—either in Moscow or in the republics—has direct responsibility for preparing or implementing the complex plans for all-round local development.

According to my calculations, of the hundreds of decrees the Soviet leadership promulgated on sundry economic questions between 1970 and 1985, only seven addressed economic issues of individual regions, and these all pertained to territories in the RSFSR. Not a single decision of the Central Committee or the Council of Ministers demonstrated interest in the economic development of non-Slavic national republics, or in the republics' broader social-economic development.

This state of affairs provokes mounting (if hidden) dissatisfaction in minority republics. Indicative is the recent demand by local elites for a clarification of article 77 to realize the rights of republics in "ensuring complex economic and social development."[4] Such assertions conveniently overlook the limitation plainly contained in the text of the article.

It would have been natural for the new constitution to inaugurate corresponding changes and clarifications in the status of republican organs of government—in particular, the republican Councils of Ministers, Gosplans and ministries. But this did not occur. The republics justly believe that their government organs will be able to "coordinate and control" the activity of all-union enterprises and to prepare their own economic policy only when they have the necessary specific rights, when the structure and practices in economic planning have been changed.

The republics have, however, built up a cumbersome administrative apparatus that, in many respects, replicates the central apparatus in Moscow. Thus, on January 1, 1985, Turkmenia had 28 ministries, 14 state committees, and 10 government agencies or domains.[5] This bureaucracy is composed mainly of national cadres, especially at leadership levels. And it is precisely they who constitute a breeding ground for discontent with the dictates emanating from Moscow. The broad zone of legal ambiguity in the interrelationship of central and republic organs created by the casuists in Moscow has retained the power of the center and left the republics impotent, thereby giving rise to protest among the latter.

Moreover, Gorbachev's statements about administrative reform stir more anxiety in the republics than in Moscow. If major retrenchments in the republic bureaucracy were made, it would be considerably more difficult for the bureaucrats to find new employment locally than in Moscow, and this is especially true for Central Asia. Insofar as the republic has no real opportunity to manage its own economy, its army of bureaucrats is of little importance, and hence a prime target for liquidation. The instinct for self-preservation has doubtless reinforced resentment within the republican establishment of Moscow's refusal to grant the republics greater authority to manage their own economies.

Gorbachev's address to the Central Committee plenum in June 1987 did not delude republican leaders. The speech must have caused republican decision makers to ask themselves the following questions:

- How will the proposed reforms in the economy and administration affect the republics' autonomy in economic planning and management?

- What changes will be made in the allocation of capital investments? Will the quota of a given republic be increased? Will the role of local leaders in the formulation of investment policy within the republic be augmented?

Gorbachev declared that, although "a series of decisions have recently been made for increasing the role of republican organs," nevertheless "the territorial aspect of administration has thus far not received proper attention and resolution. *Cardinal measures* [emphasis added] are needed here." Further, he emphasized that "the activity of territorial organs should, above all, be focused on the problem of the complex development of a region, on the most rational utilization of local resources—labor, natural resources, productive and economic resources." He then explained what he had in mind: "Strictly speaking, we have already taken some concrete steps in this direction. I have in mind the creation of the administrative organs of the agroindustrial complex, construction, the production of consumer goods and services."[6]

Thus, according to Gorbachev, the primary task of

republican administrative organs is complex development. But what powers have they been given to ensure not only that they "concentrate their activity" in this sphere, but also that this activity produces results? On this point Gorbachev remained vague. As for his references to the creation of new vertical administrative structures in agriculture, construction, and the like, such perturbations in the central apparatus (as the Soviet press bears witness) have produced changes only in the Moscow bureaucracy and the territorial branches that manage these sectors of the economy, not in the relationship between the center and the republics.

In that section of his speech devoted to "the reconstruction of the organizational structure and the work of administrative organs," Gorbachev expressed the idea that "in the future objects of direct administration from the center could become" certain integrated, gigantic enterprises. These could comprise enterprises currently under central control, which would be transformed into "production-branch, intersector, and territorial-sector combines," which would encompass "the entire cycle: scientific research, investments, production, sale, and service. Together with them, tens of thousands of middling and smaller enterprises (including cooperatives oriented toward *serving the gigantic combines* [emphasis added] and local markets can be subordinate to republican and local authorities."[7] Gorbachev also spoke about the functions of production-branch ministries, which in the future will plan the development of economic branches and control funds for the creation of new industrial capacity and the reconstruction of existing plants.

But as long as production-branch ministries in Moscow control investment and industrial capacity in the national republics, and as long as the republic governments lack the authority to regulate their own economic structure, there is not the slightest chance that the complex, proportional needs of republic economies will receive greater attention.

A dialogue between the correspondent for *Sotsialisticheskaia industriia* and the first deputy of the Council of Ministers of Tadjikistan, Georgii Koshlakov, is illustrative.[8] The interview, which was conducted at the end of 1986, dwelt on the problems that have accompanied implementation of the largest investment program in Central Asia, construction of the South Tadjik territorial production complex. This is among the most important construction projects in recent five-year plans and therefore is under the direct supervision of Gosplan. The complex is being constructed under the aegis of two union ministries—the Ministry of Nonferrous Metallurgy and the Ministry of Chemical Industry.

Koshlakov: Beginning with the ninth five-year plan, the ministries planned capital investments in the complex without taking into account overall construction [in the republic]. . . .

Correspondent: But in that case does the South Tadjik region deserve to bear the designation as a binding term in which the key word is "complex [in other words, an integrated economic system]?" No matter where you turn, there's trouble. Everywhere one encounters vested interests; under pressure from them, the interests of the republic, the population, and the employees of factories must give way. . . .

Koshlakov: Although the South Tadjik complex is planned as a separate construction project in the union Gosplan, the contours of the project are becoming increasingly blurred. Territorial [republican] organs cannot fully oversee its creation and development. In essence, everything is farmed out to union ministries. And each addresses its own, narrowly defined tasks. And the situation is not salvaged by the fact that Gosplan confirms the "entitlement" [the construction assignment] for the complex as a whole. In essence, there is no single organ overseeing the entire complex.

Correspondent: It follows that you acknowledge your helplessness? After all, the republican Council of Ministers is the chief authority on [its] territory.

Koshlakov: Its authority is nominal. The funds are not under our control. We have to be content with the sum of items that we receive when the proposals of the ministries (which, to be blunt, represent their own narrow desires) are added together. *Just try to assume the power to manipulate the resources in the interest of the complex development of the region—and nothing comes of it. . . .* [emphasis added].

From Gorbachev's statements, however nebulous they

might be, it is clear that the new leadership intends to preserve and reinforce its centralized management of the nation's economy. The liberalization concerns individual enterprises, which will be accorded somewhat greater independence. But there will be no concessions to republics in the sphere of managing all-union enterprises directly subordinate to Moscow.

At present, enterprises subordinate to republican and local authorities produce only 8 to 10 percent of the entire volume of industrial output in the USSR.[9] Judging from Gorbachev's speech at the Central Committee plenum, he does not intend to increase this share. Thus, the republics will continue to control only the relatively small enterprises that perform auxiliary service functions; yet even these have a production program that depends more on the large enterprises directed from Moscow than on the decisions of local and republican authorities. It is also obvious that planning will still be conducted on the production-branch principle and that the interests of complex economic development in the national republics will take a back seat.

Price Reform and Cost Accounting

The Soviet shift to economic methods of management and self-financing must include a restructuring of the system of price-setting. Until now, neither the theoretical nor the organizational base for this crucial step has advanced beyond an unproductive discussion stage. But it is well recognized that the prices of fuel and raw materials are substantially depressed in comparison with the prices of finished goods. In addition to distorting many economic proportions, the depressed prices discourage efforts to economize on the consumption of fuels and raw materials, although such conservation is a fundamental precondition for revitalizing the economy. The new program of the Communist Party recognizes this explicitly. In the opinion of prominent Soviet experts, the current prices of raw materials and fuel "are two or more times depressed in comparison with the socially necessary expenditures for their production."[10] It is just as universally recognized that the prices of many finished products, particularly machinery, are significantly inflated.[11] Thus, whatever new price-setting mechanism is adopted, it must provide for a significant increase in the prices of fuel and raw materials. Moreover, it must include steps to hold down inflationary increases in the price of machinery.

Price adjustments, however, have important repercussions for various regions. Thus, according to the logic of Gorbachev's economic reforms, prices should be raised on production from the Moslem republics (that is, on oil, gas, coal, metals, and cotton), while prices on manufactured goods (which come primarily from European Russia) should be lowered. Such adjustments necessarily imply a significant improvement in the role of Central Asia in the GNP, with a substantial increase in its national income. It will then be impossible to justify this region's relatively low investment quota in terms of its national income; no longer can Moscow reprimand the region for taking subsidies at the expense of the Ukraine and the RSFSR. The ambitions of the Central Asians will increase accordingly. It is possible that the opposite situation will then arise—the national income from these republics will have to be redistributed to benefit the European regions in order to implement the Gorbachev strategy of modernizing the machine-building industry. But that would only reinforce the claims of national cadres in Moscow and deepen their dissatisfaction.

Cost Accounting and the Unemployment Problem

Another aspect of the Gorbachev economic reforms—of no less consequence—is a transition to cost accounting (*khozraschet*), self-financing, and self-investment for individual enterprises. Leaving aside the likelihood of adoption, it is important to assess the feasibility of implementing this idea in a nonmarket economic system where final control rests with the party apparatus. To judge from Gorbachev's public statements, he intends to conserve this basic order. The problem nonetheless remains of assessing the impact of Gorbachev's cost accounting on the Moslem republics.

Cost accounting in its purest form (which in fact is now being postulated in public statements by Gorbachev, Ryzhkov, and other Soviet leaders) would lead to employee dismissals on a massive scale—up to one-third by my calculations. And no one takes seriously the leader's assurance that this change will not lead to unemployment. But here compromise is simply impossible: one must choose between "complete cost accounting" at individual enterprises (with employee dismissals and unemployment as an inevitable consequence) and cost accounting that is purely nominal. Nikolai Shmelev expressed the general judgment not only of Soviet economists, but of all thoughtful people on this question when he wrote in June 1987:

> We will not close our eyes to the economic harm from our parasitic confidence in guaranteed work. It seems that everyone knows that complete employment is responsible for disorderliness, drunkenness, and poor workmanship. It is necessary to discuss, in a fearless and businesslike manner, the benefits that would ensue from a relatively small reserve army of labor (which, of course, would not be left completely to its own fate by the state). . . . The real danger of losing work, of receiving temporary unemployment benefits or being obliged to work wherever one is sent—all that would be strong medicine against sloth, drunkenness, and irresponsibility. Many experts think that it would be cheaper to pay unemployment benefits to those temporarily out of work for a few months than to keep at the plant the loafers who are totally unafraid and who can destroy (and *do* destroy) any cost-accounting system, any attempt to raise the quality and efficiency of public work.[12]

Gorbachev hastened to declare that he does not concur with Shmelev on the unemployment question—politically, he cannot repudiate publicly one of the most important "achievements of socialism." Given the logic of Gorbachev's own program, however, it is difficult to believe that he does not share Shmelev's views.

Still, however compelling these ruminations about the virtues of unemployment may sound, most Soviet citizens can only abhor such talk. That reaction is natural enough in any society, but especially intense for Soviet citizens, who have been raised in the conviction that the state is obliged to provide them with jobs, that unemployment is an evil found solely in capitalist countries, that it is utterly alien to the Soviet economy—what other advantages does the Soviet system have to offer? Soviet citizens can only shiver in horror at the thought that they may lose their jobs in Moscow, Leningrad, Kiev, or even in Sverdlovsk or Omsk, where they have a place to live, child-care centers, kinsmen, and connections (absolutely essential for survival); that they will then have to look for work in some remote spot in Siberia in need of labor; and that they will have to work in some profession other than the one for which they were trained, possibly as physical laborers, and in a harsh climate, with no assurance that they will even have a place to live.

If these problems seem serious, they are much more acute in Central Asia than in European Russia. Most people in the latter areas could adjust, for they could probably find a job in the main cities of their region (even if in another speciality), with some loss in status and possibly income. But the cadres in Central Asia would face greater problems. Here cost accounting and staff reductions would create an auxiliary army of unemployed people simply unable to find work. Revealing indeed is the case of Tadjikistan during the first year of the new order (1987): demand for the training of new labor was one-third less than what had been planned.[13] In a word, the industrially developed regions of the western part of the USSR can absorb an incomparably higher volume of labor resources than can Central Asia.

Furthermore, cost accounting in its full efflorescence— meaning self-investment by the enterprise from its own profits—should, in theory, impose strict discipline on the investment behavior of enterprises, reduce their investment activity, and subordinate this to high-priority needs. Even according to official data, 13 percent of all enterprises in the Soviet Union are unprofitable. With the shift to self-financing, their number will increase significantly. Those whose financial condition is favorable will prefer, especially in the initial struggle for survival, to direct their investments not toward the expansion of productive capacity and the development of the infrastructure, but toward the liquidation of bottlenecks in technology and the upgrading of equipment.

But in Central Asia the fixed capital equipment is exceedingly old and, up to now, has undergone little replacement or renewal; hence, the need to modernize existing enterprises is much greater here than in the western areas of the country. Further, many of this region's enterprises were created during World War II, when the overriding objective was to achieve the fastest possible start-up, so that many began production on a temporary basis and in hastily constructed buildings. The magnitude of the problem is evident from the fact that of 1,500 industrial enterprises in Uzbekistan, approximately 900 require immediate reconstruction. [14]

It is impossible to determine now what kind of relationship is envisioned between investments by Moscow and by the enterprise itself. In principle, however, the latter's share should be significant. Of these investments, only a marginal part is intended for developing the infrastructure and diversifying industrial production—in other words, for upgrading the industrial structure, creating additional jobs, and improving social conditions. Priority, rather, is to be given to commercial interests. Local authorities already reprove union ministries for neglecting local requirements and investing too little to meet social needs in areas where they locate industrial plants; once cost accounting is fully introduced, this situation may worsen.

Still more fundamental is whether the Gorbachev leadership can be expected to increase the investment flow to Central Asia. Does such a surge in new capital correspond to Moscow's economic strategy?

Moscow's New Investment Strategy

In his first programmatic statement on economic questions, in June 1985, Gorbachev affirmed the need to restructure Soviet investment policy. The precise directions this restructuring should assume were adumbrated in the twelfth five-year plan:

1. An increase in the share of the national income used for investment and, correspondingly, a reduction in current consumption;
2. Diversion of investment from the creation of new enterprises to the modernization of old ones;
3. A sharp increase in the investment share for machine building and, correspondingly, a reduction in the shares of some other sectors of the economy.

Insofar as these three pillars of Gorbachev's prescription for healing the Soviet economy have ramifications for republic economies, it is important to examine them closely.

The most important political decision facing the Soviet leadership in the preparation and promulgation of five-year plans is the distribution of national income between investments in production and in the nonproducing spheres of the economy. This proportion reflects the regime's real intention to raise (or lower) consumption. From the party congresses come vows to raise the share of consumption, and in the post-Stalin era this has even found its way into the formal plans. But, to the best of my knowledge, this has always remained a dead issue; such, for example, was the case in the last (eleventh) five-year plan, for the first half of the 1980s. Tikhonov, then holding the post of premier, announced to the twenty-sixth party congress that the plan for 1981–1985 foresaw an increase in the share for consumption. This promise was not fulfilled, however; consumption's share of the national income declined from 76 percent to 73 percent between 1980 and 1985.[15]

In contrast to preceding periods, the current five-year plan foresees a reduction in consumption, as the new premier, Nikolai Ryzhkov, candidly told the twenty-seventh party congress:

Given the policy of acceleration [in economic growth], the Central Committee of the CPSU has deemed it expedient to increase the rate of growth for capital investment in production from 16 percent in the previous plan to 25 percent in the current, twelfth, five-year plan. Naturally, this entails a certain change in the proportions for the distribution of national

172

income—an increase in the share for accumulation [and, ipso facto, a reduced share for consumption]. Such shifts are essential in order to achieve both the immediate and also strategic goals. In the following [plan] it is intended to stabilize and even to reduce somewhat the share of consumption.[16]

Ryzhkov does not clarify which "immediate and strategic goals" he had in mind, nor when the share accorded to consumption can be expected to stabilize and then decline. In general, the word "intend" suggests indecision and uncertainty, in contrast to the word "plan," which (one must assume) Ryzhkov deliberately chose not to use.

A reduced consumption quota will have a particularly strong impact on the Moslem republics. The per-capita national income in these republics is substantially lower than in the USSR as a whole: in 1985 Central Asia had 4 percent of the Soviet national income, and 11 percent of its population, and the consumption share in these republics is considerably lower than the average in the USSR, as is the share of total investment devoted to the social sphere.

As for upgrading existing plants and the priority given to machine building, it is clear that this emphasis will slow economic growth in Central Asia, particularly since the territorial distribution of state investments will still be controlled by the central ministries. The key point is that at least 80 percent of the industrial output of the USSR is concentrated in the European regions of the country.[17] By contrast, Central Asia's share comprises only 4.5 percent.[18] The sharp increase in the share of investment for existing capacity envisioned in the twelfth five-year plan will inescapably lead to a reduction in the share allocated to the industry located in Central Asia. Hence, the persisting high rate of population growth, on the one hand, and the shrinking investment quota, on the other, will exacerbate the economic backwardness of this region and aggravate the problem of unemployment.

Let us examine how another change in investment policy by the Gorbachev leadership will affect the economy of Central Asia: the sharp increase in investments for machine building.

173

The main goal of Gorbachev's economic program is to achieve a leap forward in the machine-building sector. The key to understanding how, and at what price, the plan seeks to accomplish this is evident from a statement by Lev Zaikov (the Politburo member responsible for the machine-building and defense industries) in November 1986:

> The machine-building complex has been given everything that is at the disposal of our economy. *For a year or two, construction of a series of enterprises in other sectors has been halted* [emphasis added]. In a word, the absolute maximum has been provided to ensure rapid progress in one sector. In terms of the rate of growth in production, machine building is supposed to surpass the rest of industry in the USSR by 1.7 times; the growth for machine building is to be 43.2 percent, compared with 25 percent for industry as a whole.[19]

This investment capital, moreover, will not flow evenly into all the branches of machine building; rather, first priority is given to machine-tool branches and those sectors that produce advanced technology, high-technology products, and computers. The surge is enormous; investments in the machine-tool branch in 1986 represented a 42 percent increase over the previous year.[20] Evidently, a group of top-priority branches for computers and highly sensitive equipment received an analogous infusion of investment capital.[21] At the same time, the total investment increase for the entire machine-building sector was fixed in the plan at just 15 percent for 1986.[22]

European Russia accounts for approximately 90 percent of all output in machine building; Central Asia's share is only 2.4 percent.[23] Further, Central Asia's machine-building sector lacks almost completely the advanced-technology branch that now holds highest priority in Moscow's planning. In the 1970s, approximately 7 percent of the total volume of investments in machine building in the USSR was allocated to the Asian regions of the country; of this total volume, approximately 3 to 4 percent was allotted to machine building in Kazakhstan and Central Asia.[24]

To promote the full development of Central Asia's

economy, to diminish economic backwardness of this region, to address its social problems (including the need for greater employment opportunities), it is necessary to increase the role of machine building and, correspondingly, to increase that sector's share of investment. Viktor Evstigneev from the Institute of Economics of the USSR Academy of Sciences (a leading specialist on the territorial distribution of machine-building enterprises) wrote as follows on this problem:

> Effectiveness in the distribution of machine-building enterprises in eastern regions [which include Central Asia and Kazakhstan, along with Siberia and the Far East] in the immediate future, to a significant degree will obviously be linked to the resolution of social problems. The gradual shift of the center of gravity in the construction of new machine-building plants to the eastern part of the USSR is stimulated, in its economic scale, by sociological factors—in the first instance by the necessity of equalizing the level of development in the various regions, and that assumes that the eastern regions of the country be brought into economic utilization. To resolve this enormous state objective, development of machine building will play a most important role.[25]

At present, machine building is the least developed sector of the Central Asian economy.

And the Gorbachev policy, aimed at a sharp increase in the investment quota for machine building, together with an emphasis on investing primarily in existing enterprises, gives no reason to expect an increase in investment for Central Asian machine building. Indeed, one should expect that this investment will decline in relative—perhaps even in absolute —terms. From the perspective of short-term interests, there are sufficient objective grounds to base the development of machine-building capacity in the old industrial core of Russia, since that would entail much smaller outlays for infrastructure. In short, the investment activities of the twelfth five-year plan will, in all likelihood, even further diminish the southeast flow of investment capital.

In 1987 Gorbachev spoke of investing an additional 50 billion rubles in housing construction. This figure represents approximately 20 percent of annual investment in the whole economy.[26] How will this affect the investment process in Central Asia?

Generally speaking, a retreat from the strict guidelines of the investment plan, with its proportions that so manifestly contradict the specific interests of Central Asia, can only be a positive development from the region's vantage point. Is it to be expected that the emerging instability of investment parameters of the five-year plan will end up giving these areas a greater share of investment resources? To judge from Gorbachev's comments cited above, no serious shifts of investment in this direction are currently envisioned.

Declarations that local organs should be concerned with the complex, all-round economic development of their territories, with the distribution of local resources, and with the development of the social sphere are nothing new. In a style reminiscent of Brezhnev, Gorbachev asks, "Why should we not devise and introduce a system in which industrial construction is authorized for ministries and administrative bodies only in those cases where they simultaneously allocate to territorial organs the means to develop the social sphere according to established norms?"[27] This passage is exceedingly characteristic in both its form and its content. It reflects (1) Gorbachev's presumption that the allocation of investment will in the future go through union ministries, with no increased role for local authorities; (2) his reliance on old categories, since until now ministries and administrative organs have had to consider the allocation of means for the development of local infrastructure wherever they have constructed enterprises; and (3) all the talk of giving republics and local organs a greater role in shaping their economy will remain nothing more than empty rhetoric.

If one is concerned about the development of the social sphere, then why must one distribute the resources for this through union ministries engaged in construction? Why not give these resources directly to local authorities to use for the development of their territories?

The answer to such questions is, in my opinion, quite simple: first, the distribution of investment for the construction of new enterprises is strictly centralized and will remain that way; and second, investments will be made predominantly in the producer sphere, with only a subsidiary role accorded to the social sphere. Thus, there is no reason to anticipate that Central Asia will receive more funds to solve its specific problems. Gorbachev's promise of additional housing construction over that foreseen by the plan—60 million square meters between 1986 and 1990—will have little impact on the housing situation in Central Asia, which has no reason to anticipate a larger share in this supplementary allocation,[28] and whose population increase of the next five-year period will in any event nullify any effect the supplementary funds it does receive might have.

The Attitude of National Cadres

After the twenty-seventh party congress, which adopted Gorbachev's economic program revealing the grim investment prospects for Central Asia, disgruntled voices from local cadres became audible. To be sure, they were cautious in how they articulated their protests. But, amid the rising attack on Moslem nationalism that followed the congress, the defense of national republics' interests was nothing less than a direct challenge to the new leadership, however circumspect its expression.

Central Asian economists thus insist that, in planning the development of "regions with relatively high proportions of free and spatially immobile labor resources," first priority must be given to ensuring employment and meeting consumer demand.[29] Drawing on Soviet propagandists' slogan that "everything is for the person and his well-being," they demand that their republics be given a special place in Moscow's investment policy. Let us concisely state and analyze the theses propounded in the publications of the national cadres after the last party congress.

1. It is wrong for a republic's investment quota to correspond to its contribution to the country's national income, or for the volume of investment to be determined by the volume of national income produced in the republic that is reinvested. Insofar as a republic's national income is calculated in a way that fails to reflect the real contribution

to the income of the USSR (because of prices and the turnover tax), insofar as the structure and character of the economy are determined by Moscow's interests and not those of the republic, and insofar as the republic is part of an open regional economy, Moscow should invest in the republic's economy without regard to its national income. Simply put, if one artificially lowers the real output and input of a republic, that is not grounds for underinvestment in its economy.

2. It is wrong for decision makers, when evaluating the expediency of investment in one or another project, or in one or another territory, to base their decision on criteria of economic efficiency, as reflected in profit or cost indices. Rather, one should adopt as the sole criterion improvement in the economic and cultural level of the populace in a given territory. It follows that, since the population is growing faster in the Moslem republics than elsewhere, and since their social spheres currently receive the least investment per capita in the USSR (as official statistics show), the priority of these republics in the distribution of investment by Moscow is self-evident.

3. It is wrong to extend a policy for economic development that is geared primarily toward regions with a more developed economic structure to republics with high unemployment, a predominance of raw-material output in their economic structure, and a backward infrastructure. In such areas it is necessary to create new employment opportunities, which requires the construction of new plants. Moreover, these should be plants for machine building and textile production (the most labor-intensive sectors).

Creating employment should be the primary goal of investment policy, but Moscow's strategy, which focuses on intensive rather than extensive use of investment resources, works against achievement of this goal. And Gosplan intends to apply its strategy to all republics in the USSR, without exception. Thus, the plan for Uzbekistan in 1986 foresees that, of the total increase in the growth of industrial production, 85 percent is to come from improvement in existing capacity, and only 15 percent from the creation of new plants.[30] Those proportions would be appropriate in the

Central Region of the RSFSR, the Urals, Moscow, Leningrad, Sverdlovsk, or Novosibirsk, but they are inappropriate for Uzbekistan. The situation in the other republics of Central Asia is analogous.

Thus, contrary to the policy of the Gorbachev leadership, the national cadres of the Moslem republics insist on greater investment activity in their regions. In their judgment, this is necessary to balance the economic structure and labor resources, and to overcome the backwardness of the social infrastructure and consumption sphere: in other words, to remove the discrimination that Moscow, through its investment policy, has shown toward their population. The statements on this subject have left no doubt about their authors' attitude toward the scenario of economic development that Moscow has followed over many years, amounting to casting them in the role of suppliers of raw materials and labor, without regard for the planning of investment strategies appropriate to their specific demographic structure. Here are some typical judgments expressed in the period since the twenty-seventh party congress:

> The production-branch structure of the economy that has developed up to now [in Uzbekistan] does not ensure the development of a number of economic and social goals. . . .[31]

> As is well known, the tempo of growth rates of the labor force is high in Uzbekistan . . . . The employment level of the population has stabilized at 78 percent—one of the lowest rates in the country. . . . Uzbekistan lags considerably behind the country as a whole in the most important per-capita indices.[32]

> It is necessary to establish supplementary technological links in the industrial process and to strengthen those that are insufficiently developed. So that, the output shipped from the republic [Uzbekistan] will not be dominated by raw materials and only slightly processed products, it is important to provide for a processing industry that has been retarded in its development. This direction is, in our opinion, of cardinal importance in improving the structure and raising the effectiveness of social production in Uzbekistan. . . . Of primary importance is the concentration of capital investments in the main directions that

would alter the sectoral and territorial structure of the economy. . . . It is necessary to change the relationship between investments in resource-extraction, processing and consuming branches.[33]

Thus, the national cadres of the Moslem republics have their own paradigm of economic development, which contradicts the regional-economic strategy of Moscow in general and the investment strategy of the Gorbachev regime in particular. The key idea is that, in determining the vector of investment activity, one should consider less the advantages offered by modernization than the benefits accruing from improvement in the social-economic level of backward regions. Hence, investments over the territory of the USSR should be concentrated not in the western, but in the southeastern sections of the country.

Of course, such views are beneath criticism—so far as Moscow's interests are concerned—in terms of the economic and political realities of the present period. Nonetheless, this anti-Moscow stance reflects a natural reaction to the failure of efforts to carve out an independent economic policy, and likewise a response to the policies that Moscow has pursued for many years: disregard for a balanced economy in these republics, for their demographic peculiarities. The contradiction is irreconcilable. There is every reason to assume that it will become still more acute. To chart a possible scenario, we shall examine what would happen if Gorbachev's reform plans were fully implemented.

If one sums up the likely consequences of the Gorbachev reforms and present investment policies for the social-economic development of the Moslem republics, and if one weighs all the pros and cons, one comes to the conclusion that the net effect will be negative. In particular, the polarization in economic activity between Central Asia and the western regions of the USSR will become even more pronounced. The role of Moslem republics as suppliers of raw material, fuels, and semiprocessed resources will become greater, while the manufacturing and machine-building industries will become more concentrated in the old industrial core of Russia.

The raw-material orientation of economic development in the Moslem republics runs completely contrary to their demographic situation. As the Tadjik economist Rustam Mirzoev has pointed out, "Social-economic research conducted by the economists of Central Asia permits one to conclude that one of the most important ways to solve the social-economic tasks of the region is to create labor-intensive, but not capital-intensive, branches of material production [primarily in industry]."[34] The construction of hydroelectric stations, the development of raw material and fuel extraction, their primary processing by local enterprises whose technology is based on the use of large machine units with a small number of employees to service them—all this would contribute to the growth of capital-intensive production and significantly reduce the demand for labor. This is why, for example, between 1965 and 1980 in Tadjikistan, the proportion of industry in the economy increased by 8.2 percent in fixed capital, but the number of employees rose by only 1.3 percent. For the same period the corresponding figures for the USSR as a whole were 1.2 and 1.5 percent.[35] This line of industrial development thus hinders a solution to the problem of unemployment among a rapidly expanding labor pool. The predominance of a capital-intensive policy means that an ever greater proportion of the investment allocation goes toward the producer sphere of the economy, and an ever smaller share to the nonproducer sphere. The upshot is social stagnation and backwardness in comparison with other regions of the country.

Hence, there are no grounds to count on an increase in the investment quota. But it is not just a matter of the magnitude of investment. It is also important that Moscow has given the republican governments greater autonomy in the distribution of these investment resources. Naturally, the national decision makers are striving to put their regions on their "own feet," to diversify their economy. They have their own ideas about the appropriate course of economic development: more finished-goods production, with emphasis on textile manufacture and advanced machine building, and a smaller role for raw materials extraction and primary processing. That path of development would make it possible to redirect the industrial structure toward forms of production that are more labor-intensive and consume less water and energy. Contrary to Moscow's policy of shifting surplus labor from the Moslem republics to the industrially advanced areas of Russia (especially Siberia), national economists propose "to consider the relocation of a certain part of the labor demand from other regions to this republic [Uzbekistan] by shifting the construction of some planned industrial plants (especially labor-intensive ones) from regions, above all Siberia, that have a shortage of labor resources."[36] The foregoing was expressed with consummate tact, but its key idea is unmistakable: "Don't take away our labor, but give us investment capital so that we can use this labor here."

·　　·　　·　　·

The more the actual economic conditions in Central Asia deviate from the prescribed model, the more vigorous becomes the attack on "bourgeois economists" and Sovietologists in the West who analyze the situation and fail to share the exuberant enthusiasm of Soviet propagandists. Particular zealotry is displayed by some of the local cadres, who seek to prove not only their loyalty but also their absolute subservience to Moscow. Evidently, the central ideological apparatus in Moscow believes that it is more persuasive if articles about the successes in Central Asia emanate from representatives of the indigenous people and if they (not Russians) refute Western scholarship.

Apologists for Moscow's policy make the following assertions about its Central Asian policy. With respect to Central Asia, the regime has successfully achieved its goal of uplifting the various minority borderlands to the level of the center. The thesis that Central Asia remains backward and below the general developmental level of the USSR is unjustified. This is, they assert, a mere fabrication of Sovietologists who wish to distort the real record of achievement. In fact, economic and social conditions have been created in Central Asia like those in other republics. The high indices on the living standard demonstrate that the social sphere has predominated in economic development and that the populace has come to enjoy a high degree of prosperity. Thus, in brief, is the official rebuttal to Western analysts.

These counterattacks to Western scholars are not of a very high order and, in their own right, do not merit much attention. What is striking, however, is that the very theses under attack have now begun to appear in the publications of other Uzbek, Tadjik, and Kirghiz scholars. The latter, whether from the freer spirit of glasnost or their own temerity, write with surprising candor on severe economic and social problems of Central Asia. These critics of Moscow flatly contradict the sunny picture of ubiquitous progress and state forthrightly that their region grievously lags behind all the other areas of the USSR. This critical strand in Central Asia can hardly be overlooked or underestimated; it is prime testimony to the depth of disgruntlement—and potential volatility—in this minority region in the USSR.

CHAPTER 10

Conclusion

If one examines all of the problems that plague Central Asia's economy, one can identify several common elements. First, the region is richly endowed with oil and gas (the extraction of which is well developed), but only a small portion is actually used as raw materials in Central Asia. Most of these resources are shipped to European Russia. Second, the region is well endowed with rare and precious metals, but although mining is well developed, most of the output is sent to European Russia for finishing. Third, this region produces almost all of the Soviet Union's cotton, yet only a minuscule amount is processed or converted to textiles in Central Asia; the bulk is sent to European Russia for these steps.

It may be true that, for various reasons, oil, natural gas, and nonferrous metals can be more economically processed outside Central Asia. But that proposition certainly does not obtain for cotton; in this sector, surely, Central Asia has a clear claim to investment capital to expand its capacities for textile manufacturing. Nevertheless, even though Central Asian economists have argued and lobbied to persuade Moscow on this point, until now they have had no success.

All this suggests that Moscow is determined to preserve Central Asia as a peripheral region whose function is to provide mineral resources and raw materials for the advanced industrial complexes of European Russia. Moscow's policy toward Central Asia is hardly unique; an analogous picture obtains for Siberia.[1] The point is that Moscow's policy toward Central Asia is not *sui generis* but simply another extension of its economic and borderland policies.

There is, nonetheless, an enormous difference between Siberia and Central Asia, as economic/geographic regions in different phases of industrialization. The advantages of

184

Siberia lie in the scale of its energy and raw material resources. But the well-known harsh natural conditions, the unsettled state and the sparse population of its territories, pose enormous difficulties and raise the cost of extracting these resources, of creating an industrial base to process them, and of building the requisite industrial and social infrastructure. By contrast, Central Asia offers hospitable natural conditions, and indeed it now represents the main reservoir of supplemental labor in the USSR. To tap the natural resources of Siberia, it would be necessary to make enormous pioneering investments in the infrastructure to attract people and keep them there. In Central Asia, by contrast, the main goal of investment is to provide employment to the people, and it would be incomparably cheaper to create jobs here than in Siberia.

The water shortage does substantially complicate the opportunity to expand the industrial structure of Central Asia. But textile manufacturing, for example, uses relatively little water and is highly labor-intensive. And many regions in the world have more serious water problems than does Central Asia yet have achieved a high level of differentiated industrial development. In the final analysis, it all depends on capital investment.

But for Gorbachev the chief problem is not a balanced economy, higher employment, or the standard of living in Uzbekistan, Tadjikistan, and other Moslem republics. Rather, the main task is to reconstitute the corps of cadres, to demolish the local mafia that became so entrenched in the Brezhnev era. At present, Moscow is trying to uproot the old Rashidov and Kunaev cadres and to install its own people. But that is no simple task; as yet Moscow has not succeeded in creating a reliable apparatus out of the national *nomenklatura* that was previously formed. It is urgently necessary, then, for Moscow to prepare a "reserve of cadres." For that, as Georgii Razumovskii (a secretary to the Central Committee) declared in June 1987, "People have been sent from the republics of Central Asia, the Transcaucasus, and Moldavia to study in the higher Party schools on the territory of the RSFSR. At the same time, *for the first time* [emphasis added], people have been sent from areas of the

RSFSR, the Ukraine, and Belorussia to study in the Party schools of Alma Ata, Tashkent, and Baku."[2] To carry out its plans, Moscow requires new men in the national republics who will not waver in their implementation of an economic policy that transcends the narrow interests of a particular nationality or region. These new cadres will have to provide order, and that means—inter alia—that they will have to quell the ferment among national intellectuals, extinguish their dissatisfaction with Moscow and its economic policy.

      •   •   •   •

    The replacement of cadres and excoriation of "Rashidovism" are proceeding at full speed. But there is no sign of practical steps that would suggest a change in Moscow's economic policy toward Central Asia. All the economic, demographic, and ecological ills of the region are wrapped up neatly in a single parcel; it can be undone only by a coordinated social-economic conception of development that is securely based on the real resources of the region. The core of a new approach must be rejection of the idea that Central Asia is a cotton plantation and emphasis on the development of labor-intensive industries (but not those high in water consumption). Only that approach can restore the hydrological cycle of the Aral Sea, reduce unemployment, and halt the social degradation of this region.[3]

    The decree terminating work on the water-diversion project (August 1986) instructed a number of leading organs, from Gosplan to the Councils of Ministers in Central Asian republics, to prepare a "complex program of development for Central Asia."[4] The plan is to foresee development to the year 2010, "taking into account the demographic and water circumstances" and the improved economic structure of the region. The pertinent report was due April 1, 1987, but, judging from the press, that obligation was not fulfilled. In April 1988 a corresponding member of the Academy of Sciences, V. Kotliakov, wrote in *Pravda* that such a conception of development was "urgently needed."[5] Evidently, architects of the new plan encountered insuperable difficulties. And the central problem most certainly must be that the

Gorbachev leadership does not wish to (or, more precisely, cannot) address the problems of Moslem areas. One comes away with the distinct impression that this leadership simply refuses to come to grips with these problems until a full-blown emergency erupts.

NOTES

Notes for Preface

1. Goble, Paul A., "Running against the Republics: Gorbachev and the Soviet Nationality Problem," in Friedberg & Asham, eds., *Soviet Society under Gorbachev* (M. E. Sharpe, 1987).

Notes for Chapter 1

1. *Ekonomicheskie nauki*, 1986, no. 10: 19.
2. A. Samoilov, "Nekotorye voprosy sovershenstvovaniia upravleniia i khoziaistvovaniia," *Kommunist Uzbekistana*, 1985, no. 10: 27.
3. V. Kuibyshev, *Stat'i i rechi*, vol. 5 (Moscow, 1937), 102–3.
4. "Direktivy po piatomu piatiletnemu planu," *Kommunisticheskaia partiia Sovetskogo Soiuza v rezoliutsiiakh* (Moscow, 1971), 342–366.
5. M. Urinson, *Planirovanie narodnogo khoziaistva v soiuznykh respublikakh* (Moscow, 1963), 60, 84.
6. Ibid., 65.
7. A. Kosygin, *Izbrannye rechi i stat'i* (Moscow, 1974), 288.
8. *XXIII S'ezd Kommunisticheskoi Partii Sovetskogo Soiuza. Stenograficheskii otchet*, vol. 1 (Moscow, 1966), 55.
9. *Trudy osobogo mezhvedomstvennogo soveshchaniia po vyrabotke zheleznodorozhnogo stroitel'stva* (Petrograd, 1916), 17.
10. Kosygin, *Izbrannye rechi . . . .*, 288.
11. *Ekonomicheskaia entsiklopediia. Politicheskaia ekonomiia* vol. 4 (Moscow, 1980), 545–546.
12. *Voprosy ekonomicheskogo raionirovaniia SSSR* (Moscow, 1957), 102–103.
13. See for example: V. Kistanov, *Territorial'naia organizatsiia proizvodstva* (Moscow, 1981), 212–214.
14. See the map in *Air Force Magazine*, 1986, no. 3: 72–73.
15. In general, Moscow clearly did not regard the boundaries of union republics as absolute and inviolable, but modified them at will. Indeed, the program of the CPSU is quite explicit on this point: "The borders of union republics within the boundary of the USSR are continuously losing their former significance." *Materialy XXII s'ezda KPSS* (Moscow, 1961), 405.
16. L. I. Brezhnev, *Otchetnyi doklad XXIII s'ezdu KPSS* (Moscow, 1966), 50.
17. L. I. Brezhnev, *Leninskim kursom*, vol. 4 (Moscow, 1974), 93.
18. *Materialy XXV s'ezda KPSS* (Moscow, 1976) 61.
19. *Materialy XXVI s'ezda KPSS* (Moscow, 1981), 72.

20. *Ekonomicheskaia entsiklopediia. Politicheskaia ekonomiia*, vol. 3: 241.
21. A. Alekseev, "Problemy sopostavleniia urovnei ekonomicheskogo razvitiia dvukh mirovykh sistem," *Planovoe khoziaistvo*, 1962, no. 3: 15–17.
22. *Ekonomicheskaia gazeta*, 1964, no. 8: 16–17.
23. See A. Lipko and A. Misko, *Proizvodstvo i potreblenie v regione* (Moscow, 1986), 76.

Notes for Chapter 2

1. *Sredne-aziatskii ekonomicheskii raion* (Moscow, 1972), 7.
2. Ibid., 8.
3. Ibid.
4. V. Popov, "Mineral'no-syr'evye resursy strany, ikh ispol'zovanie," *Planovoe khoziaistvo* 1981, no. 4: 34. In addition, Central Asia is rich in nonferrous and rare metals, such as zinc ores, tungsten, and gold.
5. R. Rakhimov, *Problemy razvitiia narodno-khoziaistvennogo kompleksa Tadzhikskoi SSR* (Dushanbe, 1977), 67.
6. Z. Salokhiddinov, "Otsenka effektivnosti kapital'nykh vlozhenii v usloviiakh otkrytoi ekonomiki," *Ekonomika i zhizn'*, 1985, no. 10: 17.
7. Ibid.
8. *Narodnoe khoziaistvo SSSR v 1984 godu*, 385; *Narodnoe khoziaistvo SSSR v 1985 godu*, 369.
9. *Narodnoe khoziaistvo SSSR v 1985 godu*, 363.

Notes for Chapter 3

1. *Narodnoe khoziaistvo Kirgizskoi SSR v 1984 godu*, 133; *Narodnoe khoziaistvo Turkmenskoi SSR v 1984 godu*, 129; *Narodnoe khoziaistvo Tadzhikskoi SSR v 1982 godu*, 170; *Narodnoe khoziaistvo Uzbekskoi SSR v 1984 godu*, 209; *Narodnoe khoziaistvo Gruzinskoi SSR v 1984 godu*, 149; *Narodnoe khoziaistvo Armianskoi SSR v 1984 godu*, 185; *Narodnoe khoziaistvo Azerbaidzhanskoi SSR v 1983 godu*, 104; *Narodnoe khoziaistvo Litovskoi SSR v 1980 godu*, 129; *Narodnoe khoziaistvo Litovskoi SSR v 1984 godu*, 124; *Narodnoe khoziaistvo Latviiskoi SSR v 1984 godu*, 186; *Narodnoe khoziaistvo Estonskoi SSR v 1984 godu*, 127; *Narodnoe khoziaistvo Belorusskoi SSR v 1984 godu*, 121; *Narodnoe khoziaistvo RSFSR v 1984 godu*, 222; *Narodnoe khoziaistvo SSSR v 1984 godu*, 378. In some cases, where direct data are unavailable, figures are based on the author's calculations.
2. *Sredne-aziatskii ekonomicheskii raion*, 51.
3. Ibid.
4. See, for example, D. Bairamov, "Sovershenstvovanie regional'nogo planirovaniia," *Voprosy ekonomiki*, 1985, no. 8: 41.
5. A. Makarov and A. Vigdorchik, *Toplivno-energeticheskiy kompleks*

(Moscow, 1979), 204; *Sredneaziatskii ekonomicheskii raion*, 81; *Energetika SSSR v 1976–1980 godakh* (Moscow, 1977), 165.

6. M. Burkhanova and V. Golovenko, "Voprosy perspektivnogo ispol'zovaniia vodnykh resursov Tadzhikskoi SSR," *Izvestiia Akademii nauk Tadzhikskoi SSR*, 1982, no. 2: 36, 37; P. Savchenko, "Perspektivy Razvitiia," *Ekonomika i zhizn'*, 1984, no. 1: 11.

7. P. Savchenko, "Perspektivy Razvitiia," *Ekonomika i zhizn'*, 1984, no. 1: 11.

8. *Energeticheskii kompleks SSSR* (Moscow, 1983), 194–195.

9. S. Morokhin and E. Tatarintseva, *Territorial'naia organizatsiia mashinostroitel'nogo proizvodstva* (Moscow, 1984), 10.

10. K. Makhkamov, "Formirovanie i razvitie Iuzno-Tadzhikskogo TPK," *Planovoe khoziaistvo*, 1981, no. 10: 18–19.

11. E. Leont'eva, "Illiuzii po-nauchnomu," *Sotsialisticheskaia industriia*, 10 April 1986.

12. "TPK v plenu oshibok," *Sotsialisticheskaia industriia*, December 27, 1986.

13. Leont'eva, "Illiuzii."

14. Makhkamov, "Formirovanie," 23.

15. Sh. Zakorov, *Problemy ratsional'nogo razmeshcheniia promyshlennosti Uzbekistana* (Tashkent, 1972), 57–58.

16. *Promyshlennost' SSSR* (Moscow, 1957), 77.

17. One main product of the chemical industry was mineral fertilizers. Production of synthetic fibers, plastics, and other products from oil and natural gas was also started in the *sovnarkhoz* era.

18. Zakirov, *Problemy* . . . , 54.

19. Measured by its deposits and reserves of gold, copper, lead, zinc, tungsten, molybdenum, mercury, antimony, strontium, bismuth, tin, cadmium, and a host of other metals, Central Asia ranks as one of the major depositories in the USSR.

20. See, for example: S. Ziiadullaev, "Sredniaia Azia: Sovremennoe industrial'no-agrarnoe khoziaistvo," *EKO*, 1982, no. 12: 81. The author is chairman of the Council for Productive Forces of the Uzbek Academy of Sciences and a member of the Uzbek Academy of Sciences.

21. *Narodnoe khoziaistvo SSSR v 1985 godu*, 155.

22 K. Bedrintsev, "O nekotorykh regional'nykh problemakh Uzbekistana," *Ekonomika i zhizn'*, 1973, no. 4: 13.

Notes for Chapter 4

1. N. Khamraev and Zh. Bozorov, "Problemy razvitiia narodno-khoziaistvennogo khlopkovogo kompleksa," *Izvestiia Akademii Nauk SSSR*, Seriia ekonomicheskaia, 1986, no. 1: 113.

2. These oases of Central Asia include the following: the Turan Lowland, the Golodnaia Steppe, the Zeravshan Basin, Surkhan Daria, Chirchik, Murgab, Tedzhen, and the lands of the middle and,

in part, the lower course of the Amu Darya.

3. *Sredneaziatskii ekonomicheskii raion*, 148.
4. "Mirovoy rynok khlopka," *Ekonomika i zhizn'*, 1985, no. 5: 61–62.
5. *Vneshniaia torgovlia SSSR*, 1978, 28; *Vneshniaia torgovlia SSSR*, 1980, 28; *Vneshniaia torgovlia SSSR*, 1983, 28.
6. *Narodnoe khoziaistvo SSSR v 1978 godu*, 176; *Narodnoe khoziaistvo SSSR v 1983 godu*, 180.
7. *Narodnoe khoziaistvo SSSR v 1985 godu*, 146.
8. *Vneshniaia torgovlia SSSR*, 1985, 28.
9. E. Rakhimov, "Reshaiushchii faktor intensifikatsii khlopko-proizvodstva," *Kommunist Uzbekistana*, 1983, no. 9: 51.
10. *Narodnoe khoziaistvo SSSR v 1980 godu*, 232; *Narodnoe khoziaistvo SSSR v 1985 godu*, 210.
11. I. Iskanderov, "Ekonomika respubliki v ramkakh edinogo narodno-khoziaistvennogo kompleksa strany," *Ekonomika i zhizn'*, 1986, no. 2: 9.
12. Rakhimov, "Reshaiushchii faktor," 51.
13. N. Khamraev and Zh. Bozorov, "Problemy razvitiia," 116.
14. Ibid.
15. Ibid., 117.
16. A. Ul'masov, "Burzhuaznye kontseptsii ekonomicheskogo razvitiia respublik Srednei Azii," *Ekonomicheskie nauki*, 1985, no. 3: 96.
17. *Literaturnaia gazeta*, 11 Feb. 1987, 12.
18. I analyze the causes of the cotton crisis with respect to Uzbekistan, the primary producer of cotton in Central Asia. Uzbekistan's share of both the population and fixed capital in Central Asia is about 60 percent.
19. *Narodnoe khoziaistvo SSSR v 1975 godu*, 287, 367; *Narodnoe khoziaistvo SSSR v 1980 godu*, 184, 232.
20. *Literaturnaia gazeta*, 11 Feb. 1987, 12.
21. Ibid.
22. *Narodnoe khoziaistvo SSSR v 1984 godu*, 195; *Narodnoe khoziaistvo Uzbekskoi SSR v 1984 godu*, 79.
23. N. Chumanova and M. Tadzhimuratov, "Sovershenstvovanie osnovnykh proportsii vosproizvodstva v Uzbekistane," *Kommunist Uzbekistana*, 1983, no. 8: 52.
24. *Narodnoe khoziaistvo SSSR v 1975 godu*; *Narodnoe khoziaistvo RSFSR v 1975 godu*, 110.
25. I. Iskanderov, "Eshche raz o vtoroi tekstil'noi baze strany," *Ekonomika i zhizn'*, 1966, no. 3: 25.
26. K. Bedrintsev, "O nekotorykh regional'nykh problemakh Uzbekistana," *Ekonomika i zhizn'*, 1973, no. 4: 12.
27. I. Iskanderov, "Eshche raz," 25.
28. I. Iskanderov, "Ekonomika respubliki," *Ekonomika i zhizn'*, 1985, 9.

Notes for Chapter 5

1. *Sredneaziatskiy ekonomicheskiy raion*, p. 171
2. V. Panfilov et al., "Zanos na povorote,," *Novyi mir*, 1987, no. 7, 199–200.
3. Ibid., 201.
4. Ibid., 198.
5. O. Leont'ev, "Nuzhen li povorot k uproshchennomu rassmotreniiu slozhnoi problemy?" *Novyi mir*, 1987, no. 7: 194.
6. E. Laskorin and V. Tikhonov, "Novye podkhody k resheniiu vodnykh problem strany," *Kommunist*, 1988, no. 4: 91, 93.
7. P. Khabibullaev, "Spasti Aral mozhno," *Sotsialisticheskaia industriia*, 14 June 1987.
8. B. Laskorin and V. Tikhonov, "Novye podkhody," 93.
9. V. Panfilov et al., "Zanos na povorote," 205. The writer is addressing Sergei Zalygin, the chief editor of *Novyi mir*, one of the most active opponents of the plan to divert Siberian waterways toward Central Asia.
10. K. Bedrintsev et al., "A vy nam chitateliam otvet'te," *Novyi mir*, 1987, no. 7: 206.
11. P. Khabibullaev, "Spasti Aral mozhno," 87.
12. *Ekonomika i zhizn'*, 1971, no. 8: 15.
13. Pavlenko, V., *Planirovanie territorial'nogo razvitiia* (Moscow, 1985), 136.
14. V. Sokolov, "Sud'ba Arala," *Literaturnaia gazeta*, 18 Nov. 1987.
15. Ibid.
16. *Ekonomika i zhizn'*, 1972, no. 4: 53.
17. V. Sokolov, "Sud'ba Arala."
18. Ibid.
19. P. Khabibullaev, "Spasti Aral mozhno."
20. Ibid.
21. The construction of the Baikal-Amur Railway Line was also called the "project of the century."
22. *Literaturnaia gazeta*, 10 March 1982, 11.
23. See for example: G. Voropaev, "Proekt veka," *Ekonomika i zhizn'*, 1984, no. 8: 8.
24. *Literaturnaia gazeta*, 10 March 1982, 11.
25. Such statements have appeared in the press. Especially candid were the speeches of S. Zalygin and V. Rasputin at the Congress of the Writers' Union published in *Literaturnaia gazeta*, 2 July 1986.
26. *Ekonomika i zhizn'*, 1971, no. 2: 15.
27. *Pravda*, 21 Jan. 1961, 2.
28. Ibid.
29. Ibid.
30. Ibid. Khrushchev's fascination with the idea of redirecting rivers can be traced to a memorandum from Sergei Zhuk, the leading Soviet expert on hydraulic construction and an enthusiastic proponent of

canal construction in the USSR. (Zhuk was the author of the plan for Dneproges and directed its construction.)

31. Ibid.
32. Ibid.
33. *KPSS v rezoliutsiiakh*, vol. 10 (Moscow, 1972), 469.
34. *KPSS v rezoliutsiiakh*, vol. 12 (Moscow, 1978), 221.
35. *Pravda*, 27 Oct. 1984, 1.
36. *Literaturnaia gazeta*, 18 Dec. 1985 and 15 Jan. 1985.
37. See *Pravda*, 11 and 13 Feb. 1987.
38. *Sovetskaia Rossiia*, 2 Jan. 1986.
39. *Pravda*, 30 Dec. 1985.
40. *Sovetskaia Rossiia*, 2 Jan. 1986.
41. *Literaturnaia gazeta*, 10 Oct. 1985.
42. *Literaturnaia gazeta*, 29 Jan. 1986.
43. *Pravda*, 12 Feb. 1986.
44. *XXVII S'ezd KPSS, Stenograficheskiy otchet* (Moscow, 1986), vol. 1, 210.
45. *Materialy XXVII S'ezda KPSS* (Moscow, 1986), 299.
46. *Literaturnaia gazeta*, 2 July 1986.
47. Ibid.
48. *Pravda*, 20 Aug. 1986.
49. *Ogonek*, Oct. 1986, no. 43: 29.
50. Viktor Kochetkov, "Posledniaia noch' Avvakuma," *Nash sovremennik*, 1986.
51. T. Esil'baev, "Tsena samoliubovaniia," *Pravda*, 11 Feb. 1987.
52. I. Kryvelev, "Koketnichaia s bozhen'koi," *Komsomol'skaia pravda*, 30 July 1986.
53. Samizdat.
54. *Literaturnaia gazeta*, 11 March 1982, 11.
55. *Nash sovremennik*, 1985, no. 7: 141.
56. Ibid.
57. *Literaturnaia gazeta*, 11 March 1982, 11.
58. V. Dukhovnyi, "Melioratsiia: Zabota o nastoiashchem i budushchem," *Kommunist Uzbekistana*, 1985, no. 5: 58.
59. Ibid., 57.
60. Ibid., 58.
61. A. Zemtsov, "A sovershilsia li povorot?" *Novyi mir*, 1987, no. 7: 207.
62. *Pravda*, 20 Aug. 1986, 1.
63. A. Zemtsov, "A sovershilsia li povorot?"
64. P. Khabibullaev, "Spasti Aral mozhno."
65. D. Iadgarov, "Voprosy intensifikatsii i ratsional'nogo ispol'zovaniia osnovnykh fondov Karalpakskoi ASSR," *Obshchestvennye nauki v Uzbekistane*, 1987, no. 3. Karakalpakiia is an autonomous region within Uzbekistan; its population exceeds one million and its territories are contiguous with the southern shore of the Aral Sea.
66. "Sud'ba Arala—zabota obshchaia," *Sotsialisticheskaia industriia*, 1 Oct. 1987.

67. *Pravda*, 20 Aug. 1986, 1.
68. L. Drobisheva and Iu. Poliakov, "Ne bylo gotovykh obraztsov," *Izvestiia*, 22 March 1988.

Notes for Chapter 6

1. S. Ziyadullaev and R. Ubaidullaeva, "Aktual'nye problemy ratsional'-nogo ispol'zovaniia trudovykh resursov v trudoobespechennykh raionakh," *Planovoe khoziaistvo*, 1985, no. 5.
2. S. Strumilin, "Nashi trudovye resursy i perspektivy," *Khoziaistvennoe stroitel'stvo*, 1922, no. 2.
3. M. Sonin, *Vosproizvodstvo rabochey sily v SSSR i balans truda* (Moscow, 1959), 7–8; E. Kotliar, "Vosproizvodstvo rabochey sily pri sotsializme," *Ekonomicheskie nauki*, 1972, no. 4: 33–36; N. Kistanov, *Regional' noe ispol'zovanie trudovykh resursov* (Moscow, 1978), 7; P. Kosiakov, *Trudovye resursy – ekonomicheskaia kategoriia* (Sverdlovsk, 1970), 7–9; E. Kasimovskii, "Trudovye resursy, ikh formirovanie i ispol'zovanie v SSSR," *Ekonomicheskie nauki*, 1973, no. 7: 7–11.
4. N. Khonaliev, "O sushchnosti i soderzhanii kategorii 'trudovye resursy'," *Izvestiia Akademii Nauk Tadzhikskoi SSR*, 1984, no. 2: 35.
5. R. Ubaidullaeva, "Effektivnee ispol'zovat' trudovye resursy," *Kommunist Uzbekistana*, 1983, no. 11: 21.
6. Ibid.
7. Ibid.
8. Ibid.
9. Ubaidullaeva, R., "Upravleniye trudovymi resursami – vazhnoye usloviye rosta effektivnosti proizvodstva," *Kommunist Uzbekistana*, 1985, no. 8: 48–50.
10. Kostakov, V., "Zanyatost': defitsit ili izbytok?" *Kommunist*, 1987, no. 1: 88.
11. Rakhimov, R., "Problemy povysheniya effektivnosti obshchest-vennogo proizvodstva v trudoobespechennykh rayonakh," *Izvestiia Akademii Nauk Tadzhikskoi SSR*, 1980, no. 4: 45, 46; Ubaidullaeva, "Upravleniye . . . ," 50.
12. Ibid.
13. Rakhimov, "Problemy . . . ," 46; Ubaidullaeva, "Effektivnee ispol'-zovat' . . . ," 19.
14. Chamkin, A., "Skol'ko mekhanizatorov nado selu," *Ekonomika i zhizn'*, 1985, no. 3: 16, 17, 18; *Narodnoe khoziaistvo SSSR v 1985 godu*, 8, 84, 203.
15. Chamkin, "Skol'ko mekhanizatorov. . . ."
16. Ibid.
17. Umarov, Kh., "Trudoizbytochnoye selo: problemy i resheniya," *Voprosy ekonomiki*, 1986, no. 9: 99.
18. Ibid., 100.
19. Khakimov, A., "Problemy sbalansirovannosti trudovykh resursov i

rabochikh mest v Tadzhikskoy SSR," *Vestnik Moskovskogo Universiteta*, 1985, no. 6: 25.

20. Umarov, "Trudoizbytochnoye selo . . . ," 101.
21. Khakimov, "Problemy . . . ," 25.
22. *Vestnik statistiki*, 1986, no. 8: 72, 74, 77.
23. Zavulunov, A., "Promyshlennost' Tadzhikistana: nekotoryye voprosy razvitiya," *EKO*, no. 12, 94; *Narodnoe khoziaistvo Tadzhikskoy SSR v 1982 godu*, 128.
24. Gurshumov, I., Kogai, R., "Posgotovka rabochikh kadrov za predelami Tadzhikistana," *Izvestiia Akademii Nauk Tadzhikistana*, 1984, 39.
25. Zavulunov, "Promyshlennost' . . . ," 94.
26. Ziyadullaev, "Aktual'nye problemy . . . ," 101.
27. Ibid.
28. Gurshumov, Kogai, "Podgotovka . . . ," 45.
29. Nasyrov, "Professional'naia podgotovka . . . ," 29; Gurshumov, Kogai, "Podgotovka . . . ," 39.
30. Nasyrov, "Professional'naia podgotovka . . . ," 30.
31. Gurshumov, Kogai, "Podgotovka . . . ," 40.
32. I. Gurshumov et al., "Plius-minus sud'ba," *Izvestiia*, 23 Dec. 1987.
33. Kostakov, "Zanyatost' . . . ," 89.
34. Ubaidullaeva, "Upravleniye . . . ," 48.
35. A. Iakubov, "Tragediia v kishlake," *Literaturnaia gazeta*, 19 Aug. 1987.
36. Ibid.
37. Ibid.
38. T. Kirgizbaeva, "Vot ona—plata za pripiski!" *Literaturnaia gazeta*, 2 Dec. 1987.
39. See: M. Malyshev, "Postylye plody prosveshcheniia," *Nedelia*, 1988, no. 2; L. Telen', "Kakaia zhe ona, zhenskaia dolia?" *Sotsialisticheskaia industriia*, 22 Jan. 1988.
40. V. Artemenko, "Ne ukhodia ot urokov pravdy," *Pravda*, 5 Feb. 1988; E. Gafarov, "Dramaticheskie zhenskie sud'by," *Pravda Vostoka*, 6 Jan. 1988.

Notes for Chapter 7

1. M. Makhshulov, "Metodologicheskie problemy i osobennosti povy-heniia urovnia zhizni v regione," *Izvestiia Akademii Nauk Tadzhikskoi SSR*, 1982, no. 2: 45.
2. *Narodnoe khoziaistvo Uzbekskoi SSR v 1982 godu*, 73, 75, 86, 100, 115, 120; *Narodnoe khoziaistvo Tadzhikskoi SSR v 1981 godu*, 115, 116, 117, 146; *Narodnoe khoziaistvo Kirgizskoi SSR v 1981 godu*, 66, 74, 81, 83; *Narodnoe khoziaistvo RSFSR v 1982 godu*, 82, 101.
3. V. Sokolov, "Sud'ba Arala," *Literaturnaia gazeta*, 18 Nov. 1987.
4. I. Umarov, "Problemy razvitia infrastruktury v nizov'iakh Amu

Dar'yu," *Kommunist Uzbekistana*, 1985: 65–66.
5. S. Khakimova, "Nachinaiushchim zhit'," *Izvestiia*, 14 Sept. 1987.
6. A. Minkin, "Zaraza ubiistvennaya," *Ogonek*, no. 13, 1988: 26, 27.

Notes for Chapter 8

1. G. Velikhova, A. Shokhina, "Tenevaia ekonomika," *Ogonek*, 1987, 51.
2. Ibid.
3. Vladimir Treml, "Second Economy Project."
4. *Novyi Mir*, 1987, no. 11: 201.
5. *Sotsialisticheskaia industriia*, 20 Jan. 1988, 2.
6. "V Taishete u vsekh na vidu," *Sotsialisticheskaia industriia*, 25 Feb. 1988.
7. V. Ovcharenko, "Kobry nad zolotom," *Pravda*, 23 Jan. 1988.
8. Ibid.
9. D. Likhanov, "Klan," *Strana i mir*, July–August, 1987.
10. V. Sokolov, "Zona molchaniia," *Literaturnaia gazeta*, 20 Jan. 1988.
11. Ibid. The term "*Karbyshevka*" is derived from the case of General Dmitrii Karbyshev, who became a German prisoner in World War II. According to Soviet sources, Karbyshev perished after he had been doused with water during a severe frost in a concentration camp.
12. Ibid.
13. Ibid.
14. Ibid.
15. V. Ovcharenko, "Kobry nad zolotom."
16. D. Likhanov, "Klan."
17. Ibid.
18. Ibid.
19. Ibid.
20. Ibid.
21. Ibid.
22. M. Volkov, "Otvetnyi khod," *Pravda*, 7 March 1988.
23. V. Khrustalev, "Dvoedushie: nado skazat' pravdu," *Sotsialisticheskaia industriia*, 11 Feb. 1988.

Notes for Chapter 9

1. *XXVII s'ezd KPSS. Stenograficheskii otchet* (Moscow: Politizdat, 1986), vol. 1, 362.
2. *Konstitutsiia SSSR* (Moscow 1977).
3. The exceptions do not include Central Asian republics; Gosplan reviews plans for only a limited number of areas—viz., Moscow, Leningrad, the Non-Black-Soil Zone of the RSFSR, and several other areas, such as Krasnoiarsk.

4. See, for example, the following: N. Bobodzhanov, "Rol' soiuznoi respubliki v obespechenii kompleksnogo ekonomicheskogo i sotsial'nogo razvitiia ee territorii," *Izvestiia Akademii nauk Tadzhikskoi SSR. Seriia obshchestvennych nauk,* 1984, no. 3.
5. E. Kepbanov, "Konstitutsiia SSSR i sovershenstvovanie," *Izvestiia Akademii nauk Tirkmenskoi SSR. Seriia obshchestvennych nauk,* 1985, no. 1: 49.
6. *Pravda,* 26 June 1987, 4.
7. Ibid.
8. *Sotsialisticheskaia industriia,* 27 Dec. 1986.
9. V. Kvint, "Sovety narodnykh deputatov kak organizatsionnye tsentry upravleniia ekonomikoi," *Voprosy ekonomiki,* 1987, no. 6: 26.
10. A. Komin, "Finansy i tseny," *Kommunist,* 1987, no. 9.
11. V. Volkonskii and A. Vavilov, "Tseny i prirostnye zatraty," *EKO,* 1987, no. 4.
12. N. Shmelev, "Avansy i dolgi," *Novyimir,* no. 6: 149.
13. I. Gurshumov et al., "Plius-minus sud'ba," *Izvestiia,* 23 Dec. 1987.
14. B. Li, "K voprosu o perestroike struktury proizvodstva v Uzbekskoi SSR," *Kommunist Uzbekistana,* 1986, no. 12: 22.
15. *XXVI s'ezd KPSS. Stenograficheskii otchet* (Moscow: Izdatel'stvo politiheskoi literatury, 1981), 17.
16. *Pravda,* 4 March 1986.
17. See Boris Z. Rumer, *Investment and Reindustrialization in the Soviet Economy* (Boulder: Westview Press, 1984), 72.
18. See Table 2.1.
19. "Korennye zadachi mashinostroitelei," *Ekonomicheskaia gazeta,* 1986, no. 47.
20. "Mashinostroenie—Operezhaiushchee razvitie," *Stanki i instrument,* 1986, no. 2: 3.
21. "Uroki khozrascheta," *Pravda,* 4 Dec. 1987, 2.
22. E. Gaidar, "Kursom ozdorovleniia," *Kommunist,* 1988, no. 2: 45.
23. S. Mozokhin and E. Tatarintseva, *Territorial'naia organizatsiia mashinostroitel'nogo proizvodstva* (Moscow: Mashinostroenie, 1984), 10.
24. L. Gramoteeva, *Effektivnost' territorial'noi organizatsii proizvodstva* (Moscow: Mysl', 1979), 143.
25. V. Evstigneev, *Effektivnost' razmeshcheniia mashinostroeniia v vostochnych i zapadnych raionakh SSSR* (Moscow: Nauka, 1972), 245.
26. *Pravda,* 28 Jan. 1987, 2.
27. *Pravda,* 26 June 1987, 4.
28. *Pravda,* 26 June 1987, 2.
29. M. Allakhverdiev, "Regional'nye problemy sovershenstvovaniia planovogo upravleniia ekonomikoi," *Izvestiia Akademii nauk Azerbaidzhanskoi SSSR, Seriia ekonomiki,* 1986, no. 1–2: 62.
30. Salokhiddinov, "Soderzhanie i sushchnost' intensifikatsii," *Ekonomika i zhizn',* 1986, no. 6: 8.
31. B. Li, "K voprosu . . .," 18.
32. Ibid., 19.
33. Ibid., 20, 22.

34. R. Mirzoev, "Tempy, proportsii . . . ," 89.
35. Ibid., 39.
36. M. Abdusaliamov and A. Alimov, "Proizvodstvennye sily," 18.

Notes for Chapter 10

1. See B. Rumer, *Investment and Reindustrialization in the Soviet Economy* (Boulder: Westview Press, 1984), xiv, 141.
2. G. Razumovskii, "Sovershenstvovat' podgotovku i perepodgotouku rukovodiashchikh kadrov partii," *Kommunist*, 1987, no. 9: 5.
3. I shall not consider radical changes that might ensue from a general transition of the Soviet economic and political order into a pluralistic system (with a market economy). It will serve little purpose here to indulge in idle speculation about the prospects of such a radical transition in the economic and political system.
4. *Pravda*, 20 Aug. 1986, 1.
5. V. Kotliakov, "Mozhno li spasti Aral?" *Pravda*, 14 April 1988.

ABOUT THE AUTHOR

Boris Z. Rumer is Research Associate at the Russian Research Center of Harvard University. He is author of numerous articles on the Soviet economy and of *Investment and Reindustrialization in the Soviet Economy* (1984) and of *Soviet Steel Industry* (1989).

INDEX

Adylov, A., 151–3, 159
Aganbegian, A., 94, 101
Agriculture:
  and demographics, 111–14
  and energy, 48
  income from, 124–30
  job opportunities in, 112–15
  private, 113–14
  tools for, 49
  water needs of, 77, 99
  women and, 120–2
Amu Darya (river), 76–7, 81–2, 84–5, 87, 90
Andropov, Y., 71
Anti-Moslem tendencies, 96–7
Anti-Semitism, 98–9
Aral Sea, 81–5, 101
Astaf 'ev, V., 93, 98
Automobiles, sale of, 137
Avvakum, 97

BAM (Baikal-Amur railway), 7
Bartering, 145
Bedrintsev, N., 73–4
Belov, V., 91, 93–4, 96
Birthrate, 112, 139
Bogachev, V., 6
Bondarev, I., 94–6
Branch managers, 57–8
Brezhnev, L., 6, 19–20, 109
  and water problems, 90–1
Brezhnev era, 7
  and corruption, 145
  and shadow economy, 145–7, 151–3, 158–9
Budnitskii, 146
Bukinich, D., 87

Cadres, 71
  attitude of, 177–82
Cafeterias, 135
Canals, 92

Capital equipment, 171–2
Capital investment, 29, 36–40
Catering, public, 135–8
Censorship, 96–7
Centralism, vs. regionalism, 1
Chemical industry, 56, 58–60
Chernenko, K., and water problems, 90–1
Chernobyl, 49
Children, 135, 140–2
China, as cotton producer, 62–4
Clan structure, 147–9, 158–9
Climate, 27
Collectivization, Stalinist, 127–8
Comecon (Council for Mutual Economic Aid), 35
Computers, 174
Constitution, Soviet, 161–3
Construction projects, 166, 176, 178
  housing, 175, 177
Consumption, 172–3
  problems in calculating, 25–6
  share of, 35–6
Corruption, local, 146. See also Shadow economy
Cost accounting, 167–8
  and unemployment, 168–71
Cotton, 48–9, 57, 128, 141, 184
  cycle of, 71
  as export, decline of, 62–4
  harvesting, 141–2
  and irrigation, 66–8
  and labor, 64–5, 73
  production crisis of, 64–8
  quality of, 63–5, 67
  rising production of, 55
  and shadow economy, 150–4, 159
  statistics of production of, 71–2
  "tragic experiment of," 68–72
  and water needs, 60, 82–4, 88, 100
  women and, 120–2
Cotton barons, 151–4

Cotton industry, 19–20, 34–5, 48–9, 55–7, 60
  importance of, 27–8, 40–1
Crime, organized, 154–7
  and Moscow, 158–9
Crop rotation, 70–1

Demchenko, I., 87
Demographics, 28–9, 42, 135
  and agriculture, 111–14
  and health care, 138–9
Departmentalism, in industry, 55
Doctors, 139–40
Durable goods, demand for, 135–8

Economic development (or planning), 108
  equalization of, 20–2
  indices of level of, 22–3
  regional; econometric models in, 9–12; by republics, 8–9
Economic regions, 1–5, 13, 15
  and Central Asia, 17–20
  equalization among, 20–2
  overlap of with military regions, 16–17
  and planning, 8–12
  theory and practice in, 12–15
Economists, Central Asian, 109–10
Electrical energy, 44, 47, 59–60
Employment, 178, 181, 185
  illegal, 114
  rates of, 120
  and vocational training, 115
  of youth, 116, 118–19
Energy:
  electrical, 44, 47, 59–60
  hydroelectric, 44, 47–8, 51
  nuclear, 48–9
  scarcity of, 59
  uses of, 48–9
Equalization, of economic development, 20–2
Ethnic groups, in schools, 117
European Russia, 184
Evstigneev, V., 175
Exports, cotton, deline of, 62–4

Family relations, 148
Farming, private, 124–30
Five-year plans, 2–6, 37, 55
  first, 2, 14, 53–4, 106
  second, 3, 53–4

third, 3
fourth, 4
fifth, 4
sixth, 4
ninth, 166
tenth, 57, 59
eleventh, 57–9, 172
twelfth, 171–3, 175
Food-processing industry, 45–55
Food production, 112
Fraud, 70–2
Fuel, and prices, 168
Fuel industry, 44, 46–7

Gangsterism, 155–7
Gas, natural, 28, 46, 48, 60
Gidroproekt, 82–3, 87–8
Girardi, I., 90
Glasnost, 96, 121, 146, 183
GNP, and shadow economy, 145
Gorbachev, M., 21, 40, 71, 92–3, 109, 120, 146, 158–9, 169, 171
  and reforms, 161, 163–8, 171–7, 179–80, 185–7
  and Sibaral, 95–7, 102–4
Gosplan, 6, 8, 47, 52, 56, 108–9, 115, 120, 186
  and economic planning, 160–3, 166, 178
  and regional economic planning, 2–4, 10, 13–15
Growth rates, 26

Harvest, cotton, 65–6, 141–2
Health care, 138–42
Hospital facilities, 140–1
Housing:
  availability of, 130–1
  construction of, 175, 177
  and population, 130–4
Hydroelectric energy, 44, 47–8, 51
Hydroelectric power, 28, 77, 88

Income, 123–5
  from agriculture, 124–30
  per capita, 23–5, 173
  national, 31–5
  in republics, 23–5
Industrial development, 181
Industrialization:
  character of, 53–61
  problems of, 43–61
  rate of, 53–61
  vs. resources, 43

Industrial sectors, 19–20
Industry:
    chemical, 56, 58–60
    cotton, 19–20, 27–8, 34–5, 40–1,
        48–9, 55, 57, 60
    departmentalism of, 55
    electrical, 44
    food-processing, 45, 55
    fuel, 44
    light, 44–5
    structure of, 44–50
Investment, strategy of, 109
Investment capital, 174–7, 184–5
Irrigation, 27, 82–5, 89, 100, 104
    and cotton, 48, 67–8
Iskanderov, I., 74
Islam, 18, 114–15, 137, 147–8, 158
    nationalism of, 177
    and women, 122

Kaiumov, F., 71
Kasimovskii, E., 106
Kazakhstan, 18–20, 37
    water needs in, 78, 87
Khabillulaev, P., 79–80, 84, 102
Khonoliev, N., 106
Khrushchev, N., 4–5, 19, 36, 55
    and water problems, 88–9, 91
Kirghizia, 29, 126–7
Kirilets, Z., 87
Kistanov, N., 106
Kolkhozy, 69–70, 72, 74, 99
Koshlokov, G., 165–6
Kostakov, V., 106, 108–9, 119
Kosygin, A., 5–6, 8
Kotliakov, V.; 186
Kotliar, A., 106
Krasovskii, V., 6
Kuibyshev, V., 2
Kunaev, D., 148

Labor:
    and cotton, 64–5, 73
    and private farming, 127
    productivity of, 31–3
    relocation of, 182
    reservoir of, 185
    resources of, 106, 110
    shortage of, 110, 141
    surplus of, 105–11
    training of, 56
    unused, 49
Lake Baikal, 92, 96

Land, arable, 27, 111
Latvia, 147
Lemeshev, M., 93
Lenin, V., 1, 106
Likhachev, D., 94
Living standards, 123–43
    income, 123–5

Machine building, 49, 173–5
Mafia, local, 146, 157–9, 185
    features of, 147–51
Makhshulov, M., 123–4
Maniakin, S., 161
Marx, K., 106
Mathematic models, and territorial
    planning, 9–12
Medical care. *See* Health care
Metallurgy, 49, 56, 59
Migration, 65, 111
Military regions, overlap of with
    economic regions, 16–17
Miller-Shulga, A., 87
Mirzoev, R., 181
Mobility:
    of rural population, 113
    of youth, 114
Monastyrev, V., 87
Mortality rate, 140–2
    infant, 122
Moscow:
    attitude of toward Central Asia, 142,
        180, 182–3
    attitude of toward private farming,
        127
    and Central Asia, 18
    and conflict about regional economy,
        109, 161
    and economic planning, 160–1, 178
    and employment, 118–19, 178
    investment strategy of, 171–7
    and irrigation systems, 67–8
    and organized crime, 158–9
    policy of toward Central Asia, 184–6
    and regionalism, 1, 8–9, 18
    and tribalism, 148–50
Moslems, 96–7
    and nationalism, 177
Mukhamedzhanov, M., 70

Narcotics, 157
National income, 31–5
Nationalism, 158
    and ecology, 102–3

and river project, 91–102
Natural gas, 28, 46, 48, 60
Natural resources, 27–8, 184
Nedrasov, A., 99–100
Nemchinov, V., 10
Nomenklatura, 146, 148, 154, 185
Nuclear energy, 49

Pesticides, 141–2
Planning, economic, 160–1
  and republics, 161–7, 178–9
Population:
  and birthrate, 112
  of children, 135
  discrimination of, by Moscow, 179
  distribution of, 110
  growth of, 28, 42, 105, 116, 127–30,
    139, 178
  and housing, 130–4
  income of, 123–5
  migration of, 65, 111
  mobility of, 113
  poverty of, 153–4
  and private farming, 127–30
  rural, 112–13, 124, 130–1, 135
  urban, 130
  and water needs, 78
Pospelova, E., 72–3
Poverty, of populace, 153–4
Pregnancy, 139–41
Press, Soviet, on shadow economy,
  144–5
Prices, 167–8, 178
Private enterprises, 154
Problems:
  economic, 31
  elements of, 184–7
Production levels, problems of assessing,
  23–5
Productivity:
  index of, 111–12
  of labor, 31–3
Profitability, 23–4
Punishment, 145

Racketeering, 155
Rakhimov, R., 34, 109
Rashidov, S., 71
Rasputin, V., 91–2, 94, 96–7
Raw materials, and prices, 168
Razumovskii, G., 185

Reforms:
  economic and administrative, 163–5
  goals of, 174
  Gorbachev and, 161, 163–8, 171–7,
    179–80, 185–7
  price, 167–8
Regionalism:
  vs. Centralism, 1
  and economic policy, 1–26
  Moscow and, 1, 8–9, 18
Regions, *See also* Economic regions
  economic, 1–5, 13, 15, 16–17
  military, 16–17
Religion, 148: *See also* Islam
Republics, 15
  per capita income in, 23–5
  and economic planning, 8–9, 161–7,
    178–9
  equalization of economic
    development among, 20–2
  income in, 173, 177–8
  and Moscow, 161, 178
  population growth in, 178
  social problems of, 175, 179–81
Resources, 56. *See also* Water
  fuel, 46
  hydroelectric, 51
  natural, 27–8, 184
Restaurants, 135
Rivers, 76–7, 81–2
  diverting, 85–103
RSFSR (Russian Soviet Federal
    Socialist Republic), 4, 9, 11, 14,
    34–5, 37, 40
Ryzhkov, N., 172–3

Salaries, 123. *See also* Income
Savings, 123–4
Savings account, 147
Shmelev, N., 169
Second economy. *See* Shadow economy
Semenov-Tian-Shanskii, P., 7
Sewage, 131
Shadow economy, 24–5
  in Brezhnev era, 145–7
  and cotton, 150–4, 159
  features of, 147–51
  and Moscow, 158–9
  and organized crime, 154–7
Sheep raising, 113–14
Shopmen, 155–6
Sibaral (Siberian-Aral Canal), 87–101

Siberia, 149, 184
  energy in, 48
  and water diversion, 85–7
Slastenkov, E., 72–3
Social-economic structure, 147–8
Social sphere, backwardness of, 142
Soil, exploitation of, 70–1
Sokolov, V., 130, 151, 153
Solokhiddinov, Z., 35
Solzhenitsyn, A., 97–8
Sonin, M., 106
South Tadjik Territorial Production
  Complex, 50–3
Sovkhozy, 69–70, 72, 74, 99
Sovnarkhozy, 4–5, 46, 51, 55–7
  abolished, 57
  central Asian, 19
Statistics:
  on income, 123–5
  inflation of, 71–2
  lack of, 11, 25–6
  on trade, 135–6
Strumilin, 106
Syr Darya (river), 81–2, 87, 90

Tadjik, 166
Tadjikistan, 113, 115–19, 126, 170,
  181
Tashkent, 54, 58
Television sets, 137
Territorial production complexes, 6–7
  South Tadjik, 50–3
Textile manufacturing, 184–5
  exclusion from, 72–5
Tikhonov, V., 94, 172
Trade, 135–8
Treml, V., 145
Trials, 156–7
Tribalism, 147–9
Turkestan, and water, 87
Turkmenia, 124
  resources in, 28
Turkmenistan, 18
  fuel resources in, 46
  water in, 76–7, 89
Turnover tax, 24, 34–5, 45, 178

Ubaidullaeva, R., 109

Ukraine, 9, 35
Ullmasov, A., 68–9
Unemployment, 28–9, 119, 168–71
United States, 80
  as cotton producer, 62–3
Usmankhodzhaev, I., 95
Uzbekistan, 29, 34–5, 40, 178–9
  cotton production in, 62–3, 69, 71–2
  and crime, 157
  fuel reserves in, 46
  industrialization in, 54, 60
  and shadow economy, 149–51, 153
  water in, 76, 89

Vasil'ev, N., 90, 94
Vocational training, 113
  problem of, 115–20
Voropaev, G., 90
VSKNh (All-Russian Council of
  National Economy), 3

Wages, 123. *See also* Income
Water:
  and agriculture, 77, 99
  and Aral Sea problem, 81–5
  and cotton, 60, 66–8, 82–4
  economic in use of, 84–5
  problems of, 76
  as resource, 27
  shortage/scarcity of, 59, 78–81,
   185–6
  and Sibaral, 85–101
  underground, 76–7, 79
Women:
  and health care, 139–41
  plight of, 121–2
World War II, and economic regions,
  3–4

Youth:
  discontent of, 119
  and employment, 116, 118–19
  modility of, 114

Zaikov, L., 174
Zakirov, Sh., 58
Zalygin, S., 94
Zhvanetskii, N., 146

For Product Safety Concerns and Information please contact our EU representative GPSR@taylorandfrancis.com
Taylor & Francis Verlag GmbH, Kaufingerstraße 24, 80331 München, Germany

www.ingramcontent.com/pod-product-compliance
Ingram Content Group UK Ltd.
Pitfield, Milton Keynes, MK11 3LW, UK
UKHW021829240425
457818UK00006B/129